THE FAITH OF THE PEOPLE

THE FAITH OF THE PEOPLE

*Theological Reflections on
Popular Catholicism*

Orlando O. Espín

ORBIS BOOKS

Maryknoll, New York 10545

The Catholic Foreign Mission Society of America (Maryknoll) recruits and trains people for overseas missionary service. Through Orbis Books, Maryknoll aims to foster the international dialogue that is essential to mission. The books published, however, reflect the opinions of their authors and are not meant to represent the official position of the society.

Library of Congress Cataloging-in-Publication Data

Espín, Orlando.
    The faith of the people : theological reflections on popular
Catholicism / Orlando Espín.
        p.   cm.
    Includes bibliographical references and index.
    ISBN 1-57075-111-0 (alk. paper)
    1. Hispanic American Catholics—Religious life.   2. Theology,
Doctrinal—United States.   I. Title.
BX1407.H55E87   1997
282'.73'08968—dc21   97-4923
                                                                        CIP

Para Ricardo, compañero y amigo
Para Lourdes, madre por corazón
Para Alex, hijo

CONTENTS

FOREWORD

Roberto S. Goizueta

THE THEOLOGIAN AS ORGANIC INTELLECTUAL

In August 1988, a small group of theologians from around the country gathered in a retreat amid the lush, verdant mountains of Ruidoso, New Mexico. The meeting had been convoked by Arturo Bañuelas, a priest in the Diocese of El Paso who had recently received his doctorate in fundamental theology from the Gregorian University in Rome, and Allan Figueroa Deck, a Jesuit theologian and pastoral leader who was, at the time, on the faculty of the Jesuit School of Theology at Berkeley. These two priests had been immersed for years in the daily struggles of the Mexican-American communities of Texas and California, respectively. As pastors and scholars themselves, they had experienced first-hand the dire need of their communities for intellectual and, specifically, theological leaders who could accompany the communities, affirm a religious faith too often dismissed by the religious and theological institutions, and help bring the abundant riches of that lived faith into a critical engagement with those institutions. If Latin American liberation theologians had served as models, it would no longer suffice to simply import their insights and ideas into a U.S. context often quite different from theirs. Indeed, such a naive appropriation of liberation theology would contradict the fundamental methodological insight of the Latin American theologians themselves: namely, that theology must be rooted in a people's own historical praxis. We had thus been called to Ruidoso, New Mexico, to discuss how we might begin to promote more actively the development of a specifically *U.S.* Latino theology, something which had already been taking shape in the groundbreaking work of Virgilio Elizondo.

One result of that meeting was the formation of the Academy of Catholic Hispanic Theologians of the United States (ACHTUS), an association which has grown from its original eight members to well over eighty members, with its own quarterly *Journal of Hispanic/Latino Theology*. For me, that meeting also marked the beginning of personal and professional friendships which have only become stronger in the intervening years and which have, in turn, fortified me in our common endeavors.

It was in Ruidoso that I met Orlando Espín. A Cuban American like myself, he was on the faculty of St. Vincent de Paul Regional Seminary in Boynton Beach, Florida, a position he had taken after returning from doctoral studies in Brazil. During our discussions in Ruidoso, one could not help but be impressed by the warmth of his personality, the sharpness of his intellect, and, above all, the depth of his Christian commitment. As I learned over the course of those days, this was no mere Ivory Tower intellectual, for he had spent years living among the poor in the most impoverished region of the Dominican Republic. There, he had contracted diseases which would continue to afflict him until today, and had paid dearly for his commitment to the poor.

In the years since our first meeting, Espín has found new expressions for his commitment to community, Church, and academy. In addition to continuing his own prolific work in popular religion and popular Catholicism, and his accompaniment of the poor (most recently on the Mexican border in Southern California), Espín has devoted an exceptional amount of time and energy to the thankless, though essential, task of building organizational structures which will support and promote U.S. Latino theology for generations to come. His indefatigable efforts have been instrumental not only in giving birth to ACHTUS and the *Journal of Hispanic/Latino Theology*, but also in effectively nurturing and strengthening these projects so that they will continue to support and promote a U.S. Latino "teología de conjunto" well into the future.

It is in this context, then, that one should read the important essays collected in this book. They are rooted in the conviction that rigorous scholarship and passionate commitment to justice are not incommensurable enterprises but, on the contrary, are mutually implicit imperatives for the Christian theologian. The essays are rooted in the conviction that, in the words of our compatriot José Martí, "pensar es servir" (To think is to serve). In the case of Espín, moreover, it is more than a conviction; it is a lived reality which has begotten and continues to sustain his scholarly work. Orlando Espín is truly an "organic intellectual" as that notion was understood by one of his intellectual mentors, Antonio Gramsci.

A further point which should be made concerning the context of the following essays is that, while the intellectual instruments the author uses are interdisciplinary in the best sense, Espín is very clear about the explicitly theological intent of his work. That is, while popular Catholicism should be and has been analyzed from social-scientific perspectives, Espín's concern is not only with popular Catholicism as a social, cultural phenomenon, but also, more specifically, with the expressly theological significance of this phenomenon. His use of social-scientific analysis always serves a theological end. Espín is interested not only in the manifestations and sociocultural import of Latino popular Catholicism, but also, and ultimately, in how Latino popular Catholicism reveals or mediates the Triune God of Jesus Christ. This, indeed, is one of the most fascinating and significant aspects of his work: popular Catholicism ought not to be simply an object of anthropological and sociological studies (as necessary as these might be), but also a principal resource for Christian theology itself. Latino popular Catholicism is much more than a panoply of interesting, if exotic, cultural rituals; it is a privileged locus of divine revelation. Moreover, argues Espín, such an assertion is no mere intellectual flight of fancy; on the contrary, the revelatory character of popular Catholicism is a central affirmation of the larger Catholic theological tradition itself, especially insofar as that tradition accords a privileged place to the *sensus fidelium*.

Espín's scholarship thus has important implications, not only for the U.S. Latino community as it struggles to maintain the vitality of its faith and traditions in an often hostile environment, but also for the larger Church as it addresses the pastoral issues raised by the Church's increasingly polycentric, multicultural character, and for the theological academy as it attempts to bring the new polycentric reality, and the struggles of marginalized groups, to bear on the Christian intellectual tradition. One of Espín's great gifts is his profound understanding of how these audiences are interrelated: how, for instance, the future of the U.S. Latino community is linked to the ability of Latinos and Latinas to engage critically the Church and the academy. He understands that any absolute, *a priori* rejection of these institutions would amount to a self-imposed marginalization; resistance and critique presuppose engagement. And, in the words of Edward Said, effective engagement presupposes the ability to use the "same language employed by the dominant power, to dispute its hierarchy and methods, to elucidate what it has hidden, to pronounce what it has silenced or rendered unpronounceable."[1]

Wherever U.S. Latino popular Catholicism has been ignored or dismissed, what has been hidden, silenced, and rendered unpronounceable has been the Word of God. This fact should be of concern not only to those who have been unjustly silenced, but also to those who, while claiming to know, preach, and teach the Word of God, have done the silencing. Like very few scholars, Orlando Espín knows the "language employed by the dominant power" and, with a rare creativity and effectiveness, is able to challenge its hegemony in theological discourse. In so doing, he unveils for us what had for centuries remained buried under layers of theological rationalism and imperialistic dogmatism: the profound wisdom of the popular faith which sustains and empowers the U.S. Latino community. To destroy our faith is to destroy our

very lives. As Espín repeatedly reminds us, to disparage a people's faith
and culture is no mere theoretical error; it is, at bottom, a form of
genocide. The modern Western marginalization (though this is too
tame a word to describe the historical reality) of the lived faith of the
poor represents the ongoing presence of the conquest in our midst.

LATINIDAD: GROUNDING THE UNIVERSAL IN THE PARTICULAR

The postmodern suspicion of all claims to epistemological objectivity
and universality is giving us a renewed appreciation of the influence
which the sociohistorical context of the scholar has on his/her theoretical conclusions. From quantum physics to poststructuralist literary theory, across diverse disciplines, the contemporary academy is today
unmasking the pretentious, underlying claims of modern epistemologies—especially as these presuppose an autonomous subject and the
possibility of a universal knowledge. This renewed attention to the
sociohistorical context of the intellectual enterprise can engender a new
openness to the voices of "the Other," that particular human voice
which modernity had ignored as, blind to its own particularity and
sociohistorical context, modern Western thought became assumptively
identified with universal Truth. Demanding a greater intellectual humility, this "de-centering" of the modern Western subject offers exciting
opportunities for the development of a genuine pluralism, or polycen-
trism, where the particular differences that make each people unique
are not viewed as threats to the search for truth but as absolutely
essential aspects of that search.

At the same time, if modern epistemologies assumed a totalitarian,
monolithic notion of knowledge, there exists, in the postmodern emphasis on the radical particularity and contextual character of all knowledge,
an opposite and similarly dangerous tendency toward epistemological
disintegration and relativism. This tendency manifests itself in a social
fragmentation that precludes genuine dialogue and communication; the
uniqueness of each particular "social location" is sometimes perceived as
so radically different from other, equally unique "social locations" that
any communication, dialogue, or mutual understanding becomes impossible. Can a white, male Euro-American have *any* understanding of the
experience of a Latina, and vice versa? Or is the particular sociohistorical
experience of each so radically different from the other, so absolutely
incommensurable, that *any* mutual understanding is impossible?

The danger of accepting this latter proposition is that, since the possibility of critique presupposes the possibility of communication or some
level of commensurability, to presume incommensurability is—*a priori*
and *a fortiori*—to preclude critique. Such presumptive incommensurability thus serves the interests of the dominant groups, who are effectively

immunized from criticism. The dominant groups may then be quite willing to create social spaces (e.g., clubs, professional organizations, church
groups) wherein Latinos and Latinas may affirm their own particular
culture, or popular religion. "Minorities" might be encouraged to form
"their own" groups or develop "their own" religious celebrations. But,
precisely because it is assumed that "their own" are absolutely different
from "our own," it is likewise assumed that "we" can learn nothing
from "them." Thus, the responsibility of the dominant groups is
thought to have been met once the marginalized groups are accorded
"their own" spaces, where they may do "their own" thing. Thus, U.S.
Latino theology might be recognized as valuable for Latinos and Latinas
("their" theology), but as ultimately irrelevant for Euro-Americans.
Consequently, Euro-American theologians can continue to ignore the
dramatic implications of U.S. Latino theology for *their* own Euro-
American theologies. Even if individual Euro-American theologians do
learn from U.S. Latino theology, the fact remains that they *need not* do
so in order to find acceptance in the theological academy or the Church.
As all U.S. Latino, African American, Native American, and Asian
American theologians know, however, the same does not hold true for
these groups; to gain such acceptance, these theologians must learn to
do not only U.S. Latino theology, African American theology, Native
American theology, or Asian American theology, but also Euro-
American theology—and do it well.

As we U.S. Latino theologians find ourselves caught between the
totalitarian tendencies of modernity and the polarizing tendencies of
postmodernity, the significance of Espín's retrieval of Latino popular
Catholicism as *locus theologicus* should not be overlooked and can
hardly be overstated. What he calls for is not simply an "openness" to
other cultures and religious experiences, nor simply an "understanding" or "appreciation" of Latino popular Catholicism—though this is
all, of course, desired and demanded by our contemporary situation.
Rather, what he calls for is a different starting point for the theological
enterprise, the *privileging* of a different "way of being Catholic" as a
place wherein the God of Jesus Christ, about whom we Catholic theologians claim to speak, has chosen to be revealed. The privileging of
this particular starting point, moreover, in no way implies an exclu-
sivism, or absolute incommensurability which would simply reinforce
the marginalization of the U.S. Latino community. On the contrary, the
God who has chosen to be revealed preferentially in the lived faith of
the poor is a God whose love extends to all—and who, thus, privileges
the lived faith of the poor, which has for so long been dismissed and
derided, precisely to demonstrate that the Word and love of God know
no boundaries. This God knows that, in a historical context of division
and marginalization, a truly universal love cannot be a neutral love, a
universal Truth cannot be a neutral Truth, and a universal theology

cannot be a neutral theology, one incapable of adjudicating among pre-
sumably incommensurate sociohistorical locations.

An authentically universal theology can be born only among those
persons whose lives have historically been denied any theological significance; only when God's revelation is recognized and affirmed *there* can
it be recognized as, indeed, a universal revelation, a universal Truth.
Until then, any pretentions to universality will remain but legitimations
of conquest. Far from its equivalent, then, universality is the very opposite of neutrality. If silence is consent, neutrality is complicity. And theological neutrality is idolatry.

Espín's is a profoundly ecclesial project, with important implications
for a Church confronting an increasingly polycentric, multicultural, historical reality. Rather than fear a future in which Catholicism and the
Catholic faith will be increasingly defined by the lived faith of the poor,
we should recognize the character of this moment as *kairos*, a time
when the power of the living Word of God, which is good news to the
poor, may itself be freed from the centuries-old shackles with which it
has been bound by those who fear its transformative force in society
and in individual human lives. Latino Catholics have long known and
experienced that power as a source of sustenance and strength in the
midst of struggle. The unquenchable hope born in this struggle, where
we are accompanied by the crucified and risen Jesus, is what we offer
to the larger Church, academy, and society.

Thus, the relevance of Espín's writings is not limited to his own Latino community; it extends to these larger communities which, in many
cases, have lost faith, not only faith in God but faith in life itself. When
the *sensus fidelium* is displaced by arbitrary ecclesiastical dicta, when
the search for truth is displaced by an epistemological nihilism, and
when the preferential option for the poor is displaced by socio-
economic Darwinism, faith in God is displaced by a fear of life. Para-
doxically, it is among those who most intimately know the power of
death that we find the most stubborn faith in the power of life and,
therefore, in the power of the God who is the source of life. This faith
in the ultimate goodness of life, even in the midst of affliction, is at the
heart of Latino popular Catholicism. This faith is God's gift not only to
the U.S. Latino community but to the entire Church, to all peoples.

Therefore, the following essays have important ramifications not
only for a U.S. Latino community seeking a greater understanding of
the manifold ways in which God's liberating love makes itself manifest
in our own lives, but also for Euro-Americans seeking greater appreciation of how the Christian tradition can address the ecclesial, intellectual, and social crises confronting all of our communities at the dawn
of the third millennium. Espín holds the conviction that by rooting
himself in the particularity of the lived faith of his own U.S. Latino
community he will be able to speak to the larger community. This con-

viction underlies all of Espín's work and represents the possibility of a new model of pluralism, one which will promote a unity grounded in the uniqueness of the particular. For it is only in and through the particular—especially the poor—that God continues to speak today, just as two thousand years ago God spoke in and through, not a "universal" human being, but a very particular person, a Galilean Jew, the son of a carpenter.

If the particularity of our sociohistorical location imposes limits on our ability to fully comprehend the God who transcends history, that very particularity is also the condition of the possibility of our knowing *at all* the God who is revealed in history. Thus, the depreciation of a people's particular uniqueness (e.g., culture) does not bring about an increased appreciation of the universal and spiritual truths of Christianity; on the contrary, the depreciation of the particular implies the depreciation of the universal. To insist, as Espín does, that there is no such thing as an acultural, or noncultural Christian faith is to make at least two assertions simultaneously: (1) as an imperfect human construct, *every* particular culture distorts our knowledge of God, *and* (2) *every* particular culture *makes possible* our knowledge of God. Without culture there can be no faith, no revelation, since there would be no medium through which "what" is revealed could be communicated, or "revealed." Only when Christian theology is able to make both of the above assertions simultaneously, and do so for *all* cultures, will it be truly universal. And that will happen only when those cultures, which have for centuries been dismissed—when they have not been simply exterminated—for being immature, inferior, and incapable of revealing the Word of God, are recognized and affirmed as mediations of divine revelation. After all, a principal cause of Jesus' own crucifixion was the ruling elites' assumption that nothing good (i.e., no divine revelation, no universal truth) could come from Galilee.[2]

If particularity mediates universality, culture mediates the universal Church's faith. Thus, it is precisely by virtue of his insistence on *"latinidad"* as *locus theologicus*, that Espín is able to construct theological and spiritual bridges between the Latino community and the larger communities to which we all belong. By probing the Latino experiences of God, Jesus, Mary, suffering, hope, and Christian tradition, Espín brings the riches of those experiences to light in such a way that they will find echoes far beyond the Latino community, not only among other groups who find themselves on the margins of society, but also among those persons whose privileges mask an underlying alienation and despair.[3] Espín's work thus has important ramifications for theological method; it offers us a new starting point for theology, wherein fidelity to the particular—U.S. Latino popular Catholicism—makes possible an openness to the universal. Underlying Latino popular Catholicism is an unshakeable conviction in the goodness of life.

That conviction can only be a source of hope, not just for Latinos and Latinas, but for everyone.

At the same time, of course, sociohistorical particularity implies limitation. Espín's many years of experience working among the poor, together with his sophisticated understanding of popular religion, prevent him from in any way idealizing, or romanticizing U.S. Latino popular Catholicism. This is clear, especially, in his essay "Popular Catholicism: Alienation or Hope?" His answer to the question posed in the title is: "Both. And much more."

The task of the organic intellectual is always one of *critical* reflection. In his essays, as well as in the introduction to this collection, the author's interpretation of U.S. Latino popular Catholicism avoids that romanticization which is, in its own way, as dehumanizing, suffocating, and demeaning as is outright rejection. To affirm our humanity is not only to assert our dignity as mediators of divine revelation, but also, in the light of that fundamental affirmation, to acknowledge our limitations as mediators of God's Word.

UNA MÍSTICA: GROUNDING THEOLOGY IN A SPIRITUALITY OF VANQUISHMENT

Espín's writings also have very significant implications for Christian spirituality. To ground theology in U.S. Latino popular Catholicism is to ground it in a spirituality, "una mística." This is not, however, a privatized, solipsistic spirituality divorced from the everyday struggle for justice; it is a communal spirituality nurtured in that very everyday struggle to survive as full human beings and as a community, in our resistance to "vanquishment." It is thus a spirituality, a lived intimacy with God, which is born on the cross, in Jesus' own rebellion against vanquishment—"My God, my God, *why* have you abandoned me?" This paradoxical intimacy then finds its expression in the resurrection, the "fiesta," where what is celebrated is the ultimately indestructible bonds of love and solidarity that unite us to each other and, above all, to God—even when we feel abandoned by that very God. These bonds *are* life itself. Surviving even the cross, they represent the ultimate indestructibility of life, the victory of life over death, the victory of justice over vanquishment.

The spirituality which Espín outlines, most explicitly in the first chapter of this book, bridges the barriers which modern Western theologies have erected between spirituality and social justice, between both of these and the theological enterprise itself. Those barriers have had destructive consequences. Perceived by many Christians as little more than esoteric and irrelevant Ivory Tower speculation, the theological enterprise has increasingly become the purview of an intellectual elite far removed from the life and concerns of the faith community, or, for that matter, of *any* community outside our ivied walls. Where Christians seek to address their very concrete experiences of personal and social alienation, they often perceive theology and theologians not as companions in that search but as sources of alienation: in short, as part of the problem, not part of the solution. When theology becomes irrelevant to the spiritual and social concerns of Christians, these concerns, in turn, become increasingly understood and defined in isolation from critical theological reflection. Spirituality and social justice become identified, respectively, with "personal feelings" and "social action" pursued, not as the practical *ground* of theological reflection, but as *alternatives* to theological reflection, since this has been dismissed from the outset as meaningless and irrelevant. When divorced from theology and social justice, spirituality degenerates into narcissism. When divorced from theology and spirituality, social justice degenerates into social utilitarianism. When divorced from spirituality and social justice, theology degenerates into rationalism.

By grounding his theology in the *mística* of Latino popular Catholicism, Espín provides a model for retrieving the centuries-old Christian tradition of a theology born in and nurtured by the life of prayer and worship. What he calls for, however, is not an uncritical appropriation of the Christian spiritual tradition as a source for theology, but a *critical* retrieval of that tradition "from the underside." As such, this theology would find its roots less in the "official" liturgical, spiritual life of the Church, as defined primarily by clergy and religious, and more in the popular liturgical and spiritual practices of the Church, as defined primarily by the laity and, especially, the poor. Precisely because these practices emerge on the margins of society and the "official" Church, they are nurtured by the spiritual and intellectual demands of the struggle for survival, by the everyday resistance to vanquishment, by that hope against all hope through which, by reaching out to our Crucified Companion, we find a liberation defined not by an illusory autonomy but by relationships of solidarity. For all their undeniable value to Christian life, the heroic spiritualities of celibate religious "experts" here are subordinated to a spirituality of "lo cotidiano," the everyday. Here, in the everyday, common struggle for our survival as a people with a dignity bestowed on us by God, the political and the personal, the economic and the spiritual, the intellectual and the emotional, the sacred and the secular are united. At a time when the laity is assuming greater leadership in the Church, Latino popular Catholicism offers important models for a lay spirituality which will address the spiritual needs of lay Christians.

As Espín warns us, however, the integral character of U.S. Latino popular Catholicism should also alert us to the temptation of interpreting popular Catholicism as opposed to, or over against "official," or "mainstream" Catholicism. These are different, though intrinsically related and overlapping *loci*. Given its integral character, U.S. Latino popular Catholicism represents a crucial resource for bridging the barriers that often separate the theological, spiritual, and social justice concerns of the Church in the United States.

The strength of Espín's argument for the integral, or holistic, character of popular Catholicism as *locus theologicus* does not derive only from his theological and epistemological analyses—important as these are—but also from his perceptive historical analyses. To insist that Latino popular Catholicism be taken seriously as a theological source is not only to be true to the contemporary postmodern context, but to be true to the very history of Christianity. The theological retrieval of U.S. Latino popular Catholicism implies a concomitant retrieval of those pre-Tridentine forms of popular Catholicism which, for centuries, characterized European Christianity, and which were brought to the Americas by the Spanish. Despite the many differences among them, one characteristic shared by U.S. Latino popular Catholicism, pre-Tridentine Iberian popular Catholicism, indigenous American religions, and African religions is the central role each accords to communal, performative ritual—not in isolation from social life, but as the very heart of social, public life.

U.S. LATINO THEOLOGY AS A FORCE FOR UNITY

Orlando Espín's theological reading of U.S. Latino popular Catholicism—as communal, performative praxis—embodies and makes possible the re-integration of those dimensions of Christian faith and theology which have, in our contemporary Western world, become polarized. Moreover, this epistemological fragmentation—where intellectual knowledge (theology) is understood as separate from the knowledge of the heart (spirituality) and practical knowledge (social action)—is much more than a purely abstract concern. This fragmentation is mirrored in the very concrete, human, interpersonal fragmentation of the Church itself, specifically the Roman Catholic Church—where theologians, pastoral workers, liturgists, and social activists all work in isolation from each other.

As noted above, theologians have become increasingly irrelevant to the everyday lives of most Christians, especially the poor. Influenced—indeed, governed—by modern epistemological assumptions about the nature of human experience, reason, scientific analysis, and the academic enterprise, we have sought acceptance and respect as a "scientific," academic discipline. There is little doubt that the modern academy's demands for scientific, epistemological, and methodological rigor have had a profound and positive influence on Christian theologians, forcing us to take seriously the interdisciplinary context of our theology and calling forth from us a more acute attentiveness to the many ambiguities inherent in the theological enterprise itself. In the face of the great insights that have emerged and have been developed in other intellectual disciplines during the post-Enlightenment period, theologians have had to learn the virtue of intellectual humility. We are not a self-sufficient intellectual community standing "above" all other disciplines any more than the Church is a community standing "above" history.

Yet, if Christian theologians have benefited from our acceptance as full colleagues in the modern academy, the cost of that acceptance has been high. Too often, we theologians have become dissociated from the ecclesial, social, and cultural contexts of our intellectual vocations. If we have benefited from a more "professional" approach to our intellectual task as theologians, a further consequence of this professionalization has been an increasingly rationalistic approach to theological research. Theology appropriated modern scientific methodologies, with their emphasis on epistemological objectivity, or detachment, and thus their concomitant depreciation of all those forms of particularity, or sociohistorical commitment and contexts (e.g., culture, gender, race) which are perceived as introducing "subjective" elements into the scholarly enterprise, thereby "biasing" the scholars' judgments and conclusions.

Yet these contexts are no mere abstractions; they contain concrete, flesh-and-blood human beings. To have uprooted ourselves from the sociohistorical contexts in which we live, in order to do detached, "objective" research and arrive at "universal" truths is to have abandoned the persons who inhabit those "contexts." Those lives, we have presumed, do not have any bearing—indeed, *must* not have any bearing—on the theological enterprise if that enterprise is going to generate detached, objective, and universal conclusions. In the modern academy, this demand for objectivity also manifested itself in the increased separation of theology, as an enterprise presupposing a commitment to a particular faith community (i.e., "subjectivity"), from religious studies, as an enterprise presupposing epistemological detachment and objectivity.

In the long term, one of the most fruitful results of the type of theology Orlando Espín does will be in the dialogue that it will engender between theologians and scholars of religion in the United States. The following essays demonstrate the essential role that social-scientific and phenomenological studies of religion must play in any contemporary Christian theology that attempts to sink its roots in the lived faith of a people. Conversely, his work also demonstrates how such studies must be attentive to the explicitly theological significance of popular religion, as a lived *faith*, not merely a sociohistorical phenomenon.

A broader, though in some ways more intractable and destructive division that today cuts across our society, the academy, and the Catholic Church is that between "conservatives" and "liberals." Increasingly, it seems, every ecclesial, ethical, and theological issue becomes divided along conservative-liberal lines, with different individuals and groups taking a place on one side of the divide or the other. Though often unspoken, the membership criteria for these mutually exclusive groups are nevertheless quite clear. Should any of these be violated, even in the most benign way, membership is automatically transferred to the opposite group (excommunication *latae sententiae*). At times, each pole seems to demand absolute orthodoxy as the price of inclusion. Then communication becomes impossible, and dialogue degenerates into recrimination. The examples, unfortunately, are so abundant as to not require enumeration here.

If a way is to be found for the Catholic Church to move beyond this destructive polarization, the way will be found in popular Catholicism, in the faith of the people, a faith neither liberal nor conservative but rooted in a lived intimacy with the God of the poor. It is a truly radical faith, in the literal sense of the word "radical." It sinks its roots in the joys, afflictions, struggles, passions, disillusionments, and, ultimately, in the intransigent hope that characterize our lives together as Latino Catholics. So deep are those roots in our common life that, in the end, faith and life become indistinguishable: to believe in God is to believe in life, and vice versa. And, like any living reality, that faith will resist the objectification of artificial labels.

U.S. Latino popular Catholicism incarnates a faith which will confound the wise, conservative and liberal alike. If the conservative feels uncomfortable with the social-transformative implications of that faith, the liberal might feel uncomfortable with its liturgical manifestations. If the conservative is likely to look past the mestizo countenance of Guadalupe, the liberal is just as likely to be embarrassed by her Marian identity. If the conservative finds somewhat suspicious the influence of indigenous and African religious traditions in Latino popular Catholicism, the liberal might find equally supicious the influence of the Catholic tradition itself. Espín's scholarship suggests, therefore, the artificiality and meaninglessness of the conservative-liberal dichotomy in the context of U.S. Latino popular Catholicism. As such, his work points to the possibility of overcoming the conservative-liberal divisions that continue to polarize our society at every level.

Espín's work also suggests interesting and creative opportunities for fostering ecumenism among the Christian churches. The outlines of such an ecumenical movement are set forth, particularly at the end of "Popular Catholicism among Latinos." Espín challenges us to look at the increasing attractiveness of pentecostal and evangelical forms of Christianity to the Latino community not as a threat but as an opportunity to deepen our common faith, an opportunity to recover those aspects of the Christian tradition's *lived* faith which may have been forgotten in the post-Tridentine rush to erect clear and distinct conceptual barriers around the faith. The experience of an increasing number of

Latinos and Latinas is that they find their own popular Catholicism, based on the "sacramental, symbolic ethos and worldview that made pre-Reformation Christianity possible," more adequately embodied in pentecostalism than in Euro-American Catholicism. This should alert us theologians to the possibility that the greatest hope for Christian unity may lie in our ability to recognize what unites us, not necessarily at the level of theological concepts, but at the level of our lived faith. To ground theology in popular religion is, after all, to suggest that theological understanding will only take place if and when we are able to *live* our faith together, to accompany each other in our common struggles.

Where theologies divide us, our popular religion may yet forge bonds among us which, while affirming our religious diversity, would promote true ecumenism. Where one's religious faith is identified less by one's theology than by one's *way of living* that faith, ecumenical understanding will emerge, not from the theological discussions of ecumenical commissions, but from a people's common struggle to live their faith, whether Catholic or Protestant, in an environment which, whether Catholic or Protestant, is hostile to such a lived faith. It should come as no surprise that, without underestimating the very real differences, Latino Catholics often find that they have more in common with Latino Protestants than with Euro-American Catholics—and that Latino Protestants often experience a greater affinity with Latino Catholics than with Euro-American Protestants. Neither should it come as a surprise that, if Latino Catholics find that a particular Protestant church *lives* its faith in a manner more closely resembling their own popular Catholicism than does the local Catholic parish (by, for example, fostering interpersonal relationships, hospitality, and community), they will be drawn to the Protestant church—even if they also continue to participate in the local parish and, especially, in popular Catholic celebrations.

This "pluriconfessionalism" so common in the Latino community is only possible where faith is understood as *fundamentally* a way of living or being, "una manera de ser," rather than fundamentally a way of thinking, "una manera de pensar." (As mentioned above, critical theological reflection is essential, but it is not itself definitive of faith.) No amount of theological agreement will bring about mutual understanding if that understanding is not lived out in our communities of faith. If the Latino community resists the dominant culture's pressure to reduce faith to conceptual, rigidly dogmatic formulas, if we continue to value and affirm the centrality of Christian praxis in popular religion, we may yet fashion a new, more effective model of Christian unity.

By demonstrating a new way of doing theology, and uncovering the spiritual riches of popular Catholicism, Orlando Espín is issuing a prophetic call to reconciliation in Church, academy, and society. The challenge which Espín lays before us does not, however, ignore the profound obstacles to such reconciliation; indeed, it is a challenge born in the struggle against those very obstacles. Far from being a source of division, then, the preferential option for the poor, the "faith of the people," represents our only hope for reconciliation.

Notes

1. Edward W. Said, "Nationalism, Human Rights, and Interpretation," in *Freedom and Interpretation: The Oxford Amnesty Lectures 1992*, ed. Barbara Johnson (New York: Basic Books, 1993), p. 198.

2. Virgilio ˈElizondo, *Galilean Journey: The Mexican-American Promise* (Maryknoll, New York: Orbis Books, 1983).

3. Recently, a friend who had experienced "burn out" after working many years as a hospital nurse in an inner-city Latino barrio took a new job in a middle-class suburban hospital. Expecting relief from the emotional stress of tending to so many fatally wounded teenagers, victims of gang warfare, she soon discovered that, in the suburban hospital, she was also tending to fatally wounded teenagers, no longer victims of gang violence but, instead, victims of suicide.

INTRODUCTION

In 1975 I moved to the towns of Dajabón and Loma de Cabrera, on the Haitian-Dominican border. I went to serve as teacher and pastoral agent. I also went with an educational background that had offered me a solid foundation in European and Euro-American theologies. The post-Vatican II Church was alive and well then, and, in Latin America, it had undergone its own Medellín Conference. In the mid-seventies we were still optimistically preparing for what was soon to be the Puebla Conference.

In 1975, however, I also learned that the vast majority of the people I taught and served were only tangentially interested in the important ecclesial and social issues and movements of the day. The people of Dajabón, of Loma de Cabrera, and of the dozens of hamlets and villages around them, were usually Catholic, but not in the way I had been used to or trained to appreciate. Most of the people were, in my view at that time, "nonpracticing" Catholics, often living and believing in ways that my theology and convictions had taught me to deem as incorrect, insufficient, or superstitious. In 1975 I thought that what they needed was "good" catechesis, "more" religious education, "better" moral training, and so on. What they had, I thought, was a diluted and bastardized form of "real" Catholicism. They were "devoted" to saints and rites instead of "committed" to Christ and gospel. Furthermore, in my view, this bastardized form of Christianity was a very serious impediment to their understanding the social and economic forces that were oppressing them, and a real obstacle for a liberating praxis.

In 1975 I was, consequently, not inclined to understand the faith of the people in any sympathetic way. A vestige of an unfair and dehumanizing past, it was bound to disappear, and the more I did to promote its early demise, the better.

In 1996, as I write these lines, I look back on the twenty-one years that have passed since Dajabón and Loma de Cabrera. My life has changed a great deal. The Church too has changed, and I am no longer on the Haitian-Dominican border. Much has occurred in the Church and in the world, and in my theological reflection. In 1996, I am not so

1

"theologically colonizing" in reference to popular Catholicism as I was twenty years ago; but I am not so naive as to be blind to the difficulties still inherent in the people's religion. This collection of essays is a result of the changes in perspective and method that my own reflection has undergone in the past two decades.

The texts included in the present book were written and published between 1991 and 1995. They first appeared either as journal articles or as chapters in collective works. I have barely touched them in preparation for this Orbis Books edition, so the reader will find some very evident repetitions. It was my choice to leave them basically untouched because there is some value in the reader's noticing what I thought needed mentioning or explaining at every turn (e.g., the use of the terms "Hispanic" and "Latino," my fundamental outlook on what is popular Catholicism, etc.), and what I assumed (rightly or not) to be self-evident. With very few exceptions, I also left the notes and bibliographical references as they were when the essays were first published.

A number of my Latino colleagues encouraged me to gather some of my recent work and publish it in book form. They recommended some entries for this collection, but the final decision was left to me. The texts included here represent my thought on Latino popular Catholicism, and, especially, they are the texts that have acted (at least in my mind) as signs that have led my reflection in new directions.

What do these essays say? What are the few contributions that I might have made to the theological study of popular Catholicism? Someone once said that I bring passion and conviction to what I write about this deceptively simple field of study. I also hope that I might contribute a bit more. The following are some issues I have tried to point to in my theology.

• Throughout these essays I insist that the people's faith be taken seriously as a true *locus theologicus* and not solely or mainly as a pastoral, catechetical problem. If the Latino peoples' actual way of being Catholic is not important enough to merit serious theological reflection, then the American Church's theologians should explain why European or Euro-American Catholicisms merit it. Questions about the biased and ethnocentric nature and methods of American theology can then be legitimately raised.

The theological significance of Latino popular Catholicism cannot be denied. Contained (and not just implied) in it are centuries of the most crucial Christian reflection on gospel and life. The vast majority of Catholics in the history of the universal Church have always been and still are the lay poor. Consequently, given that Catholic doctrine holds that the Church is the infallible witness to revelation, then this *must* mean that the lay poor (i.e., the immense majority of the Church throughout twenty centuries) *are too* the infallible witnesses to revelation. However, the way these millions have understood, received, and expressed their faith is undeniably "popular Catholicism." The Latino peoples are no exception to this. Therefore, Christian theologians cannot simply ignore the real faith of the Church any more than they could ignore revelation. Popular Catholicism is the real faith of the real Church, whether we like to academically and institutionally admit it or not. A circle doesn't stop being round just because someone decrees otherwise. The people's Catholicism as *locus theologicus* cannot be dismissed.

• I have tried to show in my work that although the majority of Latinos are Catholic, they are usually so in a "popular" way. By "popular" I do not mean "widespread," although popular Catholicism certainly is. "Popular," rather, is the adjective to the noun "people." Thus, popular Catholicism is "popular" because it is the people's own. Although it is evident that not every single Latino Catholic person shares in this tradition within Catholicism, most Latinos do, and all of our cultures are clearly grounded in it.

Some authors in theology, in history, and in the social sciences, at times tend to identify popular Catholicism as an inimical opposite to some sort of "official" Catholicism. Sometimes academic terminology, including my own, is not as exact as we wish. Nevertheless, the supposed opposition between these two traditions is more the result of scholarly wishful thinking than a true historical reality. I don't think popular and official Catholicisms are best explained as inimical and mutually exclusive forces that confront each other on a *doctrinal* Catholic battlefield. At least not too often. However, these two traditions within the one Church do exist, co-exist, at times clash, and frequently misunderstand each other. The realities and uses of ecclesiastical and social *power and powerlessness* are more frequently responsible for the misunderstandings and clashes than any doctrinal, theological arguments. Doctrinally these two traditions are much more complementary and in agreement than theologians (and others) might care to admit.

All of this, of course, has raised a number of seriously foundational, theological questions in my mind and in my work. And as I sought to deal with them, I realized that historical and cultural studies had to be engaged, that the social sciences had to become partners in dialogue, and that the implied claims to universal validity still made by Eurocentric theologies needed to be closely examined and critiqued. It is my conviction that no serious theology may be produced today in the United States without confronting and honestly addressing the issues and difficulties raised by cultural, historical, and social-scientific studies. Cultural and historical naiveté, in Euro-American theologies of the "modern" *and* "postmodern" varieties, seems to me to have actually conspired to make Christian theology acquiesce to the silencing and the dismissal of Latinos in both Church and society.

• Ecclesiological and pastoral models are not only explained by theological (and other) assumptions; they are founded on them. If the dominant ecclesiological and pastoral models are to be examined, they must evidently be opened to the entire Church's critique. But how we define "Church" will lead us down one or another path to probably conflicting evaluations.

Even though any adequate Catholic definition of "Church" will always and necessarily include the laity, most contemporary ecclesiologies have (in my view) not been successful in their theologizing on the laity. Indeed, the most fundamental ecclesial roles of the laity—the exercise of the *sensus fidelium* and of "reception," and the crucial and indispensable role as infallible bearers of Tradition (which necessarily involves them as primary subjects of evangelization, and certainly not as mere assistants to the episcopate)—are usually treated as either afterthoughts or as somehow not foundational enough to the Church's mission and nature, or they are simply not treated at all.

It seems to me that theologians have to start taking the *real* laity of *real* Catholicism seriously (and not the *imagined* laity of so many ecclesiologies), otherwise the very understandings of "Church," of Tradition, of infallibility, and of revelation might be compromised and vitiated. "Mainstream" Catholicism is and must always be defined (by theologians and others) from within the real laity's own experience and definition. I have tried to point to these issues as evident, critical consequences to theological reflection on popular Catholicism. Furthermore, since no one in the Church (laity or clergy) live their faith outside of everyday human life, and since all human life is always and exclusively cultural, social, gendered, historical, etc., then there can be no credible ecclesiology or theology of the laity today that does not take these determining contexts seriously into account in theological method and conclusions. This is so self-evident that I wonder how we could go on doing theology as if these issues were not foundational.

• Latino popular Catholicism is foundationally dependent for its existence on the *entire community*, on the *families* within the community and, especially, on the *older women* within the families. The ministers of Latino Catholicism are primarily the older women. They are deemed wiser and usually in possession of greater personal and spiritual depth than the men. Women are the center and pillars of the families, and Latino popular Catholicism is definitely woman-emphatic. It is no exaggeration to say that older women are our people's cultural and religious hermeneuts. They are the ministers and bearers of our identity. And so this explains, at least to me (and among a number of other consequences), the Latino inclination to image and explain the divine and the religious through feminine symbols and categories, and through women-led rites. Any doubt as to why I have been interested in some of the Marian devotions so evident among Latinos?

I need not add that discussion on a significant number of issues relating to the sacrament of the ordained ministries might benefit from the theological study of popular Catholicism.

• In some of the essays in this book I mention that popular Catholicism *cannot* be simply identified with the sum of Latino devotions. Such an easy and superficial definition of popular Catholicism is ultimately dismissive and paternalizing.

Quite often the Euro-American Catholic "liberal," in his/her attempt to be in solidarity with Latinos, actually falls for the dominant culture's assumptions that popular Catholicism is an anachronism to be buried, or a "quaint" component of a people to be "aided." The horrifying and dismissive premises implied in this view are simply unacceptable. "Liberal" pastoral agents are at times the worst enemies of our people's cultural identity and faith, especially when the latter do not fit the Euro-American notion of how we should be, live, and believe. Needless to say, in the name of solidarity and progress quite a few attempts at cultural colonization and oppression are committed.

But the Euro-American Catholic "conservative" fails us just as often. The latter sees our popular Catholicism from the perspective of his/her own ecclesiastical, political agenda and wrongly assumes that our religion agrees . . . or at least can be recruited to appear to be in agreement. Latino popular Catholicism, although not necessarily subversive, can (and quite often has) surprised the conservative with confrontation and opposition. Catholic conservatives suspect that they can separate our holy symbols (especially Marian ones) from the lives and suffering of our people (thereby forgetting that much of the pain inflicted on Latinos is often the direct result of the conservative political agenda). They do not understand how much they offend our faith and our holy symbols!

There is more to this religious universe beneath its "devotional" surface! Both Euro-American liberals and conservatives forget that they are *both equally* the heirs to a post-Tridentine, "modern" Church that is *not* the main or authentic matrix of our people's Catholicism.

As time passes I am more convinced of the potentially subversive role that popular Catholicism can play, especially because of its function as our culturally authentic epistemology. I am not quite sure if I have successfully explained (in my writings) the intuition behind this last point. But I am certain that there is a great deal to be explored here, below the surface. Epistemology is cultural too. And if Latino culture is profoundly marked, at its very roots, by the assumptions and premises that shaped its popular Catholicism, then Latino epistemology cannot be exempt from the same shaping elements.

The essays in this book are not everything I have thought about or written on Latino popular Catholicism. These texts should not suggest that I might not disagree with myself in the future. In fact, I already have some reservations on a few issues I raised and supported in the articles and chapters published here. I sense that I have begun to move away from some of my own earlier thoughts.

I readily grant that my work on popular Catholicism exhibits limitations. Some of my Latino colleagues have pointed some of these out to me already, and others will do so in the future. That is part of the dialogue typical of and necessary in theology. That is how our field grows and becomes ever more vital and pertinent to human life.

Although I think that I have been sensitive to many specific perspectives, I acknowledge that I have not sufficiently concentrated on some that might have needed such emphasis in my past work (as this book proves). For example, questions of social class and class analysis appear in my writings but are not a real dominant concern. Furthermore, sometimes I wonder if I might not be viewing our people's lives and cultures a bit too optimistically, not giving enough consideration to our own acquiescence to and cooperation with sin, idolatry, and evil as these appear in religion and society. In the same vein, I have said much about the crucial role of women in Latino culture and Catholicism, but have I said enough about the cultural and religious roles of abusive patriarchy in our midst? I also suspect that some of my colleagues wished I were more comfortable with the "classical" means of theologizing. More "philosophical," in other words.

I am quite sure that the limitations are real and the criticisms reasonable and well founded. I perceive my work not as a definitive approach or contribution to the theological study of popular Catholicism (*¡qué osadía sería pensar eso!*). On the contrary, I see my theology as a growing series of "legible signs" on my chosen road (i.e., on and about Latino popular Catholicism). It is up to others to judge if these signs are clearly legible and/or if their message is significant enough.

The interpretation of the people's Catholicism advances, or so it seems, by delving into its *foundational epistemology*. Figuring out *how* Latinos could historically and culturally think and image events, doctrines, or experiences has often proved more important than *what* might have been actually thought or imaged.

The theological interpretation of one key Latino Marian devotion is a case in point. There are some questions and issues that I am currently debating in my mind in reference to the veneration of the *Virgen de Guadalupe*. I have reached no conclusion, so what follows should be read as a public snapshot of an ongoing private discussion. I am including these reflections here as an example of important new avenues of theological reflection that the study of popular Catholicism can open up for us. I don't know where these new avenues will take us, or what my position on the following questions will finally be. Sharing these thoughts with the reader might foster some interesting and fruitful discussions.

I am convinced that it is *not* the Jewish woman Mary of Nazareth, the mother of Jesus, that most Latinos speak of when they refer to the *Virgen de Guadalupe*. I am certainly not the first one to know or say this. But I am not particularly satisfied with the alternatives implicated by others and by myself in the past (e.g., the *Virgen* is Tonantzin, or another earth goddess, or some sort of personified syncretization between the Christian Mary and the Aztec Tonantzin, or Mary in Nahua cultural garb, or a new inculturated image of Christianity in *mestiza,* Marian-Nahua symbols, and so on).

Stafford Poole's book, *Our Lady of Guadalupe: The Origins and Sources of a Mexican National Symbol, 1531-1797* (Tucson: University of Arizona Press, 1995) raised a number of questions in my mind. I should make clear that I am in no way implying agreement with every one of Poole's conclusions. I do have serious objections to some of his sweeping statements, above all to his methodological decision to dismiss *un*written evidence as unimportant and unacceptable (thereby showing an extraordinary and unjustifiable disregard for much of the evidence that could contradict his conclusions). But in spite of these problems, Poole did make a strong case in favor of *his* position, even such solidly researched work as Richard Nebel's *Santa María Tonantzin, Virgen de Guadalupe: Continuidad y transformación religiosa en México* (Mexico City: Fondo de Cultural Económica, 1995), does not contradict Poole's basic case—although Nebel correctly sees that the issues are broader and require better research methods.

Poole's book, in the final analysis, challenges Latino theologians to evidentially demonstrate that the *Virgen de Guadalupe* did appear in 1531 on the hill of Tepeyac, or honestly and explicitly acknowledge that they are basing some of their writings on unproved legend at worst or on popular myth-making at best. It seems, however, that Poole's book demands that Latino theologians, *before* they engage Poole and his world in argument, must first carefully analyze what are the very foundations of the purported "objectivity" on which Poole operates and which he assumes to be universally self-evident—in other words, Poole's own culture's foundational myth and unproved legend. In other words, much deeper and prior analysis and critique needs to be done on the epistemological foundations of the dominant Euro-American world (as evidenced by seminal work of Latino theologians Roberto S. Goizueta and Alex García-Rivera, among others).

In my particular way of thinking about these issues, Stafford Poole's work made me wonder if there might not *also* be another line of thought opening for us here. Poole's book assumes that the written evidence is the only one worth considering, or at least the more "objective" one. He ignores (or at least does not take into account) that written material from colonial Mexico on Guadalupe was necessarily going to promote (for theological and political reasons) the view that the *Virgen de Guadalupe* was/is Mary of Nazareth. But *is* she? The *criollos*, as well as Hispanicized *mestizos* and natives, whom Poole quotes, were all enthusiastically promoting the notion that Mary had appeared in Mexico. Whatever their ultimate intentions in pushing this view, these colonial authors would have found it unacceptable to think of Guadalupe in other terms. They could have been accused of crypto-paganism, heresy, or something to that effect, if they had doubted that Guadalupe is just another way of referring to the mother of Jesus. Perhaps the alternative to Poole's sources' Marian enthusiasm is not crypto-paganism or heresy but traditional Christian pneumatology. Is it impossible for orthodox Christian theology to think the divine in feminine categories and images? Obviously not; but, for the literate elites in colonial Mexico, maybe yes.

Perhaps Poole's fascination with the colonial Mexican *elites* (and their written texts) made him blind to *popular* pneumatology as the foundational epistemology and hermeneutic of the Guadalupe story. He disregards as unimportant the fact that colonial New Spain was very much politically, ideologically, and ecclesiastically still dependent on Spain. And Spain, at least when the published text of the *Nican Mopohua* first appears (1649), was trying very hard to implement the Tridentine reforms and guarantee national religious homogeneity. The fear of Protestantism was still real, and talk of the Holy Spirit (in all but the most orthodox of devotional and theological terms) was not common or expected, and could indeed provoke an investigation by the Inquisition. Poole also unexplainably ignores that the Nahua culture (still very much alive, even after the Spanish conquest) would have transmitted its holiest and most fundamental beliefs and wisdom through oral means too; and especially after Nahuatl became alphabetized, orality remained a viable and frequent means of transmission among the majority of Nahuas. Indeed, Poole forgets the very notion of *traditio,* so important in Catholic theology and worldview.

After reading Poole, however, I wonder if I have taken seriously enough, in my own theology's methodology and epistemological assumptions, our people's capacity (in the colonial past as well as in the present) to think the divine in categories that can still surprise me. When I am confronted by the depth of trust and affection that Latinos have for the *Virgen*, and when I see the beautiful, reverential relationship they nurture with her, and also how deeply touched and empowered they are by her, then as a theologian I have to wonder. I cannot be blind to the extraordinary claims made for Guadalupe, the "pneumatological" relationship implicated in the devotion, etc.

Let me pose a series of questions, all related, that come to mind when theologically studying Guadalupe, *and* when the theologian's feet are kept not so much in ecclesiastical as in sociohistorical Latino realities. Why can't the *Virgen* be the Holy Spirit? Is the Mary-Guadalupe identification really the people's creation and discovery? Or is it possibly a historically understandable, defensive cover, naively (though sincerely) imposed by theological and ecclesiastical elites on themselves and on the people's symbol system? Don't we face a need to rethink the contents of these devotions in(to) pneumatological categories (i.e., *"vertir" las devociones y categorías supuestamente marianas, y sus contenidos, en categorías pneumatológicas*), instead of continuing to insist on the Mary of Nazareth connection, in spite of this connection's apparent historical absence among everyday people? If we continue to insist on the Marian interpretation of Guadalupe, are we not granting "normative" character to a dominant interpretation that, in fact, is not the everyday people's own, and, more importantly, that cannot prove itself to be the only or best interpretation? By insisting on the Marian connection are we not, consequently, disregarding or dismissing the very "popular" dimension in this important component of popular Catholicism? Why do contemporary Latino and non-Latino ecclesiastical elites continue to insist on a Marian connection, based almost exclusively on written texts (*Nican Mopohua* and others)? Is this not a parallel to Stafford Poole's arguments and, thus, flawed methodology?

Why can't we understand the "Mary" categories of Latino Catholicism as *orthodox popular pneumatology*? Is there something inherent in the divine nature of the Spirit that prevents it from being imaged, spoken of, and related with in feminine categories? If colonial Mexico (and Tridentine Spain) were not really free to choose a pneumatological language truly adequate to proper evangelization about the Spirit (and not just to superficial pneumatological ortholalia) among the natives and *mestizos* of Mesoamerica, then I could wonder if the Mexican population might not have borrowed culturally meaningful Marian language (symbols, imagery, etc.), readily available in and through Catholic speech and practice, thereby allowing orthodox pneumatology to *understandably* speak with and to them. The ecclesiastical establishment convinced itself that Guadalupe is Mary of Nazareth; but is this the more correct, orthodox, or only interpretation? Instead of an inculturated mariology, don't we have here a superbly inculturated pneumatology?

I am not implying that Mary of Nazareth (and, consequently, Marian devotion) might be just mediating the maternal or feminine face of God, as some theologians have suggested. And I am certainly *not* saying that Mary *is* the Holy Spirit. I am only asking whether it is possible that what we have here is not mariology but pneumatology, but in an unexpected and brilliantly achieved cultural mediation?

If this were so (and I am far from being satisfied with every element of my own questioning at this stage), then the theological and pastoral consequences are immense, as are the ramifications for an honest intra-Latino ecumenical dialogue (especially with pentecostals!). But then, what happened to legitimate and real Marian devotion? I am only carrying this line of questioning in relation to Guadalupe (and a few other "culturally foundational" *Vírgenes*), but I can see Marian devotions present among our people through many *other* true and traditional Mary-related symbols and language (e.g., rosary, novenas, and titles such as "*la Purísima*") that do not evoke the type of *relationship and response* that Guadalupe elicits from the people.

Where will these new avenues of research take us? I can only guess . . . and want to continue.

I cannot conclude this introduction without thanking Professor Fernando Segovia (of Vanderbilt University) and Professor María Pilar Aquino (my colleague at the University of San Diego) for their initial and insistent suggestion that I gather some of my previously published work into one book. I also want to express my appreciation to Mr. Robert Ellsberg of Orbis Books, for his constant, gentle prodding, and for his patience while I put together the pieces that form this volume.

I am very grateful to Professor Roberto S. Goizueta (of Loyola University, Chicago) for accepting the invitation to write the foreword to this book. Goizueta is a respected scholar who has taken popular Catholicism quite seriously in his own theology. It is indeed an honor for me to count on his friendship and scholarship.

I also want to thank my colleagues in the department of theological and religious studies at the University of San Diego. Most are Euro-Americans, and yet they have consistently shown sensitivity to, awareness of, and respect for U.S. Latino theology, peoples, and cultures. I could not have asked for a better and more supportive community of scholars. The same gratitude is due to many members of the Academy of Catholic Hispanic Theologians of the United States, especially Virgilio Elizondo, Arturo Bañuelas, Jeanette Rodríguez, and Sixto García.

Finally, *and most importantly*, I need to publicly thank the many Latinos/as and Latin Americans who opened up for me (and still do) the beauty, power, and depth of our peoples' faith. They have been and are my privileged teachers. They live in Loma de Cabrera, Dajabón, Santiago de los Caballeros, San Cristóbal, and Santo Domingo (all in the Dominican Republic), in Mexicali (Baja California), and also in Miami, in El Paso and Socorro, and in San Diego and Tijuana. They are too many to name. Without them I would not have written these essays. *Dios y yo conocemos sus nombres y el gran bien que han hecho en mi vida, y les agradecemos de todo corazón.*

1

THE GOD OF THE VANQUISHED
Foundations for a Latino Spirituality

Jesus of Nazareth definitively reveals God to humankind—and not only reveals but *is* himself the revelation of God.

If those two propositions are true (and in Roman Catholicism they are held to be true),[1] then I think we have the foundations of a truly Latino spirituality. This brief article will attempt to propose that if one human life—the experience of Jesus of Nazareth—can reveal who/what/how God really is, then the humanness of that life is legitimately the analogy of God's being. And furthermore, if that one human life is placed within its real sociohistorical context, it reveals not just *any* God but a caring God who is definitively sensed as true in and through the human experience of the vanquishment of Jesus the man. I will further insist that if the preceding is correct, then the vanquished neighbor is in turn the (partial) analogy for understanding Jesus' own revelatory human experience.

Having hopefully established the justification for the legitimacy of my use of the human vanquishment of Jesus as the analogy of God's being, and of the vanquished neighbor as the (partial) analogy of Jesus, I will then proceed to discuss some key components of the U.S. Latino experience and how some of Latino popular Catholicism's foundational emphases and symbols connect with elements of revelation that may be retrieved from the experience of the vanquished Jesus. We will finally gather the results of our discussion and propose in very broad strokes a U.S. Latino spirituality.

Given the nature of this article it will be impossible to give more than a brief, synthetic treatment to the several subjects touched upon here.

Originally published in *Listening: Journal of Religion and Culture*, 27:1 (1992): 70-83.

JESUS, THE REVELATION OF GOD

Jesus reveals God to humankind, according to Christians. And he is the revelation of God. *How* he reveals God, however, is of crucial importance in understanding what is meant by our opening propositions.

Even within Chalcedonian orthodoxy, it is impossible to claim that Jesus' contemporaries perceived him as anything but human.[2] What he taught, what he did, what he suffered, his death and his resurrection, were all events in a life intepreted only as human. An extraordinary life, yes, but only human.

The affirmation of the divine *of* Jesus became common Christian belief only much later. However, the affirmation of the divine *through* Jesus was Christian belief from the very beginning. Through him God was sensed or perceived as reaching and affecting humankind in a unique and definitive way. But what does it mean to say that "through him" God was sensed? It certainly cannot mean that the divine *of* Jesus was understood as somehow "manifesting itself" through his humanness so as to allow itself to be clearly perceived. It means that *through the human experience* of Jesus of Nazareth people could *sense* God in such a way so as to be able to claim for Jesus the role of the definitive revealer (and indeed *the* revelation!) of God.[3]

But if the human experience of Jesus allows humans to sense God in this revelatory way, then the truest and deepest (and thus specifically "Christian") experience of God must be somehow available in humanness. All else that is remembered, approximated, or deduced of or about Jesus in early and later Christianity can be no more than explanation or elaboration (at times normative) of what may be perceived in and through the human experience of the man Jesus. *Christian dogmas, therefore, do not have normative precedence over the human experience of the one who himself is the revelation of God.*

The above, of course, brings up some very important trinitarian, christological, and anthropological issues. But given the specific scope of this article, I cannot discuss most of them here. There are two, however, that seem very pertinent to the subject of a foundation for U.S. Latino spirituality: (1) the God revealed through the human experience of Jesus, and (2) the experience of Jesus as the analogy of God. It might seem methodologically better to change the order of our discussion and start with the theme of analogy. However, that methodological assumption (in fact, a bias) would invert the real, historical order. People first sensed God through Jesus' real-life experience and only later wondered about how to explain it. Today we blind ourselves to key dimensions of Jesus' revelation of God when we invert the historical order.

The God Revealed

Christians claim that God is definitively revealed in and through the *human* experience of one man. Therefore, one must ask the obvious question, What was the human experience of Jesus? Evidently, no answer can pretend to go beyond that which was intimated or made manifest through the words and actions of Jesus. This is the case with any human being. However, in reference to Jesus of Nazareth we are confronted with the fact that what we know of his words and actions has been filtered through the faith option of his early disciples and through their catechetical needs and cultural categories. Most attempts at rediscovering "the historical Jesus" have proven the enormous methodological difficulties of the task. And yet, Christians still insist that the human, historical experience of the man Jesus is the *locus* of divine revelation. Are we faced with no resolution to the apparent dilemma?[4]

If the quest for the human experience of Jesus is conducted as another attempt at reconstructing a life story, we either must create an imagined biography or we must admit that the attempt is necessarily doomed to fail. However, if the quest for that human experience were not expected to yield a biography, or even the barest outline of a biography, then perhaps we might be able to discern some pertinent data from the gospel texts.

There are two points on which contemporary scholarship appears to be in agreement. (1) Jesus of Nazareth seems to have centered his preaching mainly around the theme of the "Reign of God."[5] (2) His preaching and his life ended in utter failure, having been crucified. What do these points say about the human experience of Jesus? Very little indeed, but what can be reasonably deduced from these two facts seems quite interesting.

The man Jesus must have been deeply religious, since his life was risked for explicitly religious motives. He preached about the "Reign of God" to a people that (at least at that particular moment in their history) understood the phrase in religious and political terms. Since Jesus was part of that people, he could not have ignored the religious and political categories through which his listeners would have heard any preaching of the "Reign of God." This preaching, to make any sense and have any meaning, had to presume that God was intervening (or at least could intervene) in human history to radically transform it into a better reality. This better reality, however pictured, had to be a dramatic and permanent improvement over the current reality, both in religious and in political terms.

If Jesus of Nazareth's preaching centered around the theme of the "Reign of God," then the above must also be minimally assumed as part of (or as presumed by) his preaching in first-century Palestine.

He failed, however, to convince his listeners. His preaching was either not acceptable or not accepted, or both. He was put to death by the authorities. Thus, he not only failed as preacher of the "Reign," but he also became a victim of those who had the religious and political power to kill him. He was easily "disposed of," indicating his social (political and religious) insignificance.

The core of his preaching and his final failure: that is mainly what we can assert about Jesus with some degree of confidence. Yet, even admitting the very limited knowledge we have of the experience of the man Jesus, can something be sensed about God in and through the very little we know (or be reasonably deduced from what we know)? Can anything be gleaned about God from these few pieces in an otherwise unsolvable puzzle?

For Jesus, God appears to have been supremely important, a caring God.[6] But his understanding and experience of God seem to have led him down a path that ended in his becoming an insignificant victim of the powerful. For Jesus, God cared enough to intervene in human reality in order to make it permanently better, and yet the personal reality of Jesus became (as a consequence) definitely worse. His view of God and of God's "Reign" provoked his own personal vanquishment. *Jesus did not just fail, he was vanquished as insignificant.*

If, in the experience of the man Jesus, God definitively reveals who God is, then failure and vanquishment must somehow be included in all Christian attempts at understanding and imaging the divinity.[7] Christians claim—based on what can be discovered about the experience of Jesus—that God cares and intervenes in human history to make it better. Christians must also claim—based on the same data and reasoning—that that same God encounters (and experiences?) failure, insignificance, and vanquishment as He/She cares and intervenes in our human world.

To claim otherwise is, first of all, to attempt to ideologically "sanitize" the experience of Jesus, depriving it of its embarrassing, painful, "failure" component (probably the best substantiated datum we have about the historical Jesus). And this, of course, should lead one to wonder about the motives and beneficiaries of this ideological manipulation, and about the type of Christianity (triumphant and oblivious to victims) that would emerge from it.

Secondly, to insist that Jesus is the definitive revelation of who/what/how God is, but then erase from consideration as an integral part of that revelation all that might not fit preconceived (and therefore necessarily non-Christian) ideas about God, is, at the very least, a completely unacceptable route for any Christian understanding of the divinity (in trinitarian and christological terms). Thirdly, if the most public and personal experience of Jesus (his death as a failed and insignificant man) can be doctrinally dismissed or exclusively interpreted through much later dogmatic expressions, then one is led to question whether Christians really believe in the two opening statements of this article. And if they don't, then Christianity must explain why it claims a unique role for Jesus of Nazareth and his cross in human history.

In brief, the God sensed through the experience of the man Jesus is a God who cares and hence intervenes in human history to make it better. But in doing this, God encounters failure, rejection, and the victimizing treatment given the politically and religiously insignificant. Belief in the Resurrection (however it be interpreted) necessarily implies the affirmation of the ultimate significance and success of Jesus' experience and the ultimate truthfulness of the perception of who God is as sensed through the experience of Jesus.

The Experience of Jesus as Analogy of God

What has been said in the preceding section depends, of course, on the human ability to know and make truthful assertions about God. If this ability were not possible, or if it could not arrive at truthful assertions, then we could not speak of God at all, or at least not in ways that were not directly supported and allowed by divine revelation.

Karl Barth[8] strongly criticized the claims of a "natural cognoscibility" of God. For Barth God can only be truthfully known through God's own self-revelation, and nothing in humans allows them a non-revealed, correct knowledge of who/what God is. To pretend that without God's initiative humans may come to a true understanding of God is to raise natural cognoscibility to the level of revelation, dispensing with the need for the latter, and thereby turning the former into an idol. In this context Barth also strongly rejected the notion of the "analogy of being" as a theory that posits the existence of a "third entity" between God and the human creature, allowing the latter to understand God and his/her relationship with God without need of or recourse to God's self-revelation. According to Barth this theory of the "analogy of being" can only lead to and depend on human self-sufficiency and self-aggrandizing, thus further deepening the idolatrous inclination of humankind.

In the Barthian view the unavoidable consequence of the "analogy of being" is that the criterion to determine the truthfulness and correctness of the relationship between God and humankind would not be revelation but human experience. The infinite, qualitative difference between God and creation, as well as the sinful condition within which human experience exists, impede all possible theological deduction in the sense pretended by the "analogy of being." For Barth only divine revelation is the basis for all correct knowledge of God. And all human, analogous speech about God is correct only to the degree that the human speakers submit in obedience to the revelation of God and to the grace of God operating in the life of the speakers.

Without entering here into a complete discussion or critique of Barth's arguments, I do feel that his rejection of the "analogy of being" and of a "natural cognoscibility" of God are certainly well founded if these are viewed as parallel to or without reference to revelation. It seems to me that other contemporary understandings of revelation and (most especially) of grace would not allow for the (European and Protestant neo-orthodox) dichotomizing and individualism that lie behind many of Barth's premises and much of his thinking on the subject. Rejecting all knowledge of God that is not ultimately based on revelation, Barth did not pay attention to the limitations that his central European, culturally determined epistemology forced on his treatment of revelation and grace as he attempted to frame his rejection's arguments. Barth did not culturally critique his philosophical and theological premises and argumentation, thus assuming that the thought, reality-perception, and logic processes of his Western milieu were universally self-evident and correct.[9]

If Jesus of Nazareth is the revelation of God, and this necessarily and first of all means that its *locus* is the human experience of Jesus, then humanness (our common humanness experienced by Jesus) must somehow be revelatory of God, in a sense of "analogy of being." Otherwise we would be confronted with the sole alternatives of either claiming the victory of monophysitism or admitting that revelation is solely (or mainly) a body of doctrinal truths communicated by Jesus' preaching.

The question is whether *human* experience can in fact be revelatory of God. And since not all experiences are or can be so labeled, we then must turn to the human experience of Jesus as the final criterion of what we may sense who/what/how God truthfully is. This means that the real human experience of Jesus is accepted as definitively revelatory of God and, as a consequence, as revelation itself (hence, Chalcedon). This also means that the human experience of the man Jesus is admitted as "analogy" of what/who/how God *is* (hence, once again, Chalcedon). And this in turn implies that the "common entity" in the analogical process is (the Chalcedonean Christ) Jesus himself, and thus not parallel or opposed to God and revelation, as Barth feared.

We have seen that, as far as we can confidently determine, the human experience of Jesus revolved profoundly around a caring God. He risked his life by preaching the arriving "Reign" of that God. We know that, above all else, the human experience of Jesus was marked by his end as a failed, insignificant man who suffered vanquishment and death at the hands of those more politically and religiously powerful than he. So, were we to answer our question about the possibility of human experience being revelatory of God, we would have to appeal to what is sensed through Jesus. And then conclude—based on Jesus himself as revelation—that who/what/how God is *can* be perceived through Jesus' experiences, which communicate caring, which lead to commitment (risk-taking) for the sake of others, and which become one in solidarity with those who are treated as insignificant failures and are victimized by the more powerful. It seems to me *that the human experience of the vanquished, failed, insignificant Jesus of Nazareth is the analogy of what/who/how God is*, with the ambiguity inherent in all analogies (in this case, with the added and inevitable scandalous dimensions of the Christian gospel and of the Chalcedonian doctrine).

TOWARD A LATINO SPIRITUALITY

I said earlier that through the human experience of Jesus people could sense God in such a way as to be able to claim for Jesus the role of the definitive revealer (and indeed *the* revelation) of God. People, however, will glean from a human experience (including that of Jesus of Nazareth) that which culturally they can. Now, this seems self-evident, but it is not.

Culture, Experience, and the "Sensing" of God in the Story of Jesus

Without entering here into cultural theory or analysis, it is important to emphasize that all perception, learning, and understanding (including theological and religious perception, learning, and understanding) are culturally mediated and determined.[10] Societies will understand and even "see" events and "live through" experiences only to the degree that their cultures will allow. And cultures will provide the necessary perception and interpretation tools for "seeing" and "living" only based on the societies' own previous needs to cope and learn. Society's needs provide the possibility for cultural epistemological creations. And where socially shared needs have not required epistemological creations for understanding (or for "seeing" or "living") something, that something will not be seen or lived or interpreted.

When we say that God may be sensed in and through the human experience of Jesus of Nazareth, we are also implying that what may be sensed is only that which culture allows us to sense. What is commonly catalogued in our society as "human," as "experience," and as "God," is all culturally allowed. The past needs of the society have made us sense and understand in some ways and not others what is meant by those terms and (more importantly) what the limits of the reality, experience, and understanding of those terms might be. Consequently, what we might correctly sense about God through the human experience of Jesus is not just that which revelation might make possible (as in Barth), but also and more basically what our culture—in and through its complexity—might allow us to sense. Our cultures will also blind us to significant elements of the human experience of Jesus and, hence, blind us to significant dimensions of what may be sensed about who/what/how God is.

It is part of the essence and scandal of Christianity that God has not addressed humankind definitively through (universally witnessed) miraculous signs, divine dictations, or celestial interventions, much as later Christian folklore (some of it with a high degree of intellectual sophistication) might have attempted to suggest. The simple core is that an insignificant Jew in Roman-occupied Palestine went about preaching the arriving "Reign of God," and that he utterly failed to convince his people and was then killed on a cross by those who were in authority. Only the later belief in the Resurrection could turn this story of failure and vanquishment into a promise and hope of victory. But for whom? For those whose socially shared need to cope with humiliation and depredation had provided the possibility for the cultural creation of tools to "see" (and experience or sense) God through the story of the vanquished Jesus. Only those who understood vanquishment as revelatory could later interpret the resurrection of the victim as the best news in human history. If God reveals Godself in failure and pain, then the victory of the victim (definitively confirmed as infinitely valuable by God) also reveals who/what/how God is.

The core story of Jesus, his human experience, seems to have meant nothing to those who killed him. Nor did he change the lot of those who were his fellow victims in first-century, occupied Palestine. And no matter how modern scholarship might interpret the Resurrection, there seems to be little doubt that a number of Palestinian Jews (and others after them) became convinced that God had approached them in the crucified man Jesus and that who/what/how God is could be sensed in and through the human experience of that one man. The story of vanquishment thus became the *condition* for the promise of their salvation from the real, daily evil they were experiencing.

The ones who could "see" and understand God through a human story of failure and vanquishment were those who themselves experienced these in their human lives. The victors were blinded to the God revealed in and through Jesus, because ultimately their image of God included as necessary elements of power, of conquest, of grandeur, of strength. In their minds human failure, social (political, religious) insignificance, and vanquishment could not, consequently, be an analogy for the being of God.

It can be argued that the more successful Christianity became in the Roman world (and in the centuries since), the more the failure and social insignificance of Jesus had in turn to be made ecclesially, doctrinally, and socially insignificant, covered with the symbols of the victorious (whether these symbols be in politics, publicly sanctioned behavior, theology, spirituality, canon law, art, or liturgy), thus silencing the social, ecclesial need to "see," "experience," and "touch" the ongoing stories that prolong the analogy of God through other broken human lives.

The "Vanquished Neighbor" as Analogy of Jesus

If Jesus is the analogy through which we can definitively sense who/ what/how God really is, it seems to me that *the vanquished neighbor can then be understood as the ongoing analogy of Jesus.*[11] This analogy, however, can only be and always is partial, due to the sinful human inclination to turn the vanquished victim into a vanquishing victor.

Given the role of culture and sin, Christians cannot *guarantee* that their understanding of Jesus is correct unless they in turn appeal to revelation's guide, as Karl Barth would suggest. Unless we want to fall into the trap of thinking that revelation is a body of doctrinal statements communicated by Jesus and distinct from him, we must again recall that Jesus himself is the revelation of God. However, since the one who is revelation is precisely the one that needs to be understood correctly, don't we need for this purpose another analogy that cannot be apart from, parallel, or without recourse to revelation?

If failure, social insignificance, and vanquishment are indispensable dimensions of the revelatory character of the human experience of Jesus, and if the God sensed through that experience is both caring and actively intervening in history, then one may ask if there might not be some revelatory quality within other similar human experiences of innocent vanquishment. One cannot grasp or imagine what Jesus lived, felt, and understood as he confronted his final vulnerability except through grasping and understanding the pain of those who are similarly vulnerable today. The vanquished neighbor becomes thus the analogy of Jesus, and vanquishment itself is the "third, shared entity" in the analogical process.[12]

The danger, of course, is the temptation to either invent a "sufficiently sanitized" vanquished neighbor that would turn failure and social insignificance into meaningless, painless categories, perhaps even inducing religious feelings of pity; or to make the invented vanquished neighbor so heavy with sin that no connection with Jesus could ever be claimed, thus freeing one from any serious obligation toward the neighbor. Here Jesus as revelation of God must be brought in as the criterion for the truthfulness and reality of the vanquishment of the neighbor claimed as analogy. Only a vanquishment similar to Jesus' would qualify as analogy of Jesus.

Once again, however, we are faced with our lack of knowledge about the details of the experience of the historical man Jesus of Nazareth. So, what vanquishment of today could qualify as analogy of Jesus if we do not know what his was about? Or don't we?

We are confident that he was crucified. We know that he was put to death by those in authority in Roman-occupied Palestine. And we can ascertain that he was killed because of his preaching about the arriving "Reign of God" (and we saw earlier what this implied for his Jewish listeners in first-century Palestine). There are plentiful indications that he announced that the God of the Reign was a caring, parent-like God. His preaching brought him into confrontation, not because of the message itself (which was evidently not believed) but apparently because of his having been perceived as a nuisance. He failed to convince his people, and he was easily disposed of by the authorities who did not believe him or regard him as much.

If the common people turned away from him and the authorities killed him, neither group understood him to be anything but an insignificant (and thus vulnerable) and evidently mistaken preacher.

What human experiences of vanquishment would qualify today as analogy of Jesus? The ones in which humans are disposed of as insignificant, wielding their social (or religious) vulnerability against them, without regard for their personal value, intentions, or beliefs. *When and wherever people are treated as disposable nuisances of no real consequence to the dominant or generally accepted perception of reality, there we will find the analogy of Jesus.*

As a consequence of their being analogies of Jesus, through these vanquished neighbors we may sense who/what/how God is. Indeed, it is not through the experiences of those who vanquished them that we would sense God, because Jesus as criterion of truthfulness would indicate that the victors' interpretation of the gospel is (at least significantly) false.

Vanquishment in U.S. Latino Experience

The reader might be wondering what the preceding pages have to do with a U.S. Latino spirituality. Well, it seems to me that to grasp the foundations of Latino spirituality in this country, one must first step back and see how these roots are clearly parts of the tree of Christianity. The Latino experience in this country is, above all else, an experience founded on vanquishment and thus directly related to what we have been discussing here.

There are several cultural communities in the United States that are part of the larger Latino community. Statistics might describe the general Latino population through a wide range of categories, mostly showing communities suffering under prejudice, poverty, inadequate education, etc. Though this picture is not applicable to all Latino individuals or groups in the country, it does describe the reality of the majority.[13] But what statistics might make us forget is the fundamental experience shared by *all* Latino communities in the United States. And that is the experience of vanquishment.

Some Latino groups are the result of the rape of their ancestors by the conquering Spaniards, while others are the outcome of willing *mestizaje*. There are communities that trace their roots back to the violence of the *encomienda* and others to the violence of the African slave trade. Many were here when the United States militarily conquered and illegally expropriated their land in the nineteenth century. Still others came because they had become the losing victims of political and economic struggles in other lands. But in *all* cases, the Latino cultural communities are here as the result of vanquishment, of having become the losing victims of someone else's victory.[14]

All of the communities (Mexican-American, Puerto Rican, Cuban-American, etc.) are distinct, with their own histories and cultures, as well as with the shared elements of language, religious symbols, and worldview. Yet behind all the distinctions, and even divisions, there lies this common experience of vanquishment that—however they might explain it—does bind them together. The contexts and circumstances of each community's experience of victimization are different, of course, as are each community's coping response to it. But these differences do not at all cancel the one underlying fact: Latinos are in the United States as the vanquished. And the dominant Euro-American culture treats them as such.

Popular Catholicism as Religion of the Vanquished

The sources of Latino popular Catholicism in the United States are to be found in three continents.[15] From pre-Tridentine, medieval Spain Latinos received a type of Christianity that took root among them well before Lutherans, Calvinists, Anglicans, and Roman Catholics reformed European Christianity. From the native peoples of the Americas, and from the enslaved Africans brought to the Americas, Latinos inherited the cultural prisms through which they filtered and understood Spanish Catholicism.

Through the three sources U.S. Latinos also received the common experience of victimization. In 1492 Spain had just emerged victorious from the centuries-old process of the *Reconquista* against the Muslim kingdoms of the Iberian peninsula. The struggle against the "infidels," while admiring and sharing the same land with them, created that distinctly generous while intolerant national character that defines Spain.[16]

The Spaniards brought the mentality and attitudes that had seen them through the Iberian *Reconquista* to the Western Hemisphere. To claim that what started in the Americas in 1492 was merely or mainly a case of "discovery" (or even of "encounter") is to ideologically manipulate the facts. There is no doubt that the Europeans discovered a hemisphere *they* did not know existed on the other side of the Atlantic Ocean, and consequentially there was an encounter of peoples and cultures that had never seen each other before. But to pretend that this was all that happened is to forget that in the very act of discovery, at the same moment (and the period documents leave no doubt about this), the Spaniards "took possession of these lands" in the name of the Spanish crown. This was, clearly, an act of conquest.[17]

The discovery was solely *for the purpose of* taking possession of other people's lands, without regard for the native inhabitants or their rights. The subsequent meeting of cultures and peoples was not for the sake of mutual befriending and respect. The so-called encounter was solely *for the purpose of* dispossessing the natives (and later, the Africans) of what was rightfully theirs and forcing them into mandatory labor for the exclusive benefit of the Europeans.

And in this context, and not in some idealized world, evangelization began in the Americas. *The proclamation of the Christian gospel was made possible only because the evangelized had first been conquered, their lands and freedom taken from them, and their cultures invaded.* The much-discussed Christianizing aims of the Columbus voyages (and of those who followed him) always depended on conquering people first so that missionaries could announce the gospel to them later. The fact that the inhabitants had to be made victims first so as to evangelize them second seems to escape many today. We cannot avoid pointing to the terrible consequences wrought by the context of victimization both on doctrinal content and catechetical method.

The Amerindian and the African in this hemisphere received the Christian message as victims; this occured only because they had been made victims by Christians. The Europeans attempted to evangelize their victims from the position of the victors, while the depredation continued around them, somehow unaware that the social roles imposed by the conquest—added to the very important cultural differences between themselves and the Amerindians and Africans—were profoundly affecting what and how Christianity was received by their victims.[18] From the very beginning, therefore, the Christianity received and understood by the people (i.e., "popular" Catholicism) was molded by the experience of vanquishment as its constituting context. All other cultural, religious, constitutive elements of popular Catholicism (including doctrinal contents, ethical demands, and symbolic expressions) depend completely on this one context.

Latino popular Catholicism was present in Florida and the Southwest for several centuries prior to the Euro-American invasions, and it never went away. It has remained Christianity's main faith-form among U.S. Latinos. It could survive and even thrive in this country because it was (and is) designed to provide meaning and support to those who experience vanquishment. Popular Catholicism seems to be the one major component of Latino cultural reality that has not been profoundly invaded by the Euro-American dominant culture. It still acts as an indispensable bearer of values, traditions, symbols, and worldview for and among U.S. Latino communities. The importance of popular Catholicism in the cultural self-definition and self-preservation of U.S. Latinos cannot be exaggerated.[19]

The Vanquished Jesus and Popular Catholicism

Latino popular Catholicism in the United States is a very complex, elaborate, and broad religious universe. Anyone familiar with it will recall that, among other elements, some that stand out are the emphasis placed on crucifixion scenes, on very graphic depictions of the suffering and bleeding Jesus, on devotions to crucifixes and crosses, and on particular Good Friday ceremonies recalling the torture, death, and burial of Jesus as well as the sorrows of his mother. Most of the scenes and depictions clearly depend on the canonical gospel accounts of the Passion, with some secondary contributions either from extracanonical (gnostic) gospels or from the popular imagination. The doctrinal contents expressed through the symbols, however, seem to be quite orthodox even where the artistic or performative medium would not agree with current Euro-American tastes.[20]

The emphasis, then, is on Good Friday, not on Easter. On the cross, and not on the Resurrection. On vanquishment, not on victory. It could be claimed that this is due to popular Catholicism's lack of belief in the risen Jesus. However, any familiarity with the Latino religious universe would show that the people pray and deal with Jesus (even at his most extreme depictions) as a *living* person. Clearly, for the people, Jesus of Nazareth is alive today. Why then the emphasis on Good Friday, on cross and suffering?

I believe that beyond and *besides* the minimally necessary practices and beliefs—confession of faith in the death and resurrection of Jesus and on the basics of the gospel and creeds—Christians have always and will always project *their* experience of life onto Jesus of Nazareth. One of the most fundamental of Christian beliefs is that the God sensed in and through the human Jesus is in solidarity with *our* lives, whatever these might be like. Evidently, not all projections would be acceptable to Christian orthodoxy, but the fact of the projection happening is vividly substantiated in every Christian generation and tradition. U.S. Latinos and Euro-Americans are no exception.

Latinos in this country, as we have seen, bear the mark of the unwilling victim. Euro-Americans bear the sign of the victor. Among Christians, the former project onto Jesus their suffering, and the latter project their success. Latinos concentrate on the cross while Euro-Americans emphasize the Resurrection. Both groups claim to believe in the cross as much as in the Resurrection, and yet their symbolic projections express their distinct, fundamental experiences of life.

Latino popular Catholicism looks to Jesus as the suffering, vanquished human in and through whom who/what/how God is may be definitively sensed. The victimized Jesus is the vehicle through which God reaches and touches humankind, and through which humankind may somehow reach and touch God. This vanquished Jesus is the analogy through which our people sense that God really is caring, supportive, and in solidarity with their suffering and pain.

Confirming Karl Barth's assertion that only in connection with revelation can the truth about God be understood (though not necessarily confirming his views on revelation and grace), it seems clear that as long as Latino popular Catholicism keeps the victimized Jesus as the center of its sense of God, this Catholicism will speak the truth about the caring God. But when other symbols replace the suffering Jesus, be these other religious or more broadly cultural symbols, the sense of God may be vitiated.

It is important to note that the projection of victory onto Jesus by Latinos (i.e., understandings, symbols, and celebrations of resurrection) can and will come as an authentic consequence of their actual liberation from vanquishment, but not as the imposed result of ecclesiastical orthodoxy or of deculturizing evangelism. What does not authentically flow from the people's experience will sooner or later become an idol impeding their correct relationship with the true God, and thus an unacceptable analogy of who/what/how God really is.

In brief, the vanquished, failed Jesus is the analogy of the being of God among Latinos in the United States. The people have symbolically projected their experience of victimization onto him, emphasizing depictions of his vulnerability, while sensing through him the solidarity and care of God in the midst of their own vulnerability. Granted that this is not all that the Christian gospel proclaims, but to impose the projection of victory (resurrection), if not an authentic expression of experience, would only perpetuate the people's imposed role as victims.

Not Only Victims: The Hope for Tomorrow

Victimization is the common experience of U.S. Latinos. It is at the root of their birth as distinct cultures. It is at the source of the religion of the people. It would not be difficult, given these facts, to arrive at the conclusion that the role of the victim will always be part of Latino experience. And yet, that is not the authentic or inevitable conclusion within the Latino cultural milieux. The symbols of popular Catholicism do not convey such a reductionist message.

Latinos may experience life as victims, but that is not all that Latinos are or experience. Their culture and history are profoundly marked from the start by victimization, yes, but just as strongly and as early by rebellion. It would be a disastrous ideological ploy to believe that suffering and failure have no important part in the self-definition of Latinos, when social reality is and has been clearly saying otherwise. But it would be an equally cruel and disastrous ideological ploy to want to define Latinos (or for Latinos to define themselves) as capable of playing *solely* the social role of the victim. Reality does not allow such reductionism.

In the honorable quest for an adequate justification for liberative action, it would be irresponsible to portray the Amerindian or African worlds that preceded the conquest as ideal societies, free from the ravages of cruelty or injustice, and somehow surprisingly filled with all the values and elements that contemporary Western societies wish they had and fear to have lost. This idealized view of what was before the European conquest of the Americas is very far from the documented truth. I realize that sometimes even Latinos wish they could rewrite a painful history by creating a beautiful but imaginary past, from before the colonial period. However, the Amerindian or African social realities vanquished by the Europeans were seldom less cruel than the new order imposed from across the Atlantic. One may not deny the truth, and certainly not if the intent is liberation. There is no need to go beyond truth in order to justify and unveil the people's quest for another, more humane reality.

Because of the same respect for truth, one must remember that Amerindians and Africans never willingly gave up their lands and freedom. And still more important, one must note that the peoples born out of the European and Euro-American conquests sustained (and do so even today) the very explicit "doubt"[21] that the new order imposed on them (by these and all subsequent conquests) is the last, permanent word in their history.

This "shared doubt" has promoted social reinvindication movements, stirring communities and individuals into significant action. This "shared doubt" has become, not infrequently in U.S. Latino history, the force to keep hope alive, to justify the need for communal solidarity, and to create the symbols (religious or otherwise) through which to express and confirm hope and solidarity.

The "shared doubt" is ultimately founded on the lived and felt premise that the convincing abilities of European and Euro-American dominant ideologies have not erased the thirst for justice and freedom. These ideologies have not completely or sufficiently convinced the victims of the "evidence" establishing their victimization. The "doubt" denies finality to present reality. It reminds the people of the penultimate quality of their condition. And at the same time, the longer this imposed victimization is robbed of its "evident" justification and of its pretended definitive character, the more it becomes possible and credible for the people to sustain their hope in the alternative.

Popular Catholicism, through its complex symbol-making system, seems to have successfully managed to maintain the dream of a supportive, caring alternative by claiming that this hope is similar to God's sensed being, as found in the suffering, victimized Jesus. In other words, another reality is possible because it is sensed as the being of God, through Jesus. And just as Jesus has endured victimization but not been ultimately conquered, so will their suffering not lead them to be *only* victims at the end.

The symbols of popular Catholicism portray God as provident in a radically caring way.[22] The God sensed through these symbols is not the powerful, conquering divinity of the victorious and successful, but a parental (maternal!), familial, communal God whose providence is encouragement and support, shared suffering and quiet determination, and final justice-building.

The festive and aesthetic/poetic elements in all Latino cultures,[23] the people's constant and explicit reference to the future and to God's will as the determining factor of the future, their willingness to fight to maintain communal solidarity in spite of significant social woundedness,[24] their observance and faithful transmission of basic cultural values and traditions across the centuries, and so much more, point to a fundamental attitude not only of "shared doubt" vis-à-vis victimizing reality and ideologies, but of active hope for the future. It is not merely a silent, internal wish for a change of conditions, but rather an active creation of symbols and means to foster hope, to sustain communal solidarity, and to prepare for the alternative, all the while believing that only God will grant the definitive alternative.

U.S. Latino experience, in brief, is surely one of vanquishment, but also one of active hope in a good alternative from God. Popular Catholicism has symbolized these dimensions in the depictions and experience of solidarity with the suffering Jesus, as well as in the belief and expressions of God's caring providence.

A LATINO SPIRITUALITY

At the start of this article I said that at its conclusion we would gather the results of our discussions and attempt to briefly paint a U.S. Latino spirituality in some very broad strokes. I do not believe that the task is one of creating such a spirituality, since it already exists, but rather unveiling the fundamental elements that seem to compose it.

Within the Catholic tradition, a spirituality seems to be an *understanding* that emerges as the *result* of the way the same basic gospel

dimensions are *combined* in the daily life of Christians. The understanding, as I am calling it, must be clear enough to encourage a particular and distinctive way of Christian living and knowing, while at the
same time be broad or generic enough to allow for growth and individ-
uality (personal and generational). Evidently, the fact that people are
dealing with these dimensions assumes their Christian faith and basic
acceptance of the gospel and creeds.

Needless to say, popular Catholicism reads the gospel texts quite literally, enriching its interpretation of them with noncanonical traditions
and especially with commonsensical wisdom acquired throughout the
centuries. Thus, what the canonical texts do not say, popular Catholicism might supply, often with some surprisingly wise and plausible
exegeses.

The dimensions, which combined in different ways result in different
spiritualities, appear to be: (1) the way God is perceived, and how this
perception was arrived at, (2) what are believed to be the most important moments and characteristics of Jesus' life and message, (3) how
neighbor and community relate to Jesus, to God, and to the individual
Christian, and, as a consequence of the first three dimensions, (4) what
are the Christian's proper options and lifestyle.

How these elements are interpreted, related, and therefore combined
with one another will provide the shape of any spirituality. Evidently,
most persons or groups do not go about explicitly meditating on these
particular dimensions and then providing themselves with "their" spirituality. What in fact occurs is a much more fluid, long, and implicit process of growth, crises, doubts, discoveries, commitments, etc., that only
in retrospective can be identified as resulting in a specific spirituality.

With five centuries now behind them, Latinos could summarize their
distinct spirituality's understanding, in broad strokes, as follows:

In and through the human experience of Jesus of Nazareth, God may
be sensed as reaching and touching humankind in a definitive way.
However, the characteristics of this one human experience—once
understood in its sociohistorical context—make the revelatory *locus*
and the God revealed to be quite different from what might be
expected by the dominant ideologies. This is so because the medium
of revelation is the insignificant, failed, and vanquished life of a first-
century Palestinian Jew, who was easily disposed of by the authorities
of his day. Thus, the God sensed through this revelatory medium could
not authentically be one of power and victorious conquest but, rather,
one who is in solidarity with and caring for those who are insignificant
victims with and like Jesus. Later Christian reflection suggests to
Latinos that perhaps the God sensed in and through Jesus might suffer
and be victimized too.

The most correct interpretation of Jesus' life would be one in which
he is understood as caring for and being in solidarity with the poor and

suffering, especially because he himself was a victim, too. In Latino experience, a trial before the authorities, torture, cross, and burial (however these might be lived across the centuries by different peoples) would be the most fundamental moments in any life viewed as generous and selfless. The sayings and parables would only confirm the overall view that Jesus was extraordinarily compassionate toward the suffering and that he himself was a victim of suffering.

And so, if Jesus lived such a life, anyone claiming to be his follower must imitate him in this selfless solidarity with the victims. Knowledge of doctrine or of scripture, or any other "religious talent," will ultimately mean little when compared with the paramount importance of the compassionate, selfless care of the suffering neighbor. Jesus will identify as *his* only those who have acted like him, not those who claimed to be Christians only because they held to "correct belief."

Therefore, a Christian must be first and foremost a person committed to solidarity with suffering victims. And this commitment must be brought to bear in every aspect of daily life, both private and public.

A deeply symbolic and analogous ("sacramental") way of Christianity, Latino popular Catholicism reaches into its depths and there touches the experience of vanquishment, discovering from within it the caring touch of God through the victimized Jesus. For Latinos the hope for God's tomorrow relativizes the pretensions of the imposed present. Life then is lived in active expectation, without fleeing from the side of the victims. Jesus of Nazareth is still one of them.

Notes

1. See for example: Second Vatican Council, *Dei Verbum*, 2, 4; *Lumen Gentium*, 5; etc. This article was enriched by several conversations with my colleague, Dr. Patricia Plovanich, to whom I express my appreciation. The ideas expressed here, however, are my responsibility.

2. On Nicæa and Chalcedon, see Denzinger-Schönmetzer (35th ed.), nn. 125-126 and 300-303. See also, J. Pelikan, *The Christian Tradition: A History of the Development of Doctrine. Volume I: The Emergence of the Catholic Tradition* (Chicago: University of Chicago Press, 1971), 172-277; and, L.D. Davis, *The First Seven Ecumenical Councils (325-787): Their History and Theology* (Wilmington: Michael Glazier Books, 1987), 33-78, 81-131.

3. See J. Pelikan, cit. See, especially, two remarkable works: J.P. Meier, *A Marginal Jew: Rethinking the Historical Jesus* (New York: Doubleday, 1991. Anchor Bible Reference Library), vol. I; and, E. Schillebeeckx, *Jesus: An Experiment in Christology* (New York: Crossroad, 1981).

4. See E. Schillebeeckx, 62-102.

5. See C. Bravo, *Jesús, hombre en conflicto. Un estudio del evangelio de Marcos* (Mexico: CRT, 1986); J.L. Segundo, *El hombre de hoy ante Jesús de Nazaret* (Madrid: Ediciones Cristiandad, 1982), II/1, 69-250; R. Schnackenburg, "Reino de Deus," in *Diccionário de teologia bíblica*, ed. J.B. Bauer (São Paulo: Edições Loyola, 1978), II, 947-964.

6. See J. Jeremias, *The Central Message of the New Testament* (London: SCM Press, 1965); O. Hofius, "Padre," in *Diccionario teológico del Nuevo Testamento,* eds. L. Coenen, E. Beyreuther and H. Bietenhard (Salamanca: Ediciones Sígueme, 1983), III, 242-248.

7. See W. McWilliams, *The Passion of God* (Macon: Mercer University Press, 1985); F. Varillon, *The Humility and Suffering of God* (New York: Alba House, 1983); M. Hellwig, *Jesus. The Compassion of God* (Wilmington: Michael Glazier Books, 1983); G. Gutiérrez, *El Dios de la vida* (Lima: Centro de Estudios y Publicaciones, 1989).

8. On what follows, for example, see K. Barth, *Church Dogmatics* (Edinburgh: T.T. Clark, 1975 and 1978), I/1, 41, 119, 168-173, 239, 242-247, 333-347, 436-438, and I/2, 37, 43, 144. Also, I. Mancini, "Dios," in *Nuevo diccionário de teología,* eds. G. Barbaglio and S. Dianich (Madrid: Ediciones Cristiandad, 1982), I, 312-344; P.A. Sequeri, "Analogía," in *Diccionario teológico interdisciplinar,* eds. L. Pacomio, et al. (Salamanca: Ediciones Sígueme, 1982), I, 400-412; L. Scheffczyk, "Analogía de la fe," in *Sacramentum Mundi,* K. Rahner, ed. (Barcelona: Editorial Herder, 1976), I, 138-143; J. Splett and L.B. Puntel, "Analogía del ser," in *Sacramentum Mundi,* I, 143-152; G. Söhngen, "La sabiduría de la teología por el camino de la ciencia," in *Mysterium Salutis,* ed. J. Feiner and M. Löhrer (Madrid: Ediciones Cristiandad, 1969), I, 977-1049.

9. See T. McCarthy, *The Critical Theory of Jürgen Habermas* (Cambridge: MIT Press, 1985); J. Habermas, *Knowledge and Human Interests* (Boston: Beacon Press, 1971), 301-317; R.S. Goizueta, *Liberation, Method and Dialogue* (Atlanta: Scholars Press, 1988); J.C. Scannone, ed., *Sabiduría popular, símbolo y filosofía* (Buenos Aires: Editorial Guadalupe, 1984); idem, *Evangelización, cultura y teología* (Buenos Aires: Editorial Guadalupe, 1990); P.L. Berger and T. Luckmann, *The Social Construction of Reality* (New York: Doubleday, 1967); R. Wuthnow, et al., *Cultural Analysis* (London: Routledge & Kegan Paul, 1984); M. Vovelle, *Ideologies and Mentalities* (Chicago: University of Chicago Press, 1990); P. Bourdieu, *A economia das trocas simbólicas* (São Paulo: Editora Perspectiva, 1974), 3-202; A. Schutz, *El problema de la realidad social* (Buenos Aires: Amorrortu Editores, 1974), 195-316; idem, *Collected Papers II. Studies in Social Theory* (The Hague: Martinus Nijhoff, 1976), 226-273.

10. See for example, Berger and Luckmann, *The Social Construction of Reality,* cit. Also, R.A. Shweder and R.A. LeVine, eds., *Culture Theory: Essays on Mind, Self, and Emotion* (Cambridge: Cambridge University Press, 1984); R.A. Shweder, *Thinking through Cultures* (Cambridge: Harvard University Press, 1991).

11. See for example, J.I. González Faus, *Proyecto de hermano. Visión creyente del hombre* (Santander: Editorial Sal Terrae, 1987), 79-180; J. Sobrino, *Jesús en América Latina. Su significado para la fe y la cristología* (Santander: Editorial Sal Terrae, 1982; English trans. *Jesus in Latin America* (Maryknoll, New York: Orbis Books, 1987), 223-234; J. Severino Croatto, "El Mesías liberador de los pobres," in *Cristología en América Latina,* ed. Equipo Seladoc (Salamanca: Ediciones Sígueme, 1984), 235-243.

12. See E. Levinas, *Humanismo del otro hombre* (Mexico: Siglo XXI Editores, 1974); U. Vázquez Moro, *El discurso sobre Dios en la obra de E.*

30   *The God of the Vanquished*

Levinas (Madrid: Publicaciones de la Universidad Pontificia de Comillas, 1982); A. Parra, "La hermenéutica palabra-vida, hermenéutica de los pobres," in *Revista Latinoamericana de Teología*, 18 (1989), 365-377.

13. See F.D. Dean and M. Tienda, *The Hispanic Population of the United States* (New York: Russell Sage Foundation, 1987).

14. See R. Acuña, *Occupied America: A History of Chicanos* (New York: Harper & Row, 1981. 2nd ed.); M.V. Gannon, *The Cross in the Sand* (Gainesville: University of Florida Presses, 1983. 2nd ed.); W. Moquin and C. van Doren, eds., *A Documentary History of the Mexican Americans* (New York: Praeger, 1971); J.P. Fitzpatrick, *Puerto Rican Americans* (Englewood Cliffs: Prentice-Hall, 1987. 2nd ed.).

15. Popular Catholicism is quickly becoming the main *locus theologicus* among U.S. Latino scholars. From among a growing bibliography, see C.G. Romero, *Hispanic Devotional Piety* (Maryknoll, New York: Orbis Books, 1991); O. Espín, "The Vanquished, Faithful Solidarity and the Marian Symbol," in *On Keeping Providence*, eds. J. Coultas and B. Doherty (Terre Haute: St. Mary of the Woods College Press, 1991), 84-101; idem, "Tradition and Popular Religion: An Understanding of the *Sensus Fidelium*," chapter 3 below and in *Frontiers of U.S. Hispanic Theology*, ed. A.F. Deck (Maryknoll, New York: Orbis Books, 1992); idem, "Grace and Humanness," in *We Are a People! Initiatives in Hispanic American Theology*, ed. R.S. Goizueta (Minneapolis: Fortress Press, 1992); idem, "Popular Catholicism among Latinos," chapter 5 below and in *Hispanic Catholic Culture in the U.S.*, ed. J. Dolan and A. Deck (Notre Dame: University of Notre Dame Press, 1994); idem, with S. García, "Lilies of the Field: A Hispanic Theology of Providence and Human Responsibility," in *Proceedings of the Catholic Theological Society of America*, 44 (1989), 70-90; R.S. Goizueta, *Caminemos con Jesús: Toward a Hispanic/Latino Theology of Accompaniment* (Maryknoll, New York: Orbis Books, 1995); A. García-Rivera, *St. Martin de Porres: The "Little Stories" and the Semiotics of Culture* (Maryknoll, New York: Orbis Books, 1995).

16. See O. Espín, "Trinitarian Monotheism and Popular Catholicism: The Case of Sixteenth-Century Mexico," chapter 2 below and in *Missiology*, 20:2 (1992), 177-204.

17. See L. Rivera Pagán, *Evangelización y violencia. La conquista de América* (Río Piedras: Editorial Cemí, 1990); J. Höffner, *Colonização e evangelho. Ética da colonização espanhola no século de ouro* (Rio de Janeiro: Editora Presença, 1977).

18. See Espín, "Trinitarian Monotheism and Popular Catholicism," cit.

19. See O. Espín, "Religiosidad popular: un aporte para su definición y hermenéutica," in *Estudios Sociales*, 58 (1984), 41-57; idem, "Popular Religion as an Epistemology (of Suffering)," chapter 6 below and in *Journal of Hispanic/Latino Theology*, 2:2 (1994), 55-78; idem, with S. García, "The Sources of Hispanic Theology," in *Proceedings of the Catholic Theological Society of America*, 43 (1988), 122-125.

20. For a more thorough history of Latino popular Catholicism in the United States, see Espín, "Popular Catholicism among Latinos," cit. See also my "Tradition and Popular Religion: An Understanding of the *Sensus Fidelium*," cit.

21. See A. Gramsci, *Os intelectuais e a organização da cultura* (Rio de Janeiro: Editora Civilização Brasileira, 1979); H. Portelli, *Gramsci y el bloque*

histórico (Mexico: Siglo XXI Editores, 1973); R. Ortiz, *A consciência fragmentada. Ensaios de cultura popular e religião* (Rio de Janeiro: Editora Paz e Terra, 1980).

22. See O. Espín, "The Vanquished, Faithful Solidarity and the Marian Symbol," cit., and "Tradition and Popular Religion," cit.

23. See R.S. Goizueta, "Theology as Intellectually Vital Inquiry: The Challenge of/to U.S. Hispanic Theologians," in *Proceedings of the Catholic Theological Society of America*, 46 (1991), 58-69.

24. See A.M. Isasi-Díaz and Y. Tarango, *Hispanic Women: Prophetic Voice in the Church* (San Francisco: Harper & Row, 1988).

2

TRINITARIAN MONOTHEISM AND THE BIRTH OF POPULAR CATHOLICISM

The Case of Sixteenth-Century Mexico

Popular Catholicism is an omnipresent reality in almost every U.S. Latino community. Whether one is dealing with Puerto Ricans in New York or Chicanos in Los Angeles or Cuban-Americans in Miami, popular Catholicism seems to be ever-present in all the Latino cultural communities. The external symbols used to express a particular community's history might vary, but the fundamental structures and components seem to be basically the same across the country.

When confronted with this popular religious universe, most modern-day evangelizers tend to react either with disgust or bewilderment. All too often Latino popular Catholicism is denigrated as a bastardized version of "official" Roman Catholicism, a syncretic aberration of Christianity, or at best the terrible result of religious ignorance. Contemporary Euro-Americans (both Catholic and Protestant) are frequently inclined to accuse Spain's colonial missionaries of incompetence in communicating the gospel. Most often Latinos themselves are treated either as incapable of anything but a magical approach to Christianity (supposedly because the poor can do no better) or they are viewed as pagan masses who have no idea of what true Christianity is all about. Fortunately, reality is much too complex for such simplistic (and wrong!) answers.

It is my belief that Latino popular Catholicism in this country is the result of historical and cultural processes that have required religious

Originally published in *Missiology*, 20:2 (1992): 177-204.

categories and symbols in order to permit the survival of Latinos in a hostile context. Secondly, popular Catholicism is and has been the medium through which generations of U.S. Latinos have been evangelized in culturally meaningful ways, thus allowing for a specific "Latino" inculturation of the Christian gospel. However, it seems to me that *at the deepest roots of U.S. Latino Catholicism there lies a concept and an image of God.*

It seems that the introduction of Christian trinitarian monotheism in the Americas has not merited the attention it deserves. The research emphases have always been placed on either the sociopolitical and cultural dimensions of Christianity (both "official" and "popular"), or on the more eye-catching components of popular Catholicism, such as Marian devotions. And yet, at the foundation of it all, there lie the concept and images of the divine which have not yet received the necessary scholarly attention. If there can be no orthodox Christianity without trinitarian monotheist belief, then to reflect on the vehicles, contents, and degrees of proclamation and acceptance of trinitarian monotheism is of utmost importance in determining the orthodox quality of evangelization and of the resulting Christian community.

It is my contention that trinitarian evangelization and belief outside of European cultural milieux are usually too difficult if not impossible. This is due to several historical and cultural elements. First of all, the doctrines concerning the Trinity have been expressed, ever since the councils of Christian antiquity, through the cultural and linguistic vehicles of European philosophical traditions. No serious attempt has been made by the main Christian theologics to escape this cultural and linguistic straightjacket (the efforts of Jesuits Ricci in China and DeNobili in India perhaps being exceptions). And since in Western Europe these doctrines have not raised the passionate arguments among Christians that would have led to a development of thought and language beyond conciliar, creedal categories, evangelization on the Trinity in and from the West has apparently been held hostage to European linguistic and cultural thought patterns. The popularized, catechetical explanations of trinitarian doctrines have in fact confused the very contents they have tried to simplify, leading to either practical cryptotritheism or undistinguishing, strict monotheism among most European and Euro-American Christians. Church preaching on the Trinity has repeated either classic, creedal language or popularized, catechetical simplifications. Trinitarian belief apparently has little to do with the actual lives of millions of First World Christians, except as an "ortholalic" creedal statement.

A second element that impedes trinitarian monotheist belief outside of the European milieux seems to be the apparent fact that most culturally non-European human groups have not had (and found no reason to have) the thought patterns and worldviews necessary to understand and appropriate trinitarian monotheism *until they became "European-*

ized" to some degree. But this, of course, raises other important questions about cultural invasion in the name of religion and about the possibilities of inculturation of the faith.

A third element has to do with the very vehicles chosen to communicate trinitarian doctrine. There is no question that these catechetical channels of evangelization can and do determine what, to what degree, and in what way the hearers of the proclamation understand and accept it. Obviously, the cultures of the evangelizers and hearers and their prior theological understanding, or possibility of understanding, of a given component of the Christian message should lead to this or that choice of communication vehicle. Nevertheless, when cultural differences are deep between missionary and hearer the possibility of successfully finding inculturated evangelization channels seems to be highly unlikely, thereby resulting in an incomplete proclamation. And if that which is incompletely presented is the doctrine of trinitarian monotheism, then the foundations of newly planted Christianity are dangerously weak.

It would be impossible to document in a single article all the cases and arguments that would be pertinent to this discussion. I will limit myself to *one example* which, I believe, will illustrate what I have stated above. Here I will be discussing sixteenth-century Mexico and how trinitarian monotheism was taught to the native Amerindian populations. We will discover that the elements that impede trinitarian evangelization were present then and there, and that the resulting Christianity was strongly christocentric but dangerously weak in its trinitarian belief. And *since sixteenth-century Mexican evangelization stands at the root of the Christian faith of approximately half of all U.S. Latinos, then it is important to look back into this first formative period. Latino popular Catholicism was born in part out of the inadequacies of early colonial trinitarian catechesis.*

The reader should realize, however, that U.S. Latino popular Catholicism is immensely complex and that no one article of this kind (on one specific cultural group and on one moment of its history) could ever come close to a sufficient presentation or analysis of the U.S. Latino popular religious universe or of any of its contemporary components.[1]

In pointing out the inadequacies of trinitarian monotheist evangelization in sixteenth-century Mexico, I am not implying that these serious difficulties are fixed or cast in stone, so to speak. Inculturated and therefore effective evangelization is possible outside of the European and Euro-American cultural milieux, but dealing with the Trinity is far more difficult than missionaries (of whatever historical period) would care to admit. Disregarding or downplaying the absolutely crucial place of trinitarian monotheism in Christianity—usually substituting the inadequacies of preaching with christocentric emphases—is certainly not the way to confront the difficulties.

It might be added that the problems occur in the area of culture and have little to do with (mainline) denominational doctrinal differences. Catholics and Protestants all face the same dilemmas. If sixteenth-century Mexican natives had faced Protestant missionaries, the eventual result would have been some form of "popular Protestantism." *Mutatis mutandi*, this is probably one reason why *some* types of Protestantism are increasingly acceptable to Latinos today.

One last note: when researching the sources I have been struck by the frequency with which christocentric evangelization appears to flourish where trinitarian proclamation does not seem to be as successful. I point this out in the article. Without creating unacceptable doctrinal separations between christology and trinitarian theology, it might be interesting to follow this intuition through research and discover if the latter confirms the former.

A HISTORY OF VANQUISHMENT AND DOMINATION

At least half of present-day United States territory was part of Latin America for several centuries after the Columbus voyages of the late fifteenth century. Most of these lands became "American" less than 150 years ago, while Christianity had been planted in them well before the Pilgrims left Europe for the New England coast. The first Christian permanent settlement in what is now the United States was established in St. Augustine, Florida, in 1565.[2]

To understand today's Latino Catholics one must recall these historical facts: U.S. Latinos have a long history, dating back to the sixteenth century, and cannot be adequately comprehended without this heritage. Implied in what I am saying is that the history of this country cannot be *factually* told and explained without explicit reference to Latin American history, since half of our land and millions of our people had a long and rich Latin cultural heritage before forcibly joining the country.[3] Latinos are not, by definition, immigrants. Very many have certainly come this century, but these have joined an already existing mosaic of Latino communities, some dating back several hundred years (well before the British settled at Jamestown).

Very many U.S. Latinos, and definitely their lands, were militarily conquered by Euro-Americans in the nineteenth century. With the exception of the purchase of Florida (over which the population had no control either), all other traditionally Latino territories were forcibly joined to the American union.[4] The ideology of "Manifest Destiny" justified the military conquest and occupation of the western lands. The historical facts of Spain's conquest, followed by the Euro-American conquest—both instances producing vanquished peoples and occupied territories, all justified in the name of God—cannot be disregarded when considering the role of religion and especially of the concept and images of God among U.S. Latinos.

When immigrant Latinos joined the already established Latino communities, the newcomers fell under the same stereotyping and humiliating prejudices and structures created—as a consequence of the conquests —by the dominant Euro-American population. Indeed, immigration is not the common experience among Latinos in this country. What is commonly shared is the experience of vanquishment and domination.

As already stated, one must keep in mind these facts of history, with all their cruelty and pretended religious justifications. Not to contextualize the concept and images of God within this historical framework, or to soften the latter's cruelty for any purpose, is to contribute to the permanence of the conditions of discrimination and prejudice.

Let us briefly review the history of the missionary introduction of the monotheistic concept and images of God.

THE LEGITIMIZING ROLE OF THE CONQUERING GOD

The continent was not empty when the Spaniards arrived in 1492. There were native peoples here, many of whom had created quite advanced civilizations.[5] Thus, when these lands joined Europe's history they did so as conquered territories and their peoples as vanquished subjects. And when large contingents of Africans were forced to join Europe's trans-Atlantic world, they did so in chains. Therefore the birth of this continent's modern history, as we have come to know it, took place under the signs of conquest and defeat for the vast majority.[6] Only the Europeans and their successors, by and large, saw the experience as mainly a positive process. The gods of the vanquished were also defeated, and the new Christian God came to be accepted. The conquest was all too often justified by the "might" of this God.

In Favor of the Conquering God

Spain attempted, from the very beginning, to spread the Christian gospel to the peoples who inhabited its new empire. Though the motives were not always purely religious, there is no doubt that many Spaniards did sincerely feel the call to the missions and generously gave their lives and talents to the tasks of evangelization.[7] But the many who came to the Americas explicitly as missionaries were all too frequently overtaken by the many more who came for financial or political gain. These were not just the official administrators of the empire.[8] They were the common folk who came to establish themselves in the newly acquired lands in the hope of becoming wealthy (e.g., the carpenters, the butchers, the soldiers, etc.). These colonizers were just as responsible as the officially appointed missionaries were for the spread of Christianity among the Amerindian populations. But what was taught about the Christian God?

First of all, the main religious argument employed by the early evangelizers was the "conquering might" of the Christian God vis-à-vis the apparent inability of the Amerindian gods to save their worshipers from the Spaniards.[9] Thus, the first confrontation with Christianity was directly with the victorious power of the Christian God. And holding a sacral worldview, where both the conquerors and the conquered believed that God was the ultimate explanation for every aspect of reality, to see the Amerindian world come to a humiliating defeat could easily be understood by the vanquished through the same religious worldview the victors held. It must have been God's will to hand victory to Spain, and it must be that the Christian God is certainly mightier than all the traditional divinities.[10] Otherwise the conquest would not have been successful. The religious legitimation of conquest was one main component in early evangelization, and it powerfully communicated and confirmed what both the vanquished and the victors believed to be true. The Christian God was, indeed, a mighty and conquering God.

When the colonial administration was set up, so were black slavery and Amerindian *encomiendas*.[11] And once again, God was called upon to legitimize the Spanish crown's claimed rights over the new lands and their peoples and, in turn, the colonial administrators' authority. As the slow (and sometimes violent) process of *mestizaje*[12] began and developed, God's power was again used to justify the racially based legal codes of privilege for the Europeans and of discrimination against Amerindians, Africans, and the increasingly large *mestizo* populations. Racial "purity" became one of the key measures for social respect and success during the entire colonial period.

No one seems to have questioned the concept or images of God in the legitimation arguments employed to justify the colonial system. Indeed, the Christian God was the "conqueror," victorious over the traditional deities, as well as the mighty foundation for the authority and shape of colonial rule.

Missionaries and Trinitarian Monotheism

Christians are monotheists. But their monotheism is trinitarian. And as history teaches, it took several centuries, a considerable number of theological texts, numberless debates, a few riots, much imperial and ecclesiastical politics, and several ecumenical councils before the vast majority of Christians could accept the minimal statements of trinitarian belief expressed in the ancient creeds of the Church. The point I am making is that trinitarian monotheism was not arrived at and explained without much difficulty by the early and patristic Church's great theologians and bishops. The language they adopted was necessarily that of the philosophies of the eastern Mediterranean. And not all was peaceably understood and accepted, even when adopted in ecumenical councils. The so-called history of trinitarian and christological heresies is there to prove the point. And today it remains a difficult chore to explain, even at the university level, all that might have been meant by the Nicæan or Chalcedonian bishops, for example.

Keeping the patristic trinitarian battles in mind, and realizing how difficult their adopted terminology can be even today, we can certainly wonder how the Spanish missionaries managed to present the Trinity to the Amerindians during the earliest colonial period. We can wonder not only about the catechetical creativity of the missionaries, but also about the degree of their success in communicating doctrines so absolutely fundamental to Christianity. Indeed, what did their conquered hearers ultimately understand? These concerns are of utmost importance because the very being of God, as understood and expressed through the trinitarian categories, is at the very core of all that is foundational to Christianity.

The cultures of the patristic-age eastern Mediterranean employed the patriarchal language of "Father," "Son," and "Spirit" in the trinitarian controversies. And after this terminology was included in the creeds of Christian antiquity, it became part of the common heritage of all Christian traditions. We are today aware, however, of the cultural and theological limitations of this type of language. But were sixteenth-century Spanish missionaries equally sensitive to the cultural difficulties that weigh heavily on this ancient terminology? Given the religious history of the Iberian peninsula, I doubt it.

Spain's theological traditions were certainly in line with the common Western views on the limitations of all human language when referring to God.[13] So we are not dealing here with possible confusion about the role of language in theological or official doctrinal statements. Nor are we dealing with questions of the trinitarian beliefs of the official missionaries. What we are facing is another and bigger set of problems.

If, as I stated earlier, a significant part of evangelization was done at the grassroots level by the Spanish lay minorities in Latin America (i.e., the butchers, the farmers, the soldiers, etc.), and the main daily contact of most *mestizos* and Amerindians was indeed with these *colonizadores*, then one must ask what was communicated in this context about God and about the meaning of trinitarian terminology. The official missionaries certainly tried to explain what the language of "Father," "Son," and "Spirit" meant, but they could not have attempted anything besides strict orthodox (and frequently "ortholalic") preaching, given the intellectual ambience of sixteenth-century Iberian Catholicism. Their explanations must have also been interpreted (very existentially) by the other, lay, daily, and often uninterested "missionaries." The hearers' own cultures, experiences, and histories must have contributed more interpretations. What then did the key trinitarian terms mean for Amerindians of the earliest colonial period?

Some Sources of Popular Catholicism

It has been shown that we can retrieve most basic elements of what U.S. Latinos and Latin Americans have believed in the past and still hold true today by going to (and through!) the symbols of popular Catholicism as created and sustained by the common people.[14] Let me briefly mention some of the sources that I will be using here.

It will be evident that I am going to refer only to colonial Mexican "popular religious constellations" that have some importance for most U.S. Latinos.[15] It will also become clear that I have made some choices as to which sources are most representative of the cultural, religious universe we want to study. Though no one component of "popular religious constellations" can ever be treated as expressing all possibilities and contents of the popular religious universe, some key ones may in fact yield a wealth of representative material. I believe that I have chosen some of these key components.

Testerian Manuscripts

In early sixteenth-century Mexico, those Amerindian masterpieces that today are misleadingly called the "Testerian manuscripts" were produced.[16] These full catechisms and prayer books (quite distinct from other visual devices used during the same period) contained pictographs that represented the doctrinal and ethical teachings that the Spanish missionaries attempted to communicate to the recently conquered native populations. The authors of these catechisms were very frequently themselves members of the vanquished communities, who now acted as interpreters between their people and the missionaries. In these manuscripts the native authors and artists employed some traditional, preconquest pictographs as well as totally new ones to convey the doctrines of victorious Christianity. Though there seems to have been some type of control by the friars over the Amerindian authors, the fact that many of these manuscripts have glossed explanations in Nahuatl (written by the friars) that do not follow the pictorial explanations (drawn by the Amerindian authors) tends to indicate that the missionaries could not impose orthodox European concepts without the free, cultural filtering done by the native authors. And it is needless to say that since "official" doctrinal communication depended very frequently on these pictorial catechisms, and these in turn were culturally and freely drawn by Amerindians who had just entered into contact with Christianity, the message received by the native populations evangelized through these pictographs could be more than the strictly orthodox teaching of the friars.

Religious Art

Another source I will be using is religious sculpture and painting.[17] Colonial Amerindian artists quickly learned many European techniques and, combining them with their own notions of aesthetics, produced an incomparable production of magnificent Christian art. These images expressed the religious feelings and convictions of the artists, while the popularity that some of these sculptures and paintings gained among the native peoples (even those pieces created by Spaniards) could only in turn imply their own religious feelings and convictions.

Religious theater was commonplace as well, having been adopted and adapted by the native populations from Iberian models. Though Christian religious music and theater followed European patterns in the Spanish American lands of the early sixteenth-century, they soon became loci of native creativity overflowing the imported Spanish molds while expressing the people's own religious concept and images.[18]

Popular Devotions

Finally, the third source I will use is the broad field of popular devotions, which in the sixteenth century ranged from christological and mariological expressions (e.g., devotions to the crucified Jesus and to Our Lady of Guadalupe, respectively) to heterodox superstitions (e.g., belief in and appeasement of hobgoblins). The former were acceptable to "official" colonial Catholicism and were sometimes promoted by it, while the latter were rejected and often persecuted. In between these two extremes there existed a very wide array of public and personal devotions that spanned the full continuum between Christian orthodoxy and (native and European) paganism. Unfortunately, popular devotions have been commonly and wrongly identified as the sole component of Latino popular Catholicism (both in the colonial period and even today). I am afraid that this identification is too simplistic and research would not allow it to stand up to serious scrutiny.[19]

All three sources were also evangelization vehicles that communicated and presumed a set of concepts and images of God, of trinitarian monotheism, and of its terminology. What do these sources allow us to learn about what was proclaimed by the missionaries of the early colonial period (both friars and laity) and, more importantly, about what the Amerindian populations seem to have understood and believed in? In the sacral world of early sixteenth-century Spanish America, all was ultimately legitimized by appealing to the Christian God. Now we must investigate what this trinitarian God meant for the evangelized population and what consequences this might have had in subsequent religious and social life.

"I BELIEVE IN THE FATHER, THE SON AND THE HOLY SPIRIT"

Practically all Latin American catechisms of the sixteenth century included this or very similar phraseology in their sections on the Trinity. Most Catholic prayers and liturgical services started (and still start) with the invocation of the triune God. But for native populations, who could not read the written language of the conqueror's catechisms, these texts were useless pedagogic tools. The pictographic catechisms were created to fill this important void.

However, when one attempts to translate doctrinal, theological concepts born and developed in a cultural milieu that employs letter-based writing into a different cultural milieu that writes through ideograms or pictographs, one must then speak of "approximation" of concepts and doctrines and not of "translation." Furthermore, when both cultural contexts involved in the attempted approximation are using many of their cultural presuppositions as if they were universally evident and valid for the entire human race, then one is confronted not only with the extreme difficulties that the two writing systems will produce, but also with the unspoken cultural filters that will necessarily interpret contents and doctrines from the purportedly "evident" presuppositions of both groups. Hence, adequate evangelization could only have occurred in sixteenth-century Spanish America if the natives and slaves in fact understood, within their cultural milieux, that which the missionaries were trying to approximate. But did this happen?

Similar difficulties arose when much of everyday evangelizing was done through religious art displayed in homes, churches, and in many other public places. The onlookers could capture the meanings and contents expressed through religious art only through their own supposedly evident and universally valid cultural filters.

However, the more common and problematic medium of communication was perhaps the universe of popular devotions. In the world of devotions the usually orthodox theology of the "official" missionaries often clashed with the at-times heterodox (and often superstitious) practices and beliefs of the Spanish laity that had come to the Americas. In that same world the Amerindians were frequently confronted with competing Christian explanations and practices, which in turn often collided against the doctrinal contents of the formal catechesis they were being offered. The native contributions to the universe of popular devotions, to religious art, and to pictographic writing are the clues that allow us to deduce what *they* probably understood of the newly arrived Christian trinitarian monotheism.

The "Father"

In the sixteenth century they did not have the very serious objections that twentieth-century feminist and cultural theologies have raised concerning the patriarchal and Hellenic origins and use of most trinitarian terminology. In that world they sincerely repeated and believed that God was "Father," "Son," and "Spirit," with the medieval understanding of "analogy" as the main limit to any idolatrous comprehension of the terms.[20]

It is evident that the Christian meaning of "Father" in trinitarian language is rooted in the New Testament usage of the term as later understood by much of the patristic Church. This meaning was certainly intended by Spain's sixteenth-century missionaries. But was this meaning adequately communicated and, more importantly, understood by the newly conquered peoples?

The *Libro de Oraciones*

One commonly used pictographic, "Testerian" catechism of the sixteenth century was a *Libro de Oraciones* now in Mexico's National Museum of Anthropology (MNA 35-53). The preserved manuscript includes a number of prayers, confession aids, a brief summary of "Christian truths" and commandments, and the Apostles' Creed with some minor additions.[21]

In the *Libro de Oraciones* there are two different pictographs for the concept "father." One clearly communicates the idea of father as spouse, as procreator, and as authority. An element of this pictograph is the hat-like headdress that seems to have been the symbol of authority and of maleness (cf. lines 3dd, 3hh, 7aa, and 8dd, for example). This pictorial symbol of fatherhood is *never* used in reference to God.

The other pictograph is the one that is exclusively and consistently used for God "the Father." It has two main figures (cf. line 3aa, for example); one depicts "God" and the other "Father." This latter figure is clearly a Franciscan friar. It seems that the *Libro de Oraciones* was trying to communicate the Spanish word *Padre*, associated with the presbyters of the Church, as if the word could explain what it meant to affirm that God is "Father."

This pictographic catechism attempted to convey a trinitarian, doctrinal content while apparently only succeeding in saying that the "fatherhood" of God was like that of the friars. This must have been thought to be the best approximation to Christian orthodoxy, because nowhere is there a hint that the native pictograph for the family-based concept of "father" was ever used for God. This might have been due to major difficulties with the societal role of males and to the author's unwillingness to compare God to sixteenth-century native or Spanish men. But did the chosen alternative (God as friar) really do justice to trinitarian doctrine? What did the Amerindian catechumens understand about God through the chosen pictograph?

From the *Libro de Oraciones*' choice of the friar as symbol for God's "fatherhood," we could deduce that God was presented, at best, as exemplifying the virtues the native population discovered in the "official" missionaries (faith, courage, creativity, learning, care, etc.).[22] But history tells us that not all friars were admirable in conduct, that many abused and overworked the Amerindians, that some of their tactics were cruel, and that all too often their attitude toward the natives was very bigoted and condescending. If the Christian God's "fatherhood" was approximated in the *Libro*'s catechesis as being like the friars', then the communicated concept and image of God "the Father" was (to say the least!) doctrinally inadequate.

The difficulties with the pictographic representation of God "the Father" as friar, however, are not limited to the consequences of unacceptable behavior among some missionaries. How could they explain the relationship between "Father" and "Son," in trinitarian doctrine, if the celibate Franciscan priest was the definition of "Father"? The way the *Libro de Oraciones* explains this, in the section on "Christian truths" (specifically lines 10dd through 11b), is most interesting.

In trying to convey, as emphatically as possible, that there is only one God and that there are three "persons" in that one God, and that one of those "persons" became human, the catechism creates such doctrinal confusion that one wonders today how it could have become so popular in the sixteenth century without running afoul of the colonial inquisitors. Let me explain.

Through a succession of pictographs, some of which were of pre-Christian origin and use, while others were evidently taken from recently arrived Christianity (and consequently, as foreign to the natives as were the doctrinal contents themselves), the Amerindian author of the *Libro de Oraciones* attempted to present to his people what he considered to be doctrinally correct trinitarian statements. Apparently caught in a cultural and linguistic nightmare, the result is a remarkable mixture of emphatic pictorial sentences that stress orthodox Christian doctrine (e.g., in lines 10gg and 10h: "Do not say three gods, but only one God who is three") together with extremely misleading or outright heretical positions (e.g., in lines 11a, 11aa, and 11b: "We call him God who came to earth, God the Father. I say it is God the Father [who] when human is Jesus Christ, born to Mary").

This is not the place to do an exhaustive study of the theological presuppositions and implications of the *Libro de Oraciones* and of other colonial pictographic catechisms. For the purpose of this article it suffices to say that sixteenth-century catechetical texts, as exemplified by the one I have been discussing, only partially succeeded in teaching the trinitarian monotheism that is at the core of Christianity.

The pictographic medium could not have offered more than it did to the author of the *Libro de Oraciones* because, as a medium for Christian doctrinal contents, it did not lend itself to abstract philosophical or theological thought. And it seems evident, as I said earlier, that it is only when one can employ the thought patterns of European philosophy and theology that one can understand and profess the very difficult Christian trinitarian doctrines.

The *Libro de Oraciones'* image of God as "Father" did not allow for some fundamental trinitarian concepts while it successfully communicated others. More importantly, the *Libro* (by choosing to use the friar pictograph for God) says nothing as to how "the Father" is related to either "the Son" or "the Spirit," and this seems to be the most dramatic doctrinal absence in this catechism's presentation of the Trinity.

Religious Art

The few instances in earliest colonial art of representations of God "the Father" are in the Franciscan church of St. Bernardine of Siena in Xochimilco, in the church of St. Diego of Alcalá in Huejotzingo, and in the Franciscan church at Tochimilco.[23] There they portrayed "the Father" as an old, bearded man, his head frequently surrounded by a triangular halo. In some instances the symbols of authority are added (e.g., God crowned with a papal triple tiara, or holding an orb). The triangular halo, of course, would be the only hint of a trinitarian connection, but would the Amerindians have understood it? I doubt it.

Popular Devotions

As far as I have been able to discover, there were no popular devotions explicitly related to God "the Father" in sixteenth-century Mexico. At least nothing beyond what has already been said about the conquering God of Christians.

There were, however, numerous references to "God" in many other popular devotions (with no explicit trinitarian distinction) which, given the contexts, seem to have referred to "the Father." In these cases what we find are variations on three standard colonial images of "the Father."

First, there was the image of conquest and victorious might. "The Father" *was* the conquering God who overwhelmed and defeated the non-Christian divinities and handed the land and its peoples to the Spaniards. Secondly, there was also the image of the aloof God who acted as the ultimate judge and legislator, who was personally offended by human sin, and who justly and swiftly punished it. This God had to be moved to mercy by prayers, mortification, and other pious deeds. Finally, there was in these devotions the image of God as perhaps a

Deus absconditus or *otiosus* who was "out there" and was the origin of all, but about whom they did not need to worry because this God was not concerned with the personal lives or pains of poor, vanquished humans. This God would be available, if and when available, to the wealthy, the important, and the religiously "correct." The common people had the crucified Jesus instead.

"The Son"

For all that could be said about the Iberian Catholicism brought to the Americas in the sixteenth century, it cannot be denied that it was emphatically christocentric. Perhaps in ways that expressed medieval theological views more than those that have emerged after the Protestant and Catholic Reformations, the missionary and catechetical evidence of the period points to a christocentric emphasis and content in the Christianity presented to the Amerindian populations in Mexico.

This christocentric proclamation, however, did not necessarily imply that the hearers understood what was being said, nor did it mean that what they in fact grasped was what was intended by the missionaries. Moreover, the christocentric proclamation did not necessitate explicit or doctrinally orthodox trinitarian thought. Let us again turn to our three sources to discover what seems to have been taught and what seems to have been understood.

The *Libro de Oraciones*

Throughout this pictographic catechism we see references to Jesus Christ, to his birth (e.g., lines 2h, 3c, 3cc, 3d, 5e, 5f, 10hh, 11a), passion (e.g., lines 3dd, 11e), death (e.g., lines 3e, 3ee, 5g, 5gg, 5h, 11dd) and resurrection (e.g., lines 3f, 6a, 6aa). Some christological titles are used (e.g., lines 1c, 3bb, 3g, 3gg, 5cc, 6c, 6cc, 6d), as well as mentions of his being "God the Son" (e.g., lines 1c, 5b) or "the Son of God the Father" (e.g., line 3bb).

It is evident that the *Libro* identified Jesus with "the Son." There is no question about that. But besides the direct and simple affirmation of Jesus being "the Son," there was no attempt whatsoever at explaining what this means or how "the Son" might be related to "the Father." Recall that in lines 11a, 11aa, and 11b we found misleading and probably heretical doctrine about "the Father's" supposed incarnation. And given also this catechism's use of the pictograph of a friar as the means of conveying the "fatherhood" of God, there was not much room left for explaining the meaning of the "Son-Father" relationship in trinitarian terms.

The *Libro de Oraciones* does insist on Christ's divinity and on his being addressed as "Lord" and "God." It is noteworthy that throughout the text the pictograph for "Lord" carries a headdress similar to those used by some pre-Columbian Amerindian *caciques* (cf., line 1c), and the one for "God" shows a figure with three groups of feather-like lines around the head (cf., line 1c; a pre-Christian symbol related to divinity?). What, however, does the use of these two pictographs say about Christ and about his divinity?

The native rulers that preceded the Spanish conquest were often just as ruthless and inhuman as the *conquistadores* in subduing and exploiting the Amerindian populations under their control. Of course, the native rulers did not claim to have received their authority or power from a loving divinity. The Christians, however, did. And to apply the pre-Columbian symbol of the ruler's power to Christ could not have been an innocent oversight. Either the author of the *Libro de Oraciones* intentionally wanted to make the connection between the two powers, basically identifying them, or he was forced to draw "Lord" in this manner because he culturally had no other choice.

Now, if the author wanted to identify Christ's lordship with that of the former native lords, then he was certainly going beyond what the missionaries could have requested of him and, as a consequence, he was making a very strong (though guarded) denunciation of Christianity as he saw it lived. If, on the other hand, the author had no choice but to draw "Lord" through the symbols of pre-Columbian native lordship (assuming that these symbols are such), then one may wonder if he was again caught by cultural differences and found no other significant way of expressing "lordship" in a cultural milieu for which "Lord" perhaps had no (explicit) religious meaning. Was he denouncing Christian abuse or was he once more a casualty of the dramatic differences in culturally bound religious language, symbolism, and thought-patterns that separated Europeans and Amerindians? We do not know.

Throughout the *Libro*'s several sections Jesus is very often called "the son of holy Mary." Sonship here is explicitly referred to motherhood, even if Mary's conception of Jesus is consistently said to have been by the Holy Spirit. What I mean to say is that in relating "Father" to "Son" there is no indication given in the text that this might have meant anything more than a mere verbal affirmation. No doctrinal, trinitarian content is given to these pictographs of affirmation. In reference to Mary, however, Jesus is pictured as really being her son. The end result is an understanding of Jesus' relationship to his human mother while his relationship to "the Father" is left unmentioned and unexplained.

Very important to this catechism, however, is the following. The author of the *Libro de Oraciones* seems to have found only one pictograph, in every instance throughout the catechism, to convey "Jesus" or "Jesus Christ." And that was the crucifix. It seems evident that the story of Jesus was so new in sixteenth-century Mexico that only a completely borrowed Christian symbol could communicate his name and story among the native population. What is very interesting is the choice of Christian symbol.

The *Libro*'s author did actually choose European letters to convey totally new religious concepts (e.g., lines 3a, 4bb, 6e, 7f, etc.) or even created pictographs that drew the new social realities and Christian doctrines (e.g., lines 8e, 8ee, etc.). But of all possible alternatives, he chose the crucifix, and *only* the crucifix, as the exclusive way to refer to Christ. Why?

I think that two distinct currents joined in our author's experience to lead him to his choice. There was, first of all, the long medieval, Iberian emphasis on the passion and death of Jesus as the high point not only of the liturgical year, but also of the life and meaning of Christ, as well as the equally emphatic use of the crucifix as the particularly Christian symbol in the centuries of the *Reconquista*.[24] The fact that most of the early Spanish missionaries and settlers were from southern Spain (Extremadura and Andalucía)—the regions that took the longest to "reconquer"—is no insignificant element in the shaping of the Iberian Catholicism that first evangelized the Americas.[25]

Secondly, the author of the *Libro* was himself a member of the vanquished race. And he was already a Christian, although still suffering the consequences of the conquest of his land and people. In drawing his catechism for his fellow victims the author was trying to explain a new religion in which he now shared. If he wanted to picture the main character in the Christian story, and create one drawing that would symbolize Jesus better than any other, was there a more powerful pictograph than the one of a tortured and dying innocent human being? By choosing a gory depiction of the crucifixion the author of the *Libro* is not only evoking the facts of Jesus' torture and death but also, and most importantly, *defining* Jesus Christ as the suffering God. Having chosen no other pictograph to broaden his depiction or understanding of Christ, the author has locked himself onto this one image. Jesus, the Christian savior and God, is a suffering God—that was the most important message of the choice of the crucifix. And since the image of a man dying on a cross would have had no artistic or religious meaning for sixteenth-century Amerindians, this image would have probably implied that those who were unjustly treated, tortured, and killed (those "crucified") were somehow connected to the Christian savior and he to them.

By joining, in his exclusive choice of the crucifix for the depiction of Jesus Christ, the southern Iberian Catholicism he had received from the missionaries with his own and his people's experience of suffering and vanquishment, the author of the *Libro de Oraciones* probably expressed the most powerful and subversive pictographic message of his entire catechism.

Finally, from what the *Libro* says, it is evident that the divinity of Christ is clearly affirmed and his humanness is very much emphasized. On this point there is no doubt that the author is within the mainstream of Chalcedonian belief, though nothing is said about such traditional doctrines as the hypostatic union. Perhaps no one could have expected it.

Religious Art

If in reference to "the Father" we could barely find some pieces of lesser quality, in reference to "the Son" we have a wealth of expressions in early sixteenth-century Mexico.

By far the most common representations of "the Son" were those of the dying, crucified Jesus. Some early colonial churches (like the three mentioned earlier) had paintings and occasional windows depicting other scenes from the life of Jesus.[26] But these were certainly not as frequent as the crucifixes found in these and other churches, plazas, crossroads, by house doors, and even in corn fields. Most of them, as in the *Libro de Oraciones*, represented Jesus' death on the cross in as gory and realistic a fashion as possible.

It is known that the most popular and more frequently presented religious plays were those that dramatized the passion story.[27] Entire villages or neighborhoods would become involved in the passion plays. Sometimes they added scenes not found in the New Testament or in Iberian passion traditions, or changed the interpretation of those found in the sources in order to do a "popular hermeneutic" on the *real* meaning *for them* of Jesus' trial, torture, and death. Doing a popular hermeneutic, however, was an integral part of southern Spain's own passion plays and traditions. The colonial interpretations were new and different in many ways, but the right and freedom to interpret were not.

In other words, most of early colonial religious art that refers to "the Son" seems to very much emphasize the passion and death of Jesus, giving these events the key "synthesizing" and hermeneutic roles in the representation and understanding of Christianity. Religious art identified "the Son" with Jesus, and especially with his vulnerable humanness. The central events and contents of the new religion were presented as summarized and symbolized in the passion and death of Christ. But what did this emphasis say in trinitarian terms? I am afraid that religious art did not enter the field of trinitarian relations. Only pieces that tangentially represent the Trinity (as the one in Huejotzingo) perhaps might offer a clue, but not enough to draw any conclusions from them.

Popular Devotions

The Testerian catechism and the religious art we have been using indicated the importance of the crucifix in sixteenth-century Mexico.

With the presence of crucifixes everywhere it should not be surprising to discover that popular devotions to passion events and to the dying Jesus himself were extremely widespread, and, by association, so too were devotions to the cross and to the "Sorrowful Mother" (*la Dolorosa*) of Jesus.

Numerous *cofradías* (i.e. lay religious fraternities) were established among the Amerindian population, dedicated to particular passion devotions. For example, some well-known *cofradías* were dedicated to the veneration of the *santo entierro* (i.e., the events and experiences surrounding Jesus' descent from the cross and his burial). Others emphasized the devotion to Mary, the "sorrowful mother of the Lord." Yet others called themselves *cofradías de Jesús Nazareno*, though their iconography clearly meant to emphasize the torture and especially the flagellation of Jesus before his crucifixion. Needless to say that there were numerous groups dedicated to the veneration of certain passion scenes as captured or expressed in some crucifixes, crosses, or paintings.

The native population was very soon attracted to this type of popular devotion. It connected, of course, with the religious theater they had come to cherish. But more concretely, I believe that these devotions to the passion and death of Jesus spoke to their own experience of passion and death. Their non-Christian religions, now forbidden and perhaps hidden, had many powerful symbols and stories, some of profound wisdom and beauty. But few if any were as powerful and shocking as the Christian story of Jesus, the divine savior, becoming vulnerable and weak to the point of torture and death at the hands of powerful men who claimed to be acting in the name of the true God.[28] The similarities with the sixteenth-century experience of Amerindians and slaves were too obvious to be missed by them.

The colonial devotions to passion scenes, crucifixes, crosses, and the "Sorrowful Mother" had ultimately nothing to do with the scenes or the objects or the personages themselves. They had everything to do with the people's experience of vanquishment, of abuse, of being unfairly condemned and neglected by those who claimed to be acting in the name and with the authority of the true God. These devotions were and are a symbolic statement of the victims' sense of experienced solidarity with the vulnerable, crucified God, and of God's solidarity with them in and through the cross.

These devotions were not a direct or indirect denial of the Resurrection. First of all, it must be remembered that the crucified and dying Jesus was always addressed as eternally living. He was alive, as far as all of these devotions were concerned. Secondly, and more importantly, these devotions developed and grew out of the experiences of conquered, victimized peoples. What fundamental human experience would joyful resurrection have resonated with, in the midst of the cultural and societal disintegration of sixteenth-century native Middle

America? Joy and hope? In the eyes of the recently conquered Amerindians and recently enslaved Africans? Perhaps in the experience of the Europeans there was hope, but in the experience of the vanquished, there was no sign of a change or of any future other than suffering, poverty and injustice.[29] Five centuries later their fears seem to have been more than justified by historical facts. Resurrection was joyful news and a symbol of profound hope for the victors, but not for the victims. For the latter the solidarity of the suffering God was *the* good news. And this message they did receive, did accept, and did symbolize through their many crucifixes and passion devotions.

These symbols were appropriated from the Spaniards and adapted by the native people, thus serving both as vehicles of evangelization and catechesis and as "sacramental" expressions of the people's understanding of the new religion. In reference to "the Son," it seems evident that the new Christians were taught by the missionaries that one of the Trinity was sent and became human and was unjustly tortured and condemned to death, having in fact died horribly on a cross. They were taught that "the Son" had died out of love for humankind and for humankind's sake. In turn, the people seem to have understood all of this and further interpreted it from within their particular, historical experience of vanquishment and unjust treatment, thus creating these particular catechetical, artistic, and devotional expressions we have been reviewing.

Somewhat unclear, however, is whether the trinitarian relations between "the Father" and "the Son" were sufficiently or even minimally understood, in the sense of explaining (for example) how and why "the Son" is "son" in the trinitarian sense. It is also unclear whether the divinity of Jesus Christ was believed to be "of the *same* substance as the Father." Evidently, herein would lie the roots of a decision for trinitarian monotheism or for tritheism. We may accurately presume that the missionaries would have been fully orthodox in their teaching but, as we know, they were not the only ones communicating doctrine. Did the lay Spaniards who came to the Americas with other than Christian motivations express trinitarian orthodoxy in their religious dealings with the conquered peoples? If the popular, southern-Iberian milieu they so frequently came from was an example of what they would have shared in Mexico during the sixteenth century, then the answer would have to point to doubt.

"The Holy Spirit"

If the Iberian Catholicism that was brought to the Americas was christocentric, it seems not to have emphasized the Holy Spirit. Evidently, the trinitarian doctrines on the Holy Spirit were taught, but in no way resembling the emphasis placed on Christ. The Spirit was constantly named and invoked, but in manners befitting the religious ambience of sixteenth-century Spain.

It must be recalled that Iberian Christianity (especially in Extremadura and Andalucía) had just emerged victorious, at the end of the fifteenth century, from more than seven hundred years of Muslim domination. The *Reconquista* had been slow and bloody, an almost contradictory process of learning to live with and from the enemy while fighting him to the death. The *Reconquista* helped to create the equally contradictory Spanish national character displayed thoughout colonial Latin America: vicious intolerance and heroic generosity, deep and sincere commitment to Christianity and quick disregard for some very basic Christian values.

The experience of the *Reconquista* also affected religious understanding and pastoral practice, as can be expected. Basic doctrinal agreement had been needed in order to guarantee some fundamental cohesiveness to an Iberian peninsula divided into competing Christian kingdoms. Also given past European experiences with popular appeals to the authority or role of the Holy Spirit, Spain's Christians were not too inclined to dwell on the "third person" of the Trinity in their theological reflections and pastoral practices. Unity in religion was needed, and it somehow seemed to them that to emphasize the action of the Spirit (beyond that which was needed for orthodoxy) was to invite a potentially dangerous divisiveness. In the sacral world of medieval Iberia, and within the context of the *Reconquista* process, this outlook probably seemed reasonable. When the *alumbrados*[30] finally appeared on the Spanish scene, with their emphasis on the Holy Spirit, they had to face the power of the Inquisition. The few sixteenth-century *alumbrados* in the Americas were even more swiftly dealt with.[31]

In brief, in Spain any discourse on the Holy Spirit, beyond that which was necessary to guarantee doctrinal orthodoxy, was at that time interpreted to be a potential source of religious and civil disunity and a possible source of heresy; thus, as a consequence, this discourse was to be avoided in order not to jeopardize unity among Christians and their common effort against the "infidels." The same can be said of the Spanish attitude toward preaching about the Holy Spirit in Mexico, except that the "infidels" here were no longer Muslim.

Given the contexts just mentioned, it should not surprise us when, in our colonial sources, we find doctrinal teaching on the Holy Spirit that only intends to promote orthodox trinitarian belief but would not go beyond this or dwell on any other question that might refer to the Spirit. Besides, the Christian concept of the "Holy Spirit" was very foreign to the cultural milieux of the Amerindian populations. Let us again go to the three main "constellations" of popular Catholicism that we are using as examples and sources.

The *Libro de Oraciones*

The Holy Spirit is mentioned in lines 1d, 3cc, 3h, 5b-bb, 5ee, 10c, 10ee, and 10g. In two pictorial sentences the reference is to the divine conception of Christ "by the Holy Spirit" (3cc, 5ee), and in four other places it is only (and without any explanation) the affirmation of the existence and divinity of the Spirit (3h, 5b-bb, 10ee, 10g). In only two places do we find references to the Spirit's activity in the lives of Christians (an extremely brief and passing mention of the Spirit as sanctifier [1d], and an equally brief and casual remark on the Spirit's action in baptism [10c]).

Given the limited number of lines on the third "person" of the Trinity, and the paucity of content in them, it seems that we can only deduce that the author of the *Libro de Oraciones* intended to say no more than what was barely necessary to affirm that Jesus Christ was "God's son by the Holy Spirit" (thus assuring christological orthodoxy). Therefore, in order to make this affirmation, he needed to say that the Holy Spirit was divine, one of the "persons" of the Christian Trinity. The author also had to include pictographs of (and thus mention) the Spirit when teaching the *per signum crucis* and the baptismal formula.

The pictograph which the *Libro* uses for the Holy Spirit is always that of a bird rising in flight, with a hat-like halo on its head, and surrounded by lines that seem to communicate radiant, glowing light. Though birds were part of the religious pictography of the native populations before the arrival of Christianity, no known pre-Columbian drawing comes even close to the drawing that the *Libro*'s author has included in his text. The depiction of the Holy Spirit is completely taken from the Spaniards' tradition, with no apparent reference to native images.

The Amerindians would have obviously identified the drawing as a bird surrounded by light, but what else would they have understood? And that is precisely the point. The pictograph would have communicated nothing else but a mere nominal reference to the third "person" in the Christian Trinity. No relation to the other two "persons" is ever mentioned (except, in effect, as being the one responsible for the conception of Jesus). No indication is offered as to the activity of the Spirit in the Church or in the believer (but for the two very casual and superficial references indicated above).

We do not have here a denial of the existence or of the importance of the Holy Spirit. Rather, we have a consequence of the silence that came upon Iberian Christianity on the question of the Spirit for the sociohistorical reasons I explained earlier. Given the paucity of teaching on the Spirit, it is not surprising that the pictographic representation and the doctrinal content of this catechism are so limited on this point of trinitarian belief. On this issue the official missionaries and their lay counterparts seem to have been in agreement.

Religious Art

Little exists from the sixteenth century concerning the Holy Spirit. We are reduced to noticing the typical dove-like representation that has been carved in a few churches and convents, most notably two carvings in the church of St. Bernardine of Siena in Xochimilco and another in a small village church in the valley of Oaxaca.[32]

Rare and tangential references to the Trinity included the dove figure but nowhere have I found any depiction, in sixteenth-century colonial art, that moved beyond this one representation, and no particular theological or pastoral significance seems to have been attached to it.

Popular Devotions

Once again we are faced with remarkable silence in this one field that is otherwise rich in religious creativity. The second half of the colonial period, as well as the decades after independence from Spain, saw a consistent increase in awareness of and "devotion" to the Holy Spirit, but not the early sixteenth century. The later *cofradías* of the Holy Spirit would have been unthinkable in the doctrinal climate of the earlier period.

There are evident references to the Spirit in the frequent use of the *per signum crucis* and in the trinitarian invocations and doxologies in the celebrations of baptism, Eucharist, and the other sacraments. Many of the established prayers to be said in private also included trinitarian formulae. The people, therefore, were often reminded of the Spirit through liturgy and other prayers. But what did they understand? Our sources, evidently, do not allow us to say more than what we have already stated. And, given the importance of the subject, that is precious little indeed.

"Person"

In religious art and in popular devotions of sixteenth-century Mexico we do not find any explanation for the meaning of the trinitarian term "person," nor do we find anything concerning "person" beyond the simple affirmation as to there being "three persons" in the Trinity. We do not know what religious art and popular devotions might have understood about "person" and about the relations among the "three," or even about how "three persons" can be "one God." The only artistic references to the Trinity (e.g., the Franciscan church at Huejotzingo) merely represent three figures, usually sitting or standing together. Whether this kind of representation would have doctrinally meant anything to the native populations is very doubtful.

In the *Libro de Oraciones* we have the trinitarian term "person" expressed through the Western European letter "P" (e.g., lines 10ee, 10h). This same "P," however, is also used in this catechism to communicate the terms *penitencia* ("penance," line 8c), *Pascua* ("Passover," "Easter," line 8h), *pecado* ("sin," line 7f), and *primicias* ("first fruits," line 9aa). If for obvious reasons the author of the *Libro* and his missionary teachers chose not to express "person" in its trinitarian meaning through the use of pictographs of human persons, one can sympathize with their apparent loss for an alternative pictograph. The choice of the European letter "P" would clearly avoid (in the author's and the missionaries' mind) any inclination to tritheism or even modalism on the part of the native populations, but did it convey *any* doctrinal, trinitarian meaning of "person" at all? Could it have, when the same drawing depicted four other totally unrelated meanings? And more to the point, how could any trinitarian understanding of "person" have been communicated by the completely foreign medium of the letter "P" (addressing a native culture whose writing was not letter-based!) about an equally strange monotheism? But then, what else could the missionaries and the author of the *Libro* have done, considering Christianity's own difficult history of trinitarian debates, battles, and heresies?

"I BELIEVE IN *ONE* GOD"

We have seen, with a high degree of probability, what was taught and understood about each of the "persons" of the Trinity and about the very concept of "person" in early sixteenth-century Mexico. We still need to look at another doctrine, the one referring to the oneness of God, thereby making trinitarian belief monotheistic. What do our sources say about what was preached and believed in the early colonial period? In doing this we will also briefly mention what seems to be God's relationship with the human race, according to those same sources.

The Libro de Oraciones

The pictorial catechism we have been using is prolific in its references to God, as can be expected. To depict "God" it employs three different pictographs. The simplest is the use of the European letter "D" (from the Spanish word *Dios*). This letter is not just plainly written but, rather, it is either decorated (as in line 12b) or somehow made to stand out by drawing it as if in the sky (as in lines 1a and 10c). In lines 4d, 8f, 8ff, 8g, and 8gg the letter "D" is used to depict "God" but only in pictorial statements, such as "thinking of God," "speaking to God," etc. In any case, the use of "D" in this catechism is not the most frequent drawing for "God."

Much more frequent for "God" are two human figures, one facing the reader directly (e.g., line 1b) and the other facing the reader's right (e.g., line 1c). These two figures are never used together and, apparently, they are employed interchangeably. Both drawings have in common the use of feather-like rays surrounding the head or emanating from it. These two figures are used dozens of times in the *Libro*, on almost every page. By the mere use of one of these drawings, the author is probably only pictorially suggesting the term "God" and not necessarily implying anything else. Or isn't he?

It could not have escaped the Amerindian populations that the figures presented as representative of "God" had feather-like emanations (or perhaps rays of light) surrounding the heads. The use of feather headdresses was one common symbol of divinity in many of the pre-Columbian cultures of central Mexico.[33] This point is further demonstrated when the author explicitly talks about "divinity" (in line 4hh) and depicts it precisely by a figure clearly carrying or displaying feathers. Therefore, the concept of "God" employed by the author of the *Libro de Oraciones* was not new or somehow foreign to his readers (as so many other concepts were). He chose to take some of the traditional, pre-Christian images and apply them to the new religion's Supreme Being when depicting this God's divinity or when merely stating that the Christian God is "God." The fact that by doing this he might have been (inadvertently?) evoking a full array of old, pre-Christian, and perhaps inadmissible ideas of divinity did not seem to have concerned him.

In any case, the pictographs of "God" in no sense communicate either the oneness of God or any other trinitarian, monotheist teaching. The drawings only presume that God exists and that the Amerindian audience knew as a matter of fact what it meant to say "God."

To say that there is but *one* God the *Libro* simply used the pre-Columbian counting symbols, thereby drawing one circle at the base of the pictograph for "God" and thus stating that only one divine being was implied (i.e., 3cc, 5a, 7d, 10gg, 10h, 10d, and 10dd). Beyond this, no effort was made to somehow communicate or explain that there was indeed only one God, except in lines 10dd and 10gg, where this is stated directly but without explanation. These lines, together with 10h, also explicitly emphasized (again without explanation) that the three "persons" of the Trinity are not three gods but together are the one God. Therefore, in the entire catechism there are seven pictographs in which God is said to be one, and of these only three make any direct statement that the trinitarian "persons" are related among themselves in the oneness of the only God. But in no instance is there any attempt at explaining or even approximating an explanation of what these trinitarian affirmations might mean.

In cultural, religious milieux like sixteenth-century native Mesoamerica, what could the Amerindian populations have understood of the mere affirmation of trinitarian doctrine ("three persons in one God"), when the fundamental terms "God" and "person" are either pre-Christian or utterly foreign? What could they have come to believe about the Trinity? Granted that we are only dealing here with a single catechetical text from the sixteenth-century, but if we were using a wider number of religious education texts from the same period—including those in use in Spain at the time—and the *crónicas* of the missionaries, we would see that there was an apparent reticence to engage in trinitarian catechesis beyond the minimally necessary orthodox affirmations.[34]

Finally, throughout the *Libro de Oraciones* the author speaks of God as being almighty (e.g., 3g), creator (e.g., 5c), eternal (e.g., 3cc), the great teacher (e.g., 5c), a judge (e.g., 6cc), in heaven (e.g., 2cc), and glorious (e.g., 2d). However, the two most frequently presented activities of God in favor of the human race are deliverance (e.g., 1b, 2f, 5cc, 4dd, 3ee) and forgiveness (e.g., 2c, 2e, 2ee, 9c, 9gg, 8ff, 10aa). It is here, perhaps, that one can see some break with pre-Columbian notions of God, because, even though the pre-Christian divinities did indeed forgive sin and did deliver from evil, their main or more frequent activities were not these. However, given the very powerful events of defeat and vanquishment experienced by the Amerindian populations, events justified in the name of a victorious God, the subtle break with pre-Christian images of conquering divinities could not have had a lasting impact on the sixteenth-century native users of the *Libro de Oraciones*.

Religious Art

The oneness of God is not an easy subject for the artist, including the early colonial ones. Hence, there do not seem to be any pieces that would address our subject. As indicated in other parts of this article, the religious plastic art that exists usually directs us to "persons" of the Trinity. Religious theater does the same, with plentiful generic references to God (mostly implying "the Father").

Popular Devotions

In this area it seems that popular devotions followed religious art, or I should say that it probably was the other way around. The superabundance of references to "the Son" have no parallel, in any sense, in references to the oneness of God.

This is not to say that, at the popular religious level, people did not believe that the Christian God was only one. The presentation of Christianity to the native populations did include the belief in the one God. There is no question on this. The problem, as I have stated before, was not the absence of the orthodox affirmation or teaching but the absence of explanations or approximations that would have made the orthodox doctrine understandable to the dramatically different cultural and religious mentality of the natives.

The absence of these explanations might *partially* account for the Amerindian and later *mestizo* inclination to compensate an insufficiently grasped Christian trinitarian monotheism by devotions to the mother of Jesus and to the saints.[35]

THE BIRTH OF LATINO POPULAR CATHOLICISM

Christian trinitarian monotheism was introduced in the Americas at the end of the fifteenth and the very start of the sixteenth centuries. We have reviewed three sources that have allowed us to see more closely how and what was taught about trinitarian monotheism, and we have also discussed the context(s) within which the actual teaching occurred.

There is no doubt in my mind that the native peoples were taught the centrality of Christ and of his cross and resurrection. The preachers announced the message of salvation. They taught about the scriptures and about the sacraments. The missionaries pointed out what was Christian ethical behavior. And they made the people members of the Church. What the Spanish friars communicated was not lacking, in any essential doctrinal way.[36]

Christianity was announced. There is no reason to doubt it. A theological evaluation—from the perspective of our contemporary theology—would point to the very many and necessary Christian elements in the people's new faith. But that same evaluation would find that the Amerindian converts of the sixteenth century could only have accepted and understood, first of all, that which was presented to them and, secondly, that which they could culturally understand. And throughout this article we have clearly pointed to the cultural and historical limitations particularly inherent in both the presentation and the understanding of the doctrine of the Trinity in sixteenth-century Mexico.

What kind of Christianity could result if the most fundamental doctrine on God is not grasped? It would be utterly naive to pretend that the problems faced by trinitarian preaching several centuries ago were due to the fact that the missionaries were Catholic. Had they been Protestant or Eastern Orthodox the difficulty would have been the same. Because the problem lay not with denominational theologies or creeds (which were in any case mostly in agreement in reference to the Trinity) *but with the European cultural expressions and philosophies* that had so marked trinitarian thought among Christians of all traditions since the earliest centuries.

Sixteenth-century Amerindians did not think and could not think in the neo-Platonic and later Aristotelian categories employed by the trinitarian theologies of the Europeans. And they did not have to think in those categories either. After all, the burden of inculturation, of communication, and of proof was not on them, but on those Christians who had forced themselves on the Americas and insisted on announcing their new religion.[37] These European Christians were so bound to the philosophical language of their theologies that they could not have inculturated trinitarian doctrine.

If philosophy had once been the providential tool to help deal with and explain major difficulties over the Trinity in the earlier history of the Church, in sixteenth-century Mesoamerica it became a source of new difficulties. These had to do, precisely, *with the very notion of trinitarian monotheism*: there is only one God, and this God is triune.

In defense of the missionaries it must be said that neither they nor anyone else could have done any better, coming from the European theological and cultural traditions of their century. European (and Euro-American) doctrinal presentations seem always to have little success when attempting to communicate the most fundamental Christian belief in trinitarian monotheism to peoples outside the European cultural sphere. Either tritheism or undistinguishing monotheism might be the result, perhaps dressed in "ortholalia," but seldom trinitarian orthodoxy and orthopraxis. What happened in our sixteenth-century case? Popular Catholicism was born.

I am in no way implying that this popular Catholicism is a bastardized version of a European model. What I am very explicitly saying is that whenever and wherever the doctrine of the Trinity is not truly inculturated, one will see a historical, religious process leading to either (1) a very clear emphasis on Christ and a very defined image of God in the strictest monotheist mold possible, or (2) an equally strong emphasis on Christ accompanied by a distant image of divinity that joins God to a number of other beings that somehow share in God's power. Furthermore, when this process takes place within the context of conquest and vanquishment, implying profoundly wounded cultural cognitive categories, *the resulting religious reality will be in the "shape" that the vanquished found more meaningful for the affirmation and survival of their identity as a people.*

Popular Catholicism is the "shape" that Latino Christianity, doubly vanquished in history, found most meaningful for the affirmation and survival of its cultural identity and of its faith heritage and life. The evident limitations of trinitarian colonial catechesis (i.e., in missionary teaching *and* in the people's cultural understanding) made possible the process that resulted in contemporary popular Catholicism. Had there been, in the sixteenth century, a truly inculturated trinitarian catechesis, this process would have dealt with other cultural and religious images in the people's quest for meaning and identity but not with the ones that, in fact, led to modern popular Catholicism.

Once the process was under way, it was only a matter of time before symbols and concepts that could not easily fit trinitarian belief and practice became not only possible but necessary. It was only a matter of time before the vanquished projected their family and social experiences onto God, and there being no trinitarian inculturated catechesis to critique these projections, the people's God all too often resembled their earthly fathers and lords. In this context the mother of Jesus became a necessary religious symbol of compassion and care in an otherwise cruel system.[38]

In order to attempt today to reverse this long historical and religious process by an evangelization that would want to undo the inadequate symbols, concepts, and projections, the evangelizer must first address the situations of oppression and of depradation that still afflict most U.S. Latinos *and*, with equal vigor, strive to inculturate trinitarian monotheism within the *real* situation of U.S. Latinos. If this two-sided evangelization were not offered, a new conquest as deculturalizing and abusive as the one five centuries ago would be inflicted again on the people in the name of God.

Notes

1. See O. Espín, "Religiosidad popular. Un aporte para su definición y hermenéutica," in *Estudios Sociales*, 58 (1984), 41-56.

2. See M.V. Gannon, *The Cross in the Sand: The Early Catholic Church in Florida, 1513-1870* (Gainesville: University Presses of Florida, 1983, 2nd. edition); and M. Sandoval, ed., *Fronteras: A History of the Latin American Church in the United States since 1513* (San Antonio: Mexican-American Cultural Center, 1983).

3. See W. Moquin and C. van Doren, eds., *A Documentary History of the Mexican Americans* (New York: Bantam Books, 1972).

4. See Moquin and van Doren, *A Documentary History*, 211-308.

5. See F. Katz, *Ancient American Civilizations* (New York: Praeger Books, 1972).

6. See M. León-Portilla, *The Broken Spears* (Boston: Beacon Press, 1962).

7. See R. Ricard, *The Spiritual Conquest of Mexico* (Berkeley: University of California Press, 1966).

8. See T. de Benavente (Motolinía), *Historia de los indios de la Nueva España*. Critical edition of the 1541 original, with notes and introduction by Edmundo O'Gorman (Mexico: Editorial Porrúa, 1979), 13-18.

9. León-Portilla, *The Broken Spears*, 138.

10. See D. Carrasco, *Quetzalcoatl and the Irony of Empire: Myths and Prophesies in the Aztec Tradition* (Chicago: University of Chicago Press, 1982); idem, *Religions of Mesoamerica: Cosmovision and Ceremonial Centers* (San Francisco: Harper and Row, 1990); and B. Díaz del Castillo, *The Discovery and Conquest of Mexico* (New York: Farrar, Straus and Giroux, 1956).

11. *Encomiendas* were groups of Amerindians *encomendados* ("entrusted") to particular Spanish settlers by the colonial authorities. The settlers were to evangelize, feed, clothe, and offer basic education to the natives. In return for these efforts on their behalf, the natives were to work for the settlers. In practice the *encomiendas* system became a cover for very cruel enslavement.

12. *Mestizaje* is the result of the biological *and* cultural mixing of different racial and ethnic groups. *Mestizo* is the individual. The terms are commonly and exclusively applied to cases of European and Amerindian miscegenation.

13. See M. Andrés, *La teología española en el siglo XVI* (Madrid: Biblioteca de Autores Cristianos, 1976), vols. I-II.

14. See O. Espín, "Tradition and Popular Religion: An Understanding of the *Sensus Fidelium*," chapter 3 below and in *Frontiers of Hispanic Theology in the U.S.*, ed. A.F. Deck (Maryknoll, New York: Orbis Books, 1992), 62-87; idem "Popular Catholicism among Latinos," chapter 5 below and in *Hispanic Catholic Culture in the U.S.*, ed. J. Dolan and A. Deck (Notre Dame: University of Notre Dame Press, 1994). And see O. Espín and S. García, "Toward a Hispanic American Theology," in *Proceedings of the Catholic Theological Society of America*, 42 (1987), 114-119; and idem, "Sources of Hispanic Theology," in *Proceedings of the Catholic Theological Society of America*, 43 (1988), 122-125.

15. The use of a method of "constellations" in the study of popular religion was first suggested by P. Ribeiro de Oliveira, *Religiosidad popular en América Latina* (Quito: Instituto Pastoral Latinoamericano, 1972).

16. See J.B. Glass, "A Census of Middle American Testerian Manuscripts," in *Handbook of Middle American Indians*, 14 (1975), 281-296; A.W. Normann, "Testerian Codices: Hieroglyphic Catechisms for Native Conversion in New Spain" (Tulane University, doctoral dissertation, 1985); N. Sentenach, "Catecismos de la doctrina cristiana en jeroglíficos para la enseñanza de los indios americanos," in *Revista de Archivos, Bibliotecas y Museos*, 4:10 (1900), 599-609.

17. See A. Cabrillo y Gariel, *Autógrafos de pintores coloniales* (Mexico: Universidad Nacional Autónoma de México, 1953), 147-165; J. McAndrew, *The Open-Air Churches of Sixteenth-Century Mexico* (Cambridge: Harvard University Press, 1965); F.A. Schroeder, "Retablos mexicanos," in *Artes de México*, 106 (1968), 11-28; and E.W. Weismann, *Mexico in Sculpture: 1521-1821* (Cambridge: Harvard University Press, 1950).

18. See E. Rull Fernández, *Autos sacramentales del siglo de oro* (Barcelona: Plaza y Janés, 1986); and M. León-Portilla, *Pre-Columbian Literatures of Mexico* (Norman: University of Oklahoma Press, 1969).

19. See Espín, "Religiosidad popular . . . ," 45-51.

20. See D.B. Burrell, "Analogy," in *New Dictionary of Theology*, ed. J.A. Komonchak et al. (Collegeville/Wilmington: Liturgical Press/Michael Glazier Books, 1987), 14-16.

21. In this article I use the line identification system employed by Carolyn S. Dean. Though I have also followed her translation of the pictographs, there are instances in which I depart from and correct her rendering. Dean's article also includes copies of the extant pages of the *Libro de Oraciones*. Basich de Canessi's 1963 publication of the *Libro* is the textual source both for Dean and for me. See C.S. Dean, "Praying with Pictures: A Reading of the *Libro de Oraciones*," in *Journal of Latin American Lore*, 15:2 (1989), 211-273; and Z. Basich de Canessi, *Un catecismo del siglo XVI* (Mexico: Editorial Offset, 1963). The *Libro de Oraciones* was probably made in Toluca, sometime in the sixteenth century, for use among the Mazahua population. The region had been within the Nahua sphere of cultural influence.

22. See R. Ricard, *The Spiritual Conquest of Mexico*, 128-132.

23. See F.A. Schroeder, "Retablos mexicanos," 11-28.

24. *Reconquista* is the term commonly used to refer to the Christian effort in the Iberian peninsula to "reconquer" the land from the Muslims. The Muslim occupation began in the first decade of the eighth century C.E., and only ended the same year (1492) as Columbus's first voyage to the Americas. Hence the *Reconquista* lasted more than seven hundred years.

25. See T. Mitchell, *Passional Culture: Emotion, Religion, and Society in Southern Spain* (Philadelphia: University of Pennsylvania Press, 1990).

26. See F.A. Schroeder, "Retablos mexicanos," cit. I have seen similar representations of "the Son" (and of the "Father" and "Holy Spirit") in early colonial churches in the city and valley of Oaxaca.

27. See R. Ricard, *The Spiritual Conquest of Mexico*, 194-206.

28. Some myths surrounding Quetzalcoatl were probably the closest pre-Columbian link to the crucified Jesus, but the *Libro* makes no connection—overt or implied—between the two.

29. See O. Espín, "Vanquishment, Faithful Solidarity, and the Marian Symbol," in *On Keeping Providence,* ed. B. Doherty and J. Coultas (Terre Haute: St. Mary of the Woods College Press, 1991), 84-101.

30. *Alumbrados* ("the enlightened") were members of a spirituality movement in early sixteenth-century Spain (but with earlier antecedents) which claimed an intense and unique direct access to the Spirit and decried all mediations—ecclesial, sacramental, or otherwise. The movement was accused of being heretical and was severely persecuted.

31. See M. Andrés, *La teología española en siglo XVI*, vol. II, 227-259, 601-603; B. Llorca, et al. *Historia de la Iglesia católica* (Madrid: Biblioteca de Autores Cristianos, 1967), vol. III, 601-640; L. Lopetegui and F. Zubillaga, *Historia de la Iglesia en la América española* (Madrid: Biblioteca de Autores Cristianos, 1973), vol. I, 438-445.

32. See F.A. Schroeder, "Retablos mexicanos," cit.

33. See D. Carrasco, *Religions of Mesoamerica*, cit.; and see also the *Codex Mendoza*, a Nahua pictographic manuscript [c. 1537] in the Bodleian Library, Oxford (Fribourg: Productions Liber, facsimile edition of 1978, with commentaries by K. Ross); and the *Codex Nuttall*, a Nahua pictographic manuscript [prior to 1521] in the British Museum, London (New York: Dover Publications, facsimile edition of 1975, with an introduction and commentaries by Z. Nuttall). In her commentary to the *Libro de Oraciones* ("Praying with Pictures," cit.), C. Dean interprets these pictographs for "God" as showing not headdresses but rays of light emanating from the figures' heads. A comparison with pre-Columbian manuscript renderings of divine headdress feathers will show that, in some instances, the feathers have been stylized into simple, short straight lines, like the ones we find used in the *Libro*. It is possible that Dean might be right in her interpretation, but I believe that the rendering I present here is better founded than hers.

34. See J.G. Durán, ed., *Monumenta Catechetica Hispanoamericana* (Buenos Aires: Universidad Católica Argentina, 1984 and 1990), vols. I-III; J. Metzler, ed., *America Pontificia. Primi saeculi evangelizationis. 1493-1592* (Vatican City: Editrice Vaticana, 1992), vols. I-II; and J.L. González, C.R. Brandão, and D. Irarrázaval, *Catolicismo popular. História, cultura e teologia* (Petrópolis: Editora Vozes, 1993).

35. See O. Espín and S. García, "Lilies of the Field: A Latino Theology of

Providence and Human Responsibility," in *Proceedings of the Catholic Theological Society of America*, 44 (1989), 68-90.

36. See R. Ricard, *The Spiritual Conquest of Mexico*, 83-132; and T. de Benavente (Motolinía), *Historia de los indios de la Nueva España*, 77-111.

37. See O. Espín, "Inculturación de la fe. Planteamiento del problema teológico-pastoral," in *Estudios Sociales*, 62 (1985), 1-31; and L. Hanke, *Aristotle and the American Indian: A Study in Race Prejudice in the Modern World* (Bloomington: Indiana University Press, 1969).

38. See O. Espín, "Vanquishment, Faithful Solidarity, and the Marian Symbol," cit.; idem, "Tradition and Popular Religion," cit.; and M. León-Portilla, *Endangered Cultures* (Dallas: Southern Methodist University Press, 1990), 55-83.

3

TRADITION AND POPULAR RELIGION

An Understanding of the Sensus Fidelium

It is practically impossible to study any Latino community in the United States, regardless of disciplinary point of departure or methodology followed, without encountering popular religion. Whether it be to denigrate it and lament its omnipresence in the Latino milieux, or to encourage and defend it as a sign of cultural affirmation, scholars sooner or later have to take a stand vis-à-vis popular religious beliefs, practices, and worldviews.

Popular religion (or "religiosity")[1] is indeed omnipresent in the Latino universe. And it is one of the few core elements shared by all Latino cultural communities in the country. Variations do exist, depending on the specific cultural history of each of the communities,[2] but some basic structures and symbols seem to appear as constants from coast to coast.

Popular religion has all too frequently been considered an embarrassment to Catholicism. It has been derided as the superstitious result of religious ignorance, a product of syncretism, a vestige of the rural past, and an ideologically[3] manipulated tool in the hands of those who would abuse simple folk. These accusations (and many others) do point to real issues and do express serious concerns. But when popular religion is only or mainly viewed through the prism of these accusations the result can only be prejudiced and distorted.

Theologians have usually stayed away from the study of popular religion, preferring to leave the field to anthropologists and other social

Originally published in *Frontiers of Latino Theology in the United States,* ed. A.F. Deck (Maryknoll, New York: Orbis Books, 1992), pp. 62-87.

scientists. Even liberation theologians have tended to downplay popular religion's role in the Church.[4] It is no exaggeration to say that, in Catholic theological circles, popular religion is either treated as an example of what should *not* be, or it is simply ignored as of no value for the serious theological enterprise.

It will be argued in this chapter that popular religion can be theologically understood as a cultural expression of the *sensus fidelium*, with all that this understanding would imply for the theology of Tradition in the Roman Catholic context. To this end (and as an extended example) we will show how two core symbols of Latino popular religion in fact convey essential contents of Christian Tradition. We will also insist that—since these symbols do no more than act as vehicles for the people's "faith-full" intuitions—the broader issue of the *sensus fidelium* must be paid closer attention in theology. We start, however, with more general but pertinent observations on Tradition that will help us set the context for our argument.

TRADITION AND *SENSUS FIDELIUM*

Within the overall theological discussion of revelation and the development of doctrine, with many ramifications into other theological areas, there lies the study of Tradition.[5] Though this is not the place for a thorough reflection on the meaning, importance, and role of Tradition in Roman Catholicism, some basic observations must be made on the subject.

In the past some authors used to consider Tradition, together with but distinct from the scriptures, as a "source" of revelation.[6] This "two-fonts theory," however, was discarded as the theology of revelation correctly came to emphasize that Jesus Christ is *the* revelation of God, and that this revelation is not primarily the "communication of doctrinal truths" but rather the outpouring of God's love and self in human history.

The two-fonts theory also failed when the relation between the biblical text and Tradition was carefully examined. It is evident that the scriptures have a privileged position as the inspired and normative witness to God's revelation. Tradition is correctly valued as the context within which the biblical texts came to be written and within which the very canon of the scriptures came to be fixed and accepted as inspired.[7] Tradition is also the ecclesial (and sometimes normative) interpretation of the scriptures. The fixed texts of the Bible are proclaimed, explained, applied to life, and correctly interpreted by Tradition for every Christian generation. This role of Tradition is guided and protected from error by the Spirit of God who also inspired the biblical texts.[8]

Scripture is the normative, written expression of a preceding Tradition that proclaims and witnesses to the revelation of God to Israel and in Christ, and from him through the apostolic community for the universal, postapostolic Church. Scripture, therefore, communicates all the essential contents (gathered in the biblical canon and received by the Church) necessary for complete, true, and saving faith. Scripture, which must always be interpreted in the light of the Tradition that precedes and accompanies it, is the norm for the Church's preaching and faith.[9]

Postapostolic Tradition, on the other hand, is essentially interpretation and reception of the one gospel of God which has found its concrete, written expression in scripture. The common content of scripture and Tradition is, simply put, their normative witness to the God revealed in Jesus Christ. The Bible and Tradition share the same content in the sense that Tradition, *through postapostolic expressions, symbols, and language*, recognizes and confesses (Creed), refines correct meaning against falsehood (dogmas), and witnesses to that same truth which scripture communicates *through the language, expressions, and symbols of Israel and the apostolic Church*. Scripture has been received and its canon fixed forever, while Tradition is necessarily living in and through history.

One could speak of Tradition as exemplified in the definitions of the great ecumenical councils of Christian antiquity, as expounded by the Fathers of the Church, and as communicated and witnessed to by the ecclesial magisterium and by the theologians throughout history.[10] Tradition is certainly expressed in and through all these means. Theologians studying Tradition usually concentrate on *written* conciliar documents, patristic texts, episcopal or papal declarations, etc. Quite correctly, this written material (as also the text of scripture) is very carefully examined and the methods of textual interpretation applied to it. Most theologians are aware of the need to properly understand a written document within its linguistic, cultural, political, historical, and doctrinal contexts. Without this careful study the interpretation of the text could be prejudiced or inaccurate and, as a consequence, yield wrong conclusions that could mislead other theological research dependent on the proper interpretation of Tradition's texts.

However, just as important as the written texts of Tradition (or, in fact, more important) is the *living witness and faith* of the Christian people.[11] However, they do not seem to be taken as seriously by those who study Tradition.[12] It is difficult to limit the object of one's study when the latter is supposed to be found mainly at the experiential level in every community of the faithful. Cultural differences, diversity of languages, and all sorts of other variations make the actual theological study and interpretation of the life and faith of real Christian people a very difficult task indeed. And to complicate things even further, the object of the study (though expressed through cultural categories, languages, etc., that run the full gamut of human diversity) is to be found at the level of *intuition*. It is this "faith-full" intuition that makes real

Christian people *sense* that something is true or not vis-à-vis the gospel, or that someone is acting in accordance with the Christian gospel or not, or that something important for Christianity is not being heard.[13] This intuition in turn allows for and encourages a belief and a style of life and prayer that express and witness to the fundamental Christian message: God as revealed in Jesus Christ. This "faith-full" intuition is called the *sensus fidelium* (or *sensus fidei*).[14]

The whole Church has received the revelation of God and accepted it in faith. And, as a consequence, the whole Church is charged with proclaiming, living, and transmitting the fullness of revelation. Therefore, the necessary task of expressing the contents of scripture and Tradition are not and cannot be limited to the ordained ministers of the Church. The whole Church has this mission, and the Spirit was promised to the whole Church for this task.[15] Members of the Christian laity, consequently, are indispensable witnesses and bearers of the gospel—as indispensable as the magisterium of the Church. Furthermore, because the foundational origin of the *sensus fidelium* is the Holy Spirit, it can be said that this "sense of the faithful" is infallible, preserved by the Spirit from error in matters necessary to revelation.[16] In other words, the "faith-full" intuition (*sensus fidei*) of real Christian laypersons infallibly transmits the contents of Tradition and thus infallibly senses the proper interpretation and application of scripture.

The main problem with the study of the *sensus fidelium* as a necessary component in any adequate reflection on Tradition is, precisely, its being a "sense," an intuition. This sense is never discovered in some kind of pure state. The *sensus fidelium* is *always* expressed through the symbols, language, and culture of the faithful and, therefore, is in need of intense, constant interpretive processes and methods similar to those called for by the written texts of Tradition and scripture. Without this careful examination and interpretation of its means of expression, the true "faith-full" intuition of the Christian people could be inadequately understood or even falsified. This is where theology and the magisterium must play their indispensable hermeneutic roles, though, as we shall see, this process is not without its own limitations and problems.

The means through which the *sensus fidelium* expresses itself are extremely varied, showing the cultural wealth of the Christian people. Given the global demographics of today's Church, the means tend to be more like they have been throughout most of Christian history: *oral, experiential, and symbolic*. These expressions also show (because of their origin in human culture) the wound of sinfulness, capable of obscuring (but never destroying) the "faith-full" and infallible intuitions of the Christian people. The interpretation and discernment needed in the study of the *sensus fidelium* must, therefore, try to ascertain the authenticity of the intuitions (i.e., their coherence and fundamental agreement with the other witnesses of revelation) and the appropriateness of the expressions (i.e., their validity as vehicles for the communication of revelation, realizing that no human expression is ever totally transparent to God and the gospel). This process calls for at least three confrontations.

The first of these confrontations must be with the Bible, because that which claims to be a necessary component of Christian revelation must prove itself to be in fundamental coherence with the scriptures. Although not everything that Christians hold to be truly revealed is expressedly stated in the text of scripture,[17] nothing held to be revealed can ever be against scripture or incapable of showing its authentic development from a legitimate interpretation of scripture.

The second confrontation must be with the written texts of the Tradition. By these I mean conciliar definitions of doctrine (dogmas), the teachings of the Fathers of the Church, the documents of the magisterium of the Church, the history of the development of doctrines, the various theological traditions and authors, etc. Throughout twenty centuries of Christian history, the Church has reflected on God's revelation, has come to a number of fundamental decisions on the proper understanding of some dimensions or elements of that revelation, and has made these decisions normative for itself and for all following generations of Christians.[18] As a consequence, all intuitions that claim to be "faith-full" (as well as all means of expression of those intuitions) must be in basic agreement with those normative decisions of the Church, and must also show some degree of coherence with the general doctrinal and spiritual thrust of the history of the Church.

The third confrontation must be with the historical and sociological contexts within which these "faith-full" intuitions and their means of expression appear. If a sense of the faith is to be discerned as a true or false bearer of Tradition, it must be capable of promoting the *results expected* of the Christian message and of Christian living.[19] In the same way, the vehicles through which the intuition of faith expresses itself (given the fact that all of these means are cultural, historical, and sociological) must somehow be coherent with Christianity's necessary proclamation and practice of justice, peace, liberation, reconciliation, etc., as indispensable dimensions of a world according to God's will. The expressions of the *sensus fidelium* must facilitate and not hinder the people's participation in the construction of the Reign.[20] This third confrontation, evidently, will demand of the theologian an awareness of culture and of economic and political reality, as well as awareness of his/her hidden (but certainly present) class and ethnocultural biases and interests which may blind him/her to dimensions of revelation present precisely in the "faith-full" intuitions he/she is studying. This latter danger seems most evident among many theologians trained in the North Atlantic presupposition that European or Euro-American theologies are the truly profound, systematic, real, and normative theologies, the ones—they claim—which effectively dialogue with the truest and most fundamental issues of human existence.[21] Of course, these North Atlantic theologies assume (very often implicitly) that their cultural, political, and economic contexts *define* what is truest and most fundamental for the human race, while considering that definitions from other contexts are either inconsequential or merely tangential to the tasks of their pretended "real" theologies. This third confrontation, obviously, calls on the theologian to become aware of the cultural and ideological limitedness and bias of the very theological tools he/she is employing in the study of the *sensus fidelium*.

If the infallible, "faith-full" intuitions of the Christian people can only be expressed through culturally given means, then it is possible that the *same* intuition could be communicated by different Christian communities through *different* cultural means. It is in this context, and as a consequence of what we have been discussing, that I believe Latino popular religion is the culturally possible expression of some fundamental intuitions of the Christian faith. Popular religion is indeed a means for the communication of many Latino Christians' *sensus fidei*.

THE ROOTS OF LATINO EVANGELIZATION

The Latino peoples of the United States have diverse origins, both ethnically and historically. Many of the communities are the result of immigration (some recent and others dating back to the nineteenth century), while large numbers of Latinos were already in present-day U.S. territory when American armies invaded and captured the populations together with their lands.[22] It is important to remember that the Latino Catholic Church was well established in today's United States two hundred years *before* John Carroll was elected first bishop of Baltimore.[23]

Latino communities with roots in the Northeast, Florida, or the Spanish-speaking Caribbean tend to be the result of *mestizaje*[24] between Spaniards and Africans. Those communities with roots in the West and Southwest or in Mexico and Central America tend to be the outcome of *mestizaje* between Spaniards and native Amerindian populations. In other words, U.S. Latinos are culturally (and very often racially as well) *mestizos* at their origin. In fact, it is this very *mestizaje* which distinguishes them from both the Spaniards and the Amerindian and African peoples; it is what binds them together as a community of communities distinct from all other segments of the U.S. population.

The very presence of Amerindian or African elements in all U.S. Latino communities points to another important fact which has serious consequences for the subject of this chapter: Latino origins are profoundly marked by slavery, plunder, and suffering. Were it not for the African slave trade, with all its horrors, or for the cruel system of the *encomiendas*,[25] the Latino peoples would not have come to exist. True,

Latinos did receive from Spain many components which provided the various *mestizajes* with a cultural richness they still cherish. However, Spain's greatest contribution was evangelization.

Christianity came to the Americas at the end of the fifteenth century. In a few decades numerous dioceses had been established, schools and several universities had been opened, parishes and mission stations appeared everywhere, and holiness and martyrdom accompanied the entire effort.[26] The missionary efforts of Franciscans, Dominicans, Augustinians, and Jesuits cannot be underestimated. They began the massive evangelization of the continent and were, in general terms, quite successful.[27] So successful, indeed, that today's Catholicism in Latin America and among U.S. Latinos is very much the direct heir to the one proclaimed and planted by the early missionaries.

Historical facts, however, remind us that together with these heroic efforts at evangelization there were enormous sins of injustice committed. As typical Europeans of the period, the Spaniards who came to the Americas believed themselves to be superior to all other peoples and their religion the only one worth professing. The same intransigent attitude that led to devastating wars of religion in Europe became the common attitude of Europeans confronted with Amerindian or African populations and their cultures and religions. The European invasion and conquest of the Americas did not take place for purely humanitarian or Christian reasons, but not without them either.[28]

The Christianity that was proclaimed in this continent, and that stands at the origin of U.S. Latino Catholicism, was the complex result of several distinct, historical elements. First of all, Spain had conquered the last Muslim-held territories in the Iberian peninsula the same year (1492) that Columbus arrived in the Americas. The process of driving the Muslims out of the Iberian peninsula had taken more than seven centuries and had made Muslims and Christians profoundly influence each other's culture. These Christians, who for hundreds of years had fought non-Christians, had developed a style of Christianity that was militant and attracted to the heroic, but it was not known for its tolerance of religious or ethnic diversity. National self-definition, indeed, had depended on the conquest and expulsion of those who were different. Not surprisingly the same militant, heroic, and intolerant attitudes were brought to the Americas by the Spaniards and were present in the process of evangelization and colonization.

Another element to keep in mind is the medieval fascination with saints, shrines, relics, images, miracles, and religious storytelling.[29] The Spaniards of the late fifteenth and early sixteenth centuries were still medieval in their approach to religion. Theirs was a Christianity that communicated the gospel by means of graphic symbols (verbal or not).

Though there had been much scholarly and theological learning in Spain's Muslim and Christian lands, this learning seldom filtered down to the majority, rural populations. The united Spain of the sixteenth century, though continuing the tradition of high scholarship, did not go beyond the best medieval models of education.[30] The Christian catechesis available to the rural majority tended to emphasize religious story-telling (often Bible stories or lives of saints) and religious dramas (*autos sacramentales*).[31] The observance of the liturgical seasons and the arrival of the occasional itinerant preachers gave the rural poor a necessary sense and knowledge of the fundamentals of Christianity. Social and religious traditions among the people of the villages also communicated some fundamental expectations of Christian living.

I am in no way implying that Iberian Catholicism was free of most of the very serious limitations of the pre-Reformation Church. What I am implying, however, is that in spite of the difficulties Spanish Catholics were certainly not ignorant of the gospel. In other words, the Catholicism that came to the Americas was one used to catechizing through symbols, stories, and dramas, a Christianity that bore the mark of the European Middle Ages and of Spain's long and recent militant anti-"infidel" past. And it was also a Christianity that, in spite of misconceptions to the contrary, depended mostly on lay leadership at the local level.

Once the Protestant and Catholic Reformations began,[32] much of Spain's religious efforts in the colonies would be devoted to keeping Lutheran and Calvinist ideas out. The Catholic Reformation in the Americas would in practice be reduced to the creation of seminaries and schools (mainly for Spaniards and the white *criollo* elite), to the implementation of the new standardized liturgy, and to stopping some major abuses.[33] But for most of the population on this side of the Atlantic, the Catholic Reformation would mean the affirmation (and thus the *continuation*) of that which was held to be *the* Catholic tradition of the continent: the Iberian fifteenth- and sixteenth-century Catholicism I have just very briefly summarized.

One last point must be mentioned and added to the picture. Though many members of religious orders came to the Americas as missionaries, I believe that most of the actual communication of Christianity was done by the lay Spaniards who came to this continent (and these were, by and large, Spain's poor) and, as time went on, by the Amerindian, African, and *mestizo* populations that entered the Church.

The end result of the combination of elements mentioned in this brief summary of the background of Latino evangelization is a type of Catholicism that can be called "popular" because it truly reflects the faith and practice of the majority of people. It does not show the sophistication of the educated elites, and it shows little awareness of the issues brought to the center stage of all Christian theology by the Protestant and Catholic Reformations. This popular Catholicism displays the medieval predilection for the visual, the oral, and the dramatic, and it is emphatic about certain dimensions of Christianity that tend to be overlooked or pushed aside by post-Reformation North Atlantic theologies, both Catholic and Protestant.

BEARERS OF THE CHRISTIAN GOSPEL: SYMBOLS OF POPULAR RELIGION

The Christian gospel preached in the Spanish-speaking Americas had earlier been filtered and interpreted by Spain's own peoples. The preached gospel was in turn re-interpreted, understood, and accepted in faith by Latin Americans and U.S. Latinos. This was as it should have been, since the gospel is either inculturated, and thus internalized, and allowed to transform a people's worldview from within, or it becomes a foreign, sterile message. And, evidently, in order to inculturate one must interpret, understand, and then accept, allowing oneself (and one's culture and previous worldview) to be challenged by the very gospel one is interpreting, understanding, and accepting. This entire process, leading from proclamation to acceptance, can only occur by means of symbols and other cultural categories in order to be a truly human process (because, even under the guidance of the Spirit, the hearer of the Word remains human and thus bound by all the normal processes of humanness). It is, therefore, very pertinent to remember here the distinction recalled in section 1, above, between the *sensus fidelium* as intuition and the various cultural expressions historically employed to communicate and witness to that "faith-full" intuition. It is also important to remember that what is the infallible bearer of revelation is the discerned, intuitive sense of the faith and not the many symbolic and historical ways employed as its inculturated expressions.

There are many symbols employed in Latino popular Catholicism. Most of them had their origin in the Church's liturgies (including Mozarabic liturgies, late medieval Iberian sacramental rites, and the sixteenth century Pius V—or Tridentine—eucharistic rite).[34] Other symbols were borrowed from Spanish medieval or mendicant piety, and still others were contributed (with totally or partially modified meaning) by Amerindian and African peoples.

As can be expected, not all symbols have the same importance within the popular religious universe. For our purposes, I have chosen two that appear as central and organizing symbols in Latino popular Catholicism: the crucified Christ and Mary. These two symbols are present in every Catholic Latino community in the United States with very similar functions and meaning, giving us a religious connecting link in the midst of Latino diversity. Finally, as can also be expected, our discussion of these two symbols can only be done in general strokes that in themselves summarize a much more detailed study of each of the symbols.

If these two devotions, so central to Latino Catholicism, are capable of communicating true elements of Christian Tradition, they may justifiably be called bearers of the *sensus fidelium*. Furthermore, since these two devotions are so important, they might offer us an entrance to the gospel preached in the Spanish-speaking Americas since the late fifteenth century. I will be devoting more space to the symbol of the Virgin of Guadalupe than to the crucified Christ because the latter's link with Tradition is so much more evident.

The Crucified Christ

Latinos give the iconography[35] of the crucifixion a very realistic quality. The crucified Jesus is painted or sculpted to appear in horrible pain. The crown of thorns, the nails, the blood, all are made to communicate real suffering, real torture, and real death. The dying Jesus, however, is not only represented nailed to a cross. The entire passion is expressed through numerous and well-known sculptures and paintings of the flagellation, of the crowning with thorns, of the descent from the cross, etc. Though many of these images or paintings may have true artistic value in themselves, the religious value is usually conveyed not by beauty itself but by the work's ability to elicit feelings of solidarity and compassion.

The passion is also enacted through religious drama, not within the confines of a theater building or a church but out in the streets. The *Santo Entierro*,[36] with its *Virgen Dolorosa* and its *Jesús Nazareno*, is one of the oldest traditions of Latino Good Friday. Some communities are known to accompany *La Dolorosa* as the procession moves through the streets, comforting her with their *pésames* at the death of her son. Needless to say, Good Friday is very important in the Latino liturgical year. There are many other popular devotions to numerous *cristos* that portray some scene of the passion story in one or another graphic way.

The Christ of Latino passion symbolism is a tortured, suffering human being. The images leave no room for doubt. This dying Jesus, however, is so special because he is not just one more human who suffers unfairly at the hands of evil men. He is the divine Christ, and that makes his innocent suffering all the more dramatic. He is prayed to as one speaks with a living person, not merely mourned or remembered as some dead hero of the past. In his passion and death he has come to be in solidarity with all those throughout history who have also innocently suffered at the hands of evildoers. In other words, it seems that Latino faith intuitively sensed the true humanness of Jesus, like ours in all things except sinful guilt. It sensed his resurrection as an intuition that he is alive now (and forever). And it also sensed that Jesus' innocent death speaks of compassionate solidarity with suffering men and women. The expressions used to convey these faith intuitions are culturally authentic, though they could conceivably be modified as

Latino cultures develop and adapt to new contexts in the future.[37] However, is there any doubt as to the truth of the intuitions or their infallible character?

Christian preaching in the Spanish-speaking Americas used the available catechizing tools and cultural symbols to convey the centrality of the cross. It emphasized the entire passion narrative and not merely the actual death. It underlined Jesus' innocence as well as his compassionate solidarity with all those who suffer. The people understood, they believed, and they interpreted, and among the results were the inculturated expressions of popular religion we have mentioned.

These expressions are not part of the normative Tradition of the Church. But the faith intuitions behind them most certainly are. Iconography has adequately communicated revelation, with contents authentically coherent with the text of the Bible and with other written documents of the Tradition. Furthermore, the passion symbols of Latino popular Catholicism not only do not hinder the building up of the Reign but, in fact, preach solidarity and compassion as attitudes of the Crucified God that are also expected from Christians. Thus, when confronted with scripture, other texts of Tradition and sociohistorical contexts (see the Tradition and *Sensus Fidelium* section above), the passion symbols of Latino popular religion can claim to witness to revelation and, therefore, to communicate the "faith-full" intuitions of the *sensus fidelium*.

Mary

Latino popular Catholicism frequently stresses the importance of Mary. It is difficult to find, besides the crucified Christ, another more powerful religious symbol. If on one hand it is not hard to discover "faith-full" intuitions behind devotions to the dying Jesus, on the other hand it appears that Marian beliefs and practices, especially as they are expressed in popular Latino contexts, are the farthest away from the Christian gospel (and, as a consequence, suspect as bearers of the *sensus fidelium*).

I have chosen to look more closely at only one Marian title and story, because practically every Latino cultural community has (at least) one title and story for Mary. These titles and stories (similarly structured accounts of apparitions of the Virgin or of discovery of her statue, connected to a confirmatory miracle) function as foundations for the Marian devotions of specific cultural communities.[38] The devotion I have chosen to address is the one to the Virgin of Guadalupe, which is probably the most widespread in the U.S. Latino universe.

The title *de Guadalupe* is a Spanish mispronunciation (and transference of an older Iberian toponym)[39] of the ancient Nahuatl term *Tecoatlaxope*, which means "She will crush the serpent of stone."[40] The story tells of a recently converted Amerindian called Juan Diego who, in December of 1531, saw and was addressed by a Nahuatl-speaking, Amerindian woman on the hill of Tepeyac, outside Tenochtitlán. It also mentions that the woman wanted a temple built on that site and that the Spanish church authorities in sixteenth-century Mexico did not believe him until a miracle occurred.[41]

That is the title and that is the story, yes, but this brief recounting does not communicate the context and symbols understood by Juan Diego, by his conquered fellow Amerindians, or by the Spaniards who had invaded Mexico. It was the context and symbols, and not just the historical outline, that created one of the most powerful Marian devotions in the history of the Catholic Church.

The context of early sixteenth-century Mexico pitched a multitude of native peoples against a smaller number of Spanish soldiers, administrators, colonizers, and missionaries. The ancient Nahua religion, and most ancient native ways, were seen by the Spaniards as unacceptable creations of ignorance, superstition, and demonic powers.[42] Though there were indeed some very forceful defenders of the native populations among the Spaniards (and especially among the missionaries), none of the defenders believed that the native religion was worth preserving (luckily, the missionary *cronistas* described for posterity the ancient Nahua religious universe that they knew was disappearing).[43]

Among the important ancient deities there was one Tonantzin, "our mother," as she was called by the Nahuas.[44] She was frequently said to be pregnant or to be carrying a small child on her back or arms. When depicted as pregnant the religious symbol representing the fundamental reconciliation of opposites was placed over her womb. Her sacred place had been precisely on the hill of Tepeyac. She dressed in a particular type of tunic, wore a mantle, and was connected in myth to the serpent high god. The woman that spoke with Juan Diego (in his native Nahuatl) did so on the hill of Tepeyac, wore that particular style of dress with a mantle, appeared to be pregnant, and had the symbol of the reconciliation of opposites over her womb.

I am in no way implying that Juan Diego saw the goddess Tonantzin, however. Though the similarities are too striking to be dismissed, the differences are also too evident to be ignored. Nahua Tonantzin had a mythology stressing her inclination to inflict cruel punishment on her worshipers. The goddess was quite capable of sending (and often did) all kinds of diseases and disgraces on her people. She was not, in any sense, a loving parent who could easily symbolize divine tenderness or warm affection. Tonantzin was also, under the title of Cihuacóatl, the wife of the serpent god.

The woman seen by Juan Diego was very pointedly kind and tender, with no trace of cruelty or anger. Her gestures were explicitly those of peacefulness. And the very title used (*Tecoatlaxope*) clearly indicated opposition to the serpent. These and other religious symbols present in Juan Diego's apparition do not allow us to identify Mary with Tonantzin. How do we explain the similarities and the differences?

Juan Diego, a recent convert to Christianity, interpreted what he believed himself to have experienced and seen through the cultural categories available to him. He was now a Christian, but his cultural milieu—of which he remained a part—was still in the process of assimilating the shock of the conquest. As it was and is common among many peoples, reality in sixteenth-century Mexico was understood in religious terms. And the conquest, followed by the arrival of Christianity, was a part of Juan Diego's reality that had to be explained, understood, and assimilated in *his people's* religious terms. Many were Christians now, but the traditional Christian religious symbols the natives received from the missionaries were Spanish, foreign to them.[45] Guadalupe seems to be the birth of the inculturation of Christianity in colonial Mexico. In other words, precisely *because* Juan Diego claimed to have seen Mary *the way* he did, we can say today that this is a sign that the Christian gospel was in fact announced and accepted in early colonial Mexico, in spite of all the betrayals of the gospel that can also be documented.

Mary is seen through religious symbols of motherhood and of the reconciliation of opposites, and for this Tonantzin's symbols were used, but without Tonantzin. Mary is also perceived as opposed to the serpent high god, without whom there could be no Nahua religion. She is pointedly tender and kind, a behavior not expected of Tonantzin. Juan Diego's Mary assumes the symbols that are useful for Christianity but rejects those that could identify her with the old religion or that appear to at least condone it. In this the Virgin of Guadalupe followed a long history of Christian appropriation and use of symbols from newly converted peoples.[46]

The devotion to Our Lady of Guadalupe, especially among Mexicans and Mexican-Americans, has remained central throughout the centuries since Juan Diego's visions. The Guadalupe symbol was immediately judged to belong to the poor, since the educated and the wealthy had their Virgin of Remedios. And for over four centuries Guadalupe has belonged to the vast majority of the people.[47]

The inculturation of Mary through the religious symbols of ancient Mexicans does not alone justify our calling it an inculturated *Christian* symbol. Mary herself must in turn be the symbol. Catholic pneumatology and ecclesiology should have little difficulty today in affirming this role for Mary.[48] But can we say the same thing of pre- and post-Tridentine Mexico? Were the Marian symbols of sixteenth-century Mexico capable of communicating, to the native peoples of that period and place, the meaning of Christ and his unique role in salvation, as well as other indispensable contents of the gospel?

To answer these questions one first needs to ask other more fundamental ones. Can analogy (semantic and cultural, *not* ontological) legitimately help us speak (in the manner of the semantic, cultural analogy) of God and the Christ?[49] Could Mary be considered, in that sense, an analogy of *some* dimensions or attributes that Christians have discovered—as a gift of the Spirit—in the one they call God? If Mary can be a semantic, cultural analogy of the Church in Catholic theology, could she be the same in reference to God? These are issues, it seems to me, at the core of all mariology. And also at the heart of our questions about sixteenth-century Mexican popular mariology.

But just as important are other issues about development in the understanding of Christian revelation. Obviously, the core of the gospel (its most indispensable content, upon which all others rest) is God's self-revelation and self-donation in Jesus Christ. But it is more than evident that the complete meaning of this revelation was not fully understood and explicated at the beginning of the Church. The history of doctrine is clear proof of development in Christian perception and progressive acceptance of the revelation of God.[50] What might be *clearly* true and/or accepted at a given age or a given place in Church history might not have been so at an earlier period *or at a different place* in that same history, sometimes provoking (or having been provoked by) confrontation about a (better) understanding of truth or about the way the latter is being expressed.

Could it be possible that sixteenth-century Mexican natives, recently converted to Christianity, intended to say something very true but (given their particular cultural and sociological context, and Spain's style of Catholicism) could only express it through the symbols that surrounded Juan Diego's Marian visions? Could the Virgin of Guadalupe be understood as a step—albeit an extremely important one—in the inculturation of the Tradition in Mexican (and later Mexican-American) history? Need all Christian communities share the same steps and moments in the development of doctrine, at the same time in history, in order to perceive or accept each other as orthodox?

Is Mary of Guadalupe the cultural, historical expression of "faithfull" intuitions of the *sensus fidelium*? I believe she is and, as a consequence, she is also open to doctrinal development that might or might not reaffirm all the Guadalupe-related symbols (though all development, in this sense, must be culturally authentic among those who historically have employed these Marian expressions in order to witness to the Tradition; cultural inauthenticity would disqualify as bearer of Tradition any development of doctrine or of expression).

Now, *if* it could be shown that Mary may be perceived as semantic, cultural (never ontological) analogy of some divine attributes—which is another way of asking if she could be interpreted as a culturally legitimate means to express some content of the Christian gospel—which of these contents would the Virgin of Guadalupe be communicating and witnessing to?

The history of this devotion especially emphasizes two intimately related aspects. First of all, Mary of Guadalupe has always been perceived by the people as a tender mother, always compassionate, accepting, supportive, and forgiving. And secondly, she is seen as protector, identified with her people but most especially with the weakest and most in need. She procures justice for the oppressed and takes up their cause.

Now, is it possible to truthfully refer to the Christian God as tender, compassionate, accepting, supportive, and forgiving? Is it possible to experience God as protector, committed to the liberation and defense of the weak and oppressed?[51] Is God really incarnate ("inculturated," therefore)? Can a Christian also refer to God as "mother," using in private devotion, liturgy, and theology the language and symbols of motherhood as validly as those of fatherhood?[52] But more to our point, must the revelation of these attributes of God be communicated *exclusively* through Jesus? Scripture does *not* allow us to answer this last question affirmatively. Though Jesus Christ is the final and definitive revelation of God—*the* revelation in the strict sense of the term—nowhere is it affirmed that *only* through Christ has God revealed Godself. As a matter of fact, the exact opposite has been a constant in orthodox Christian Tradition.[53] What one must affirm with the Tradition is the uniqueness and finality of the revelation in and through Christ, and the impossibility of its being repeated. But these affirmations do not exclude other means of revelation, only that these must never appear to compete with or add something *new* to the fullness of Christ's revelation.

This being the case, we can now ask whether it is impossible to understand that, in a given cultural and historical context, certain contents of revelation may be expressed through Marian symbols? As long as what is expressed through Mary is consonant with the gospel (and it is, as we have just seen), is there any theological difficulty in seeing the truth of the "faith-full" intuitions communicated through the devotion to the Virgin of Guadalupe as cultural *embodiments* of the *sensus fidelium*?

Elements of Christian Tradition

If we tried to briefly explicate through words (as distinct from devotional symbols) the elements of the Tradition (i.e., elements of revelation) communicated through these two popular Latino devotions, what would we find?[54] From the first of these symbols we discover these "faith-full" intuitions: (1) Jesus' true humanness, (2) his compassionate solidarity with the poor and suffering, (3) his innocent death caused by human sin, and (4) his (implied) resurrection and divinity. Through the Guadalupe devotion we find these other "faith-full" intuitions: (5) God's compassion and solidarity with the oppressed and vanquished, and (6) God's maternal affirmation and protection of the weakest. (7) From both devotional symbols we can retrieve a clear sense that if God and the gospel are to be heard and accepted, they must be inculturated ("incarnated"), as they have been, in the world and through the symbols of the poor and the disregarded (Jesus as a tortured Galilean peasant, and Mary as a member of a conquered race). And finally, (8) implied in both stories we might also discover that there results a lack of faith and a rejection of the truth and of God where the symbols of the poor (*and* the poor of the symbols!) are rejected.

But could we find the same eight or similar elements present in other Latino contexts and in other expressions of popular religion? I believe we can.[55] Even though a complete and thorough theological examination of Latino popular religion is yet to be done, the few studies that have appeared and those in progress all seem to confirm our thesis.

Much more important, however, is to question whether these eight affirmations, which may be retrieved from the two core devotions of Latino popular religion, are in fact contained in the Tradition. It is necessary to know if these affirmations (which are linguistic transpositions of symbolized and/or experienced intuitions of faith) can be said to be an integral part of the Christian gospel. If we brought these affirmations, retrieved from the symbols of the crucified Christ and of the Virgin of Guadalupe, to the three-fold confrontation with scripture, with the texts of the Tradition, and with the sociohistorical context (as suggested in section 1, above), we would have to conclude that within contemporary Roman Catholic theology no one, in good conscience, can deny that the eight faith intuitions are, without doubt, elements of Christian revelation, clearly and universally taught by the magisterium and, more importantly, witnessed by the texts of scripture and the Tradition.

And still, in contemporary theology, there is an evident reticence in the acceptance of popular religion as a valid field of study and of theological reflection on Tradition. Perhaps other, nontheological reasons (often hidden in religious language) are at the root of this reticence.

THE LIMITATIONS OF POPULAR RELIGION
AS *SENSUS FIDELIUM*

I have been arguing in favor of the study of popular religion as an authentic bearer of the *sensus fidelium*, and for that purpose I have reviewed the roots of Latino popular Catholicism and attempted to interpret and retrieve doctrinal contents from its two main symbols. Given the importance that the Spirit-given "faith-full" sense of the

Christian people has for theology (especially in Catholicism), and given the appeals to it at the hour of justifying theological, dogmatic, or even disciplinary statements in the Church, it will be important to look a little closer at the fundamental limitations of the expressions or vehicles of the *sensus fidelium* as transmitted in popular religion. Our discussion, though prompted by and applicable to Latino popular Catholicism, will not be limited to it.[56]

All expressions of the "faith-full" intuitions of the Christian people are, of necessity, not equal to the intuitions they communicate. The expressions are *human* means through which the Spirit leads the whole Church to a deeper and clearer understanding of revelation. As human means these vehicles of understanding are subject to the same conditioning limitations of all things human. The limitations I am referring to can be grouped in two categories.

Human, Contextual Limitations

There are those limitations, in the first place, that come from the cultural, sociopolitical, linguistic, and even economic contexts within which the Christian gospel is proclaimed, understood, and lived.[57] The Spirit-suggested "faith-full" intuitions, when expressed, will evidently employ the means made available through the people's cultural and linguistic codes. But the Christians who communicate their sense of faith will also exhibit in their expressions the privilege or the oppression to which they are subjected in society. Their faith will be *their* response to the gospel, and this means that their history, their struggles, failures, and victories, their social class, etc., will *necessarily* act as vehicles (or as contributors to the vehicles) of God-inspired affirmations of Christian truth. The whole of their social, human reality becomes involved as a filter offering means of expression to the gospel. But if the Christian people's reality is mainly a wounded and invaded context, the truth that the Spirit stirs within them will then express itself in a wounded and invaded manner. It is certainly the function of the entire Church (and more specifically of theologians and of the magisterium) to discern the truth amidst its wounded expressions. However, it is crucial that this discernment not be guided by or based on the presupposition that the poor's expressions of faith are of a lesser Christian quality than those of the intellectual, ecclesiastical or political elites. Were this evidently false presupposition to be operative in the discernment, the latter would itself be vitiated as a vehicle for discerning revelation's truth.[58]

In the universe of popular religion, sociohistorical and cultural reality has offered opportunities and also created limitations. The experience of poverty and injustice, for example, seems to have inclined Latino religious imagery to symbols and devotions that have explicitly to do with compassion and suffering. The same can be said of the

Latino emphasis on the extended family and on other social networks. These moved the people to conceive symbols and devotions that stress solidarity, community, and even family-like networks with the living and the dead. Many features of the Latino family have been projected onto the religious realm.[59]

The active presence of these sociohistorical and cultural dimensions among U.S. Latinos has indeed created adequate vehicles for the *sensus fidelium*, as we have been seeing, but—when not properly understood and received, or when wounded by an unfair reality—could also produce doctrinal exaggerations and deviations. However, the only discernment that can help avoid doctrinal deviation (as I mentioned before) is the three-fold confrontation with scripture, the texts of the Tradition *and* the sociohistorical context itself.[60] And, one must add, this discernment must also confront the implied racist or class ideologies (frequently expressed through theological, ecclesiastical, or pastoral categories) of those who either by training or ecclesial function might be conducting the discernment.

Limitations of Any Bearer of the Sensus Fidelium

The second group of limitations facing popular religious expressions of the *sensus fidelium* are those inherent to the very idea and reality of the *sensus fidelium*.

As I have pointed out several times, the *sensus fidelium*, strictly speaking, is not the expressions or vehicles through which it makes itself known. It is the "faith-full" *intuition* of the Christian people, moved by the Spirit, that senses, adheres to, and interprets the Word of God.

It is evident that no intuition may be had or may be expressed in human reality without somehow being mediated. This mediation, as we have seen above, will involve the reality of the ones experiencing the intuition. This is just as true of Latino popular religion as it is of the expressions of *all* the other bearers of the *sensus fidelium* in the Church. Even if difficult to discern in actual practice, it is theoretically possible (and even necessary) to affirm that the "faith-full" intuitions of Christians are not co-extensive or equal to the expressions they employ as vehicles for those intuitions. However, what is left of the intuition after distinguishing and discerning it from its expression? What is an intuition without some mediation to make it understandable or, indeed, even perceivable even at the preconceptual stage?[61]

Evidently, when discerning the truth behind the expression we must use some kind of symbolic means in order to understand. But the instant a symbolic code is appealed to as mediation (i.e., as expression), is this still considered an intuition in the strict sense of the *sensus fidelium*? Are then the mediating expressions of the *sensus fidelium* also granted the gift of infallibility?[62] The seriousness of these questions should be obvious since so many culturally given, ideologically tainted and socially wounded mediations are considered in today's Church to be vehicles of the intuitions of *sensus fidelium*.

These issues cannot be addressed here, but sooner or later professional theology will have to address them because the days when the *sensus fidelium* was an academic appendix to studies of Tradition seem to be coming to an end. The social sciences and non-European theologies have begun to uncover for us the complex and socioculturally bound structures and functions of religion and theology (and of the ideological uses of Tradition).[63] They have also begun to uncover the limitations of *all* bearers of Tradition, including the *sensus fidelium* and its popular religion expressions.

CONCLUSIÓN COMO APERTURA

Within the Church some seem to be arguing that the faithful need their faith protected. But if the Christian people's "faith-full" intuitions are infallible, Spirit-given witness to the gospel, it seems rather strange to claim that they are practically defenseless against error. On the other hand, to deride the use of the people's defense as a mere ecclesiastical political ploy is not to face the issue directly. Can the people's *sensus fidelium* and/or its expressions be misled? Why? What is the theologically adequate understanding of the relationship between faith intuition and mediation, given the results of the social sciences? Does the *sensus fidelium* witness to all of revelation? Does *any* of the bearers of Tradition ever witness to the whole of revelation?

And even more importantly, do the Christian people *actually* play a role in *today's* transmission of the Tradition, beyond being paid lip service for their "reception" of truth? What is their actual, real-life role in that transmission in our real-life Church? Are they supposed to be mere mouthpieces or mirrors for the expressions of the faith of the intellectually sophisticated (whether these be theologians or the magisterium)? Do they in fact contribute (what and how) to the ongoing process of deepening the Church's understanding of revelation?[64] Obviously, to claim that only the theologians or the bishops really understand revelation and, as a consequence, that only they should speak and express the faith in order to avoid deviations and error is to dismiss the *sensus fidelium* outright, to ignore too many facts in the actual history of the development of doctrine (and doctrine itself), and especially to come uncomfortably close to disregarding the incarnation of the One who is at the heart of the Christian gospel. There is need for a systematic, historically factual, intellectually honest, and detailed study of the relationship between the bearers of Tradition and their indispensable interdependence.

This chapter has not been the place to enter into some of the questions that I have been raising throughout. I have also tried to avoid comparing the limitations and contributions of the *sensus fidelium* with those of the magisterium, theologians, and other bearers of the Tradition (liturgy, for example). This would have led us too far from our subject. Instead I have insisted on the legitimacy of popular religion as a vehicle for the *sensus fidelium* and, as a consequence, as a valid (and necessary) area of theological reflection.

The presence of limitations in the expressions of popular religion (insofar as they express the contents of the Tradition) cannot be an acceptable argument against popular religion's role as bearer of the Tradition. Limitations apparently have not challenged the fundamental legitimacy of the other witnesses to Christian Tradition.

Perhaps one contribution Latinos can make to the American Church is to bear prophetic witness—in the name of God—to those elements of the Tradition[65] essential to Latino faith intuition that are not seriously regarded by the Euro-American Church, starting with the very legitimacy of popular religion.

Notes

1. For a comprehensive review of different approaches to and definitions of popular religion, see O. Espín, "Religiosidad popular: un aporte para su definición y hermenéutica," *Estudios Sociales*, 58 (1984), 41-56. Popular religion is not necessarily co-extensive with popular Catholicism in the U.S. Latino context. In fact, a number of Latino communities in Florida and the Northeast would recognize as theirs religious expressions that are certainly not Catholic (e.g., Santería, etc.). However, in this chapter we will use "popular religion" as synonymous with "popular Catholicism." In my aforementioned article there is an extensive bibliography on the subject, but it needs to be complemented by P.W. Williams, *Popular Religion in America: Symbolic Change and the Modernization Process in Historical Perspective* (Urbana: University of Illinois Press, 1989). See also my more recent study on the history of Latino popular religion in the United States, "Popular Catholicism among Latinos," chapter 5 below and in *Hispanic Catholic Culture in the United States*, ed. J. Dolan and A.F. Deck (Notre Dame: University of Notre Dame Press, 1994), 308-359; and the collection of essays edited by A.M. Stevens-Arroyo and A.M. Díaz-Stevens, *An Enduring Flame: Studies on Latino Popular Religiosity* (New York: CUNY/Bildner Center, 1995).

2. The distinctiveness of each Latino community in the United States is more than evident. The different cultural groups cannot be naively grouped together or thought of as having the same history, culture, etc. However, there are some fundamental similarities that allow for valid generalizations. The best example is probably the common structures, function and features of popular Catholicism. The *mestizaje* of all Latino cultures is also a binding force. See, for example, R.J. Cortina and A. Moncada, eds., *Hispanos en los Estados Unidos* (Madrid: Ediciones de Cultura Hispánica, 1988).

3. By "ideology" I mean the theoretical (conscious or not) explanation or justification of a held option or position, previously chosen (again, consciously or not) for other reasons which cannot be openly acknowledged. Ideology is created and held by social classes or groups as a tool to promote their interests in the context of their interaction with other social classes or groups. A particular ideology is disseminated in society according to the number, extension, and pervasiveness of the means of socialization (schools, mass media, churches, etc.) available to the social class or group that created the ideology in question. See A. Gramsci, *Il materialismo storico e la filosofia di Benedetto Croce* (Rome: G. Einaudi Editore, 1955), 868-873, 1319-1320.

4. See S. Galilea, "The Theology of Liberation and the Place of Folk Religion," *Concilium*, 136 (1980), 40-45; and J.C. Scannone, "Enfoques teológico-pastorales latinoamericanos de la religiosidad popular," *Stromata*, 40 (1985), 33-47. M.R. Candelaria, *Popular Religion and Liberation: The Dilemma of Liberation Theology* (Albany: State University of New York Press, 1990) presents an interesting and suggestive study of the views of popular religion taken by two highly representative liberation theologians: Juan C. Scannone and Juan L. Segundo.

5. See P. Lengsfeld, "La Tradición en el período constitutivo de la revelación," in *Mysterium Salutis: Manual de teología como historia de la salvación*, ed. J. Feiner and M. Löhrer (Madrid: Ed. Cristiandad, 1974), I, 287-337; J. Feiner, "Revelación e Iglesia. Iglesia y revelación," ibid., I, 559-603; M. Löhrer, "Sujetos de la transmisión de la Tradición," ibid., I, 607-668; K. Rahner and K. Lehmann, "Historicidad de la transmisión," ibid., I, 794-851; K. Rahner and J. Ratzinger, *Revelación y Tradición* (Barcelona: Ed. Herder, 1971); Y. Congar, *Tradition and Traditions* (London: Burns and Oates, 1966); J. Geiselmann, *The Meaning of Tradition* (New York: Herder and Herder, 1966); R.P.C. Hanson, *Tradition in the Early Church* (London: SCM Press, 1962); J. Walgrave, *Unfolding Revelation* (Philadelphia: Westminster Press, 1972).

6. The "two-fonts theory" seems to have resulted from a misunderstanding of Trent. See P. Lengsfeld, "Tradición y Sagrada Escritura: su relación," in *Mysterium Salutis*, I, ed. J. Feiner and M. Löhrer, 527-535.

7. See ibid., I, 535-555.

8. See Vatican II's *Dei Verbum*, nn. 7-11.

9. See *Dei Verbum*, nn. 9, 12. Also, G. O'Collins, "Revelation Past and Present," in *Vatican II: Assessment and Perspectives*, ed. R. Latourelle (New York: Paulist Press, 1988), I, 125-137.

10. It is common in contemporary theology to include other less "ecclesiastical" means as legitimate transmitters of Tradition. For example, the arts. See H.U. von Balthasar, "Arte cristiano y predicación," in *Mysterium Salutis*, I, ed. J. Feiner and M. Löhrer, 774-792.

11. I think that the discussion of the relationship between "literality" and "orality" is pertinent to the study of the *sensus fidelium* as distinct from the written texts of the Tradition. See J. Goody, *The Interface Between the Written and the Oral* (Cambridge: Cambridge University Press, 1987); idem, *The Logic of Writing and the Organization of Society* (Cambridge: Cambridge University Press, 1986); M. Vovelle, *Ideologies and Mentalities* (Chicago: University of Chicago Press, 1990).

12. As will be stated immediately in the main text, the reluctance to study that which is transmitted orally or through popular symbols is partly due to the difficulty in limiting the object of study. This is why the oral or symbolic communication of the Tradition (with the exception of the official liturgies) has not received the attention it deserves in theology. And this might have also contributed to the often superficial view of popular religion held by many theologians. In interpreting popular religion one needs to appeal to the interdisciplinary approach, just as it is the accepted procedure in the study of scripture and of the other texts of the Tradition. Popular religion is a very complex reality that cannot be reduced to any one category such as "devotionalism," and cannot be explained by the simplistic appeal to ignorance or syncretism caused by social conditions of poverty. See O. Espín, "Religiosidad popular: un aporte . . . ," 44-52.

13. As we will see in the section Bearers of the Christian Gospel, pages 71–78, popular religion insists on the solidarity and compassion of God, and it emphasizes the reality of the incarnation of the Son and his true humanness. Popular Catholicism expects God's affection and care for humans to be maternal and engaged. It sees Christianity as "familial" and it stresses justice, freedom, and equality as part of God's plan for humankind. Evidently, the texts of the magisterium of the Church and of much of Catholic scholarship clearly agree with these emphases of popular religion. But since the agreements are mostly set out in written texts and are all too often watered down in practice, they do not appear as bearers of true Tradition in the eyes of very many of those whose sincere faith is expressed through popular Catholicism. The permanence and vigor of Latino popular religion for close to five centuries in the United States, in spite of frequent efforts to "educate" or eradicate it, might be partially due to the people's Spirit-led insistence that the fullness of Tradition be heeded and put to practice (and not just in written texts). Events and unexplained episcopal silences vis-à-vis blatant injustices have recently hinted at the frightening depth of racism in the U.S. Church. Latinos all across the country are all too aware of the prevalence of anti-Latino racism and discrimination at the diocesan and (especially) the parish levels, often couched in religious or pastoral language. Justice and equality are paid lip service in chanceries and rectories, but reality tells a different story in most places. Popular Catholicism, it seems, will continue insisting on some gospel values being ignored or pushed aside by so many of the ordained ministers of the American Church.

14. These two expressions are practically equal in their use and meaning in the Church. See K. Rahner and K. Lehmann, "Historicidad de la transmisión," in *Mysterium Salutis*, I, ed. J. Feiner and M. Löhrer, 843.

15. See Vatican II's *Lumen Gentium*, nn. 3-4, 12.

16. See *Lumen Gentium*, n. 12.

17. See J. Pelikan, *Development of Christian Doctrine* (New Haven: Yale University Press, 1969); G.A. Lindbeck, *The Nature of Doctrine: Religion and Theology in a Postliberal Age* (Philadelphia: Westminster Press, 1984). Also, *Dei Verbum*, n. 9.

18. See T. Citrini, "Tradición," in *Diccionario teológico interdisciplinar*, IV, eds. L. Pacomio et al. (Salamanca: Ed. Sígueme, 1983), 523-542; J.H. Leith, "Creeds," in *Westminster Dictionary of Christian Theology*, ed. A. Richardson and J. Bowden (Philadelphia: Westminster Press, 1983), 131-132. Also, *Dei Verbum*, n. 8.

19. See Third General Conference of Latin American Bishops (1979), *Puebla Document*, nn. 388, 476, et passim.

20. It seems contradictory to profess belief in the indispensable nature and value of the *sensus fidelium* and then use its intuitive character as an excuse to dispense with it in theology or in official Church statements. Unfortunately this line of thought appeals to the fear of error in order to justify its own mistaken position. Equally contradictory is the admission of the *sensus fidelium* while actually disregarding the people's "faith-full" sense in pastoral practice.

21. See R.S. Goizueta, "U.S. Hispanic Theology and the Challenge of Pluralism," in *Frontiers of Hispanic Theology in the United States*, ed. A.F. Deck (Maryknoll, New York: Orbis Books, 1992), 1-22.

22. See, for example, M. Sandoval, ed., *Fronteras: A History of the Latin American Church in the United States since 1513* (San Antonio: MACC, 1983); M.V. Gannon, *The Cross in the Sand: The Early Catholic Church in Florida, 1513-1870* (Gainesville: University Presses of Florida, 1965); P. Castañeda Delgado, E. Alexander, and J. Marchena Fernández, eds., *Fuentes para una historia social de la Florida española* (Madrid: Fundación España en USA, 1987); W. Moquin and C. van Doren, eds., *A Documentary History of the Mexican Americans* (New York: Bantam Books, 1972); R. Acuña, *Occupied America: A History of Chicanos* (New York: Harper & Row, 1981). For a recent and very important contribution, see the 1994 three-volume University of Notre Dame Press series on U.S. Latino Catholic history: J. Dolan and G. Hinojosa, eds., *Mexican Americans and the Catholic Church* (vol. I); J. Dolan and J.R. Vidal, eds., *Puerto Rican and Cuban Catholics in the U.S.* (vol. II); and J. Dolan and A.F. Deck, eds., *Hispanic Catholic Culture in the U.S.* (vol. III).

23. After several failed attempts dating back to 1513, the first permanent (and still functioning) settlement of Spanish Catholics occurred at St. Augustine, Florida, on September 8, 1565. See M.V. Gannon's *The Cross in the Sand* for the history of Latino Catholicism in Florida during the entire colonial period and well into the nineteenth century. Missionaries and settlers began penetrating today's American Southwest from Mexico as far back as the 1530s— well before the British settlement at Jamestown.

24. *Mestizaje* is the process through which one becomes a *mestizo*, a person of mixed races. During the colonial period, and perhaps still today, persons of exclusive European ancestry looked down on the *mestizos* as half-breeds. So did the Amerindian or African groups that tried to reject everything from the oppressor. The *mestizo* among them was a living reminder of the rape and violence that accompanied their condition. Colonial legislation often denied civil rights to *mestizos*, and the ordained ministry was closed to them. In many places there is still a strong sense of prejudice against these persons of mixed blood. (The *mestizo* of Spaniard and African is usually called *mulato* in Spanish.) I am using the term *mestizaje* here more in reference to *cultural* rather than to biological mixing, though the latter obviously happened and in some places very much so. For a theological and pastoral use of *mestizaje* in the United States see the works of V. Elizondo. For example, *Galilean Journey: The Mexican-American Promise* (Maryknoll, New York: Orbis Books, 1983) and *The Future is Mestizo* (Bloomington: Meyer Stone Books, 1988). After Elizondo most U.S. Latino theologians have incorporated the category of *mestizaje* as foundational to their theological reflections.

25. The *encomiendas* were groups of Amerindians "entrusted" (i.e., *encomendados*) to a Spanish settler. The latter was supposed to evangelize them, teach them a trade, some rudimentary European arithmetic, and Spanish reading and writing. In return for these benefits the Amerindians were to show their gratitude by working (for only lodging and food) for the Spaniard. The system was, in fact, a way of theoretically preserving the natives' freedom while in fact subjecting them to slavery. Very few Spanish settlers carried out their commitment to evangelize and teach, while most were eager to put the natives to work in the mines and fields. See translations of some pertinent original documents in: H. M. Goodpasture, *Cross and Sword: An Eyewitness History of Christianity in Latin America* (Maryknoll, New York: Orbis Books, 1989). Also, B. de Las Casas, *En defensa de los indios. Colección de documentos* (Seville: Editoriales Andaluzas Unidas, 1985); O.K. Uya, *Historia de la esclavitud negra en las Américas y el Caribe* (Buenos Aires: Ed. Claridad, 1989).

26. Besides the work by H.M. Goodpasture mentioned in the preceding note, see the following: M. Sandoval, ed., *Fronteras*, cit.; E. Dussel, *Historia general de la Iglesia en América Latina*, vol. I (Salamanca: Ed. Sígueme-CEHILA, 1983); L. Lopetegui and F. Zubillaga, *Historia de la Iglesia en la América española. Desde el descubrimiento hasta comienzos del siglo XIX*, vols. I and II (Madrid: BAC, 1965). Florida was the first place, in today's United States, to see Christians martyred, see M.V. Gannon, *The Cross in the Sand*, 10-14.

27. See, for example, R. Ricard, *The Spiritual Conquest of Mexico* (Berkeley: University of California Press, 1966). For the lands that are now part of the United States, see, among others: M. Sandoval's *Fronteras* and M.V. Gannon's *The Cross in the Sand*.

28. For translation of the early colonial documents, once again see H.M. Goodpasture's *Cross and Sword*.

29. See B. Ward, *Miracles and the Medieval Mind* (Philadelphia: University of Pennsylvania Press, 1982); R. and C. Brooke, *Popular Religion in the Middle Ages* (London: Thames and Hudson, 1984).

30. See M. Andrés, *La teología española en el siglo XVI*, vols. I-II (Madrid: BAC, 1976). As Andrés clearly explains, the contents of Spanish theology and philosophy did develop (remember the Dominican scholars in Salamanca and Alcalá, for example), but the educational methods were still medieval.

31. *Autos sacramentales* were free dramatizations of Bible scenes, performed in the atrium in front of the church building or, less frequently, inside. The laity acted in these dramatizations, which were often quite elaborate. The *autos sacramentales* were commonly used in the evangelization of the Americas. For example, see R. Ricard, *The Spiritual Conquest of Mexico*, 194-206. For Spain's popular religion at that time, see W.A. Christian, *Local Religion in Sixteenth-Century Spain* (Princeton: Princeton University Press, 1981); and idem, *Apparitions in Late Medieval and Renaissance Spain* (Princeton: Princeton University Press, 1981).

32. It is usual to refer to the Catholic Church's activities in the sixteenth century (and beyond) as the "Counter-Reformation." I think the "counter" dimension, which was certainly there too, does not fully explain what was actually happening in and through the Church. See F. Martín Hernández, *La Iglesia en la historia* (Madrid: Ed. Atenas, 1984), II, 83-170.

33. See E. Dússel, *Historia de la Iglesia en América Latina* (Mexico: Mundo Negro-Esquila Misional, 1983), 91-115. The *Patronato Regio* (i.e., "Royal Patronage") had the colonial Church firmly under control. No Tridentine or pontifical document could be executed in any of Spain's territories without the royal *exequatur*. This system, which determined even minutiae of Church government and customs, ended with either Latin American independence (though some of the new republics attempted for a while to continue the colonial control of the Church) or with incorporation into the United States (as was the case of Florida).

34. See L. Maldonado, *Génesis del catolicismo popular* (Madrid: Ed. Cristiandad, 1979). See also C. Dehne, "Devotion and Devotions," in *The New Dictionary of Theology*, ed. J.A. Komonchak, M. Collins and D.A. Lane (Wilmington: Michael Glazier, 1987), 283-288.

35. By "iconography" I mean the sculptures, paintings, dramatizations, and stories used in the Latino context graphically to communicate or symbolize a biblical scene, a doctrine, or a religious disposition or feeling. It is thus only tangentially related to the Eastern Orthodox meaning of the word.

36. The *Santo Entierro* is a Good Friday public procession wherein statues of a grieving Mary (*La Dolorosa*, or "sorrowful one") and of a dead Jesus are carried about. Sometimes there are other statues of passion scenes included in the procession, such as one of Jesus being flagellated. The *pésames* are words of sympathy offered to the grieving Mary, and they are either set phrases sanctioned by custom or spontaneous ones. The *cristos* are either crucifixes of various styles or statues of Jesus suffering other torments.

37. There has been some discussion as to the future of Latino popular Catholicism in the United States. It is argued that the forces of secularizing modernity will extinguish the need for it and the worldview upon which it depends. It seems to me, however, that indications of the effect of secularization on Latino popular religion do not allow us to forecast its early demise. The symbols might be transformed and/or reinterpreted, as has already happened in the past, but this would be a sign of health and not of impending death. See M.R. Candelaria, *Popular Religion and Liberation*. The *Puebla Document*, nn. 460-469, addresses this very issue.

38. For example, the story of the discovery of the statue of the Virgin of Charity (for Cubans and Cuban-Americans) and the legend of the origins of the painting of the Virgin of Altagracia (for Dominicans and Dominican-Americans) have the same function as the one involving Guadalupe. The names, places, and other details are different, of course, but there seems to be a certain *structure* that is *culturally set* to convey precisely the religious meaning intended and to elicit the desired faith response. See W.A. Christian, *Apparitions in Late Medieval and Renaissance Spain*, 10-25, 203-214; and also V. and E. Turner, *Image and Pilgrimage in Christian Culture* (New York: Columbia University Press, 1978).

39. See J. Lafaye, *Quetzalcóatl and Guadalupe: The Formation of Mexican National Consciousness, 1531-1813* (Chicago: University of Chicago Press, 1976), 217-224.

40 The term *Nahua* refers to a people that settled the central valley of Mexico. They had a highly evolved, literate, and sophisticated culture, centered around cities. Some of these became dominant in time over the other Nahua

cities, thereby creating federations under the rule of one city-state. About a century before the arrival of the Spaniards, the city of Tenochtitlán, site of a Nahua people who called themselves *Mexicas*, became the dominant city-state, and it spread its rule well beyond the traditional Nahua territories. The term *Nahuatl* refers to the common Nahua language.

41. See F.J. Perea, *El mundo de Juan Diego* (Mexico: Ed. Diana, 1988); and J. Lafaye, *Quetzalcóatl and Guadalupe*, 211-300.

42. See R. Ricard, *The Spiritual Conquest of Mexico*, 35-38.

43. Well known are the chronicles (i.e., *crónicas*, hence *cronistas*) of the Franciscans Toribio de Benavente (a.k.a., "Motolinía") and Bernardino de Sahagún, and of the Dominican Bartolomé de Las Casas.

44. See J. Lafaye, *Quetzalcóatl and Guadalupe*, 211-237. Also, L. Sejourne, "La antigua religión mexicana," in *Historia Religionum. Manual de historia de las religiones*, eds. C.J. Bleeker and G. Widengren (Madrid: Ed. Cristiandad, 1973), I, 645-658.

45. See R. Ricard, *The Spiritual Conquest of Mexico*, 83-96, 264-283.

46. See P. Brown, *The Cult of the Saints: Its Rise and Function in Latin Christianity* (Chicago: University of Chicago Press, 1981); J. LeGoff, *The Medieval Imagination* (Chicago: University of Chicago Press, 1988); C. Saldanha, *Divine Pedagogy: A Patristic View of Non-Christian Religions* (Rome: Ateneo Salesiano, 1984).

47. See J. Lafaye, *Quetzalcóatl and Guadalupe*, 238-300; R. Ricard, *The Spiritual Conquest of Mexico*, 188. As Lafaye points out, the Virgin of Guadalupe became the symbol of Mexican nationality and independence. Ricard explains the devotion of the Spaniards to Our Lady of Remedios almost as being in conscious opposition to the natives' and *mestizos'* devotion to Our Lady of Guadalupe. In the United States César Chávez and his followers have explicitly evoked the symbol of Guadalupe in their struggle for farm workers' rights.

48. From a growing body of literature, see, as examples: L. Boff, *O rosto materno de Deus. Ensaio interdisciplinar sobre o feminino e suas formas religiosas* (Petrópolis: Ed. Vozes, 1979); P.D. Young, *Feminist Theology/ Christian Theology. In Search of Method* (Minneapolis: Fortress Press, 1990).

49. See D.B. Burrell, "Analogy," in *The New Dictionary of Theology*, ed. J.A. Komonchak, M. Collins and D.A. Lane, 14-16; idem, *Analogy and Philosophical Language* (New Haven: Yale University Press, 1973); J.S. Martin, *Metaphor and Religious Language* (Cambridge: Oxford University Press, 1986); P.A. Sequeri, "Analogía," in *Diccionario teológico interdisciplinar*, I, ed. L. Pacomio et al., 400-412.

50. See Z. Alszeghy, "The *Sensus Fidei* and the Development of Dogma," in *Vatican II: Assessment and Perspectives*, I, ed. R. Latourelle, 138-156. See also the works mentioned in note 17, above.

51. The references to the Bible, to texts of the Tradition and of the magisterium, and to the works of spiritual writers and theologians could be countless. The point is that all agree in affirming this possible way of experiencing and imaging God. Merely as a recent and good example, see M.K. Taylor, *Remembering Esperanza: A Cultural-Political Theology for North American Praxis* (Maryknoll, New York: Orbis Books, 1990).

52. After the contributions of feminist theology it is very difficult to deny this.

53. It is interesting to remember the Church's reaction to the Marcionites' attempt to reject the Hebrew Scriptures, because the Church considered these a vehicle of God's revelation. It is also pertinent to recall that the Church has always believed that, though intimately connected to Christ, the apostles and other authors of the New Testament were inspired when writing their texts. The modern exegetical sciences do not allow us to think that the New Testament authors were literally reporting events or words. See the very nuanced article by G. O'Collins, "Revelation Past and Present," in *Vatican II: Assessment and Perspectives*, I, ed. R. Latourelle, 125-137. On Marcionites, see R.B. Eno, "Marcionism," in *The New Dictionary of Theology*, ed. J.A. Komonchak, M. Collins, and D.A. Lane, 623-624.

54. For background on a method of retrieval of content from popular religion, see O. Espín and S. García, "Hispanic-American Theology," *Proceedings of the Catholic Theological Society of America*, 42 (1987), 114-119; idem, "Sources of Hispanic Theology," *Proceedings of the Catholic Theological Society of America*, 43 (1988), 122-125.

55. Each devotion or symbol will have its uniqueness, as can be expected, but a systematic retrieval of contents across cultural communities would yield similar results. As an example of the work done with other symbols, see O. Espín and S. García, "Lilies of the Field: A Hispanic Theology of Providence and Human Responsibility," *Proceedings of the Catholic Theological Society of America*, 44 (1989), 70-90.

56. Given the demographics of present and future Catholic population growth in the United States and in the world at large, and also given that popular religion is very much present and alive among U.S. Latinos and in Latin America, Africa, and Asia (continents where, together, the largest number of Catholics live), one is led to wonder if *popular* Catholicism isn't in fact the *real* faith of the majority of Catholics.

57. Pertinent here is a careful consideration of P.L. Berger and T. Luckmann, *The Social Construction of Reality* (New York: Doubleday, 1966). Suggestive also are: H. Portelli, *Gramsci y la cuestión religiosa* (Barcelona: Ed. Laia, 1977); P. Bourdieu, *A economia das trocas simbólicas* (São Paulo: Ed. Perspectiva, 1974); R. Ortiz, *A consciência fragmentada. Ensaios de cultura popular e religião* (Rio de Janeiro: Ed. Paz e Terra, 1980).

58. The magisterium and the theologians must also look at *their* own stereotypes, *their* biases and prejudices, perhaps even *their* own racism. Without a clear awareness of these limitations, bishops and theologians run the risk of blocking within them the voice of the Spirit speaking through the poor. What would result, then, of their discernment if they are deaf to the Spirit?

59. See O. Espín and S. García, "Lilies of the Field: A Latino Theology of Providence and Human Responsibility," 76-79; O. Espín, "Hacia una teología de Palma Sola," *Estudios Sociales*, 50 (1980), 53-68; idem, "Religiosidad popular: un aporte para su definición y hermenéutica," 41-56.

60. This also means that there is an urgent need among the people for a culturally respectful biblical catechesis, for promoting awareness of and critical reflection on Church history and sociohistorical reality. This will evidently require a socially engaged Church to grant this process real credibility.

61. See P.L. Berger and T. Luckmann, *The Social Construction of Reality*; and also S.J. Hekman, *Hermeneutics and the Sociology of Knowledge* (Notre

Dame: University of Notre Dame Press, 1986). The sociology of knowledge is a pertinent contributor to this discussion.

62. Do the racism, biases, and prejudices embedded in the mediating code affect the intuition or the perception of the intuition being mediated by the code?

63. Perhaps more theological dialogue should be conducted with the social sciences, especially those that directly deal with studies of culture.

64. The theological answers to these questions might at first appear evident. But it is difficult to have these theological answers actually fit the practices that they, in the first place, are supposed to be describing and explaining. There is a terrifying gap here that needs to be addressed.

65. See the section Elements of Christian Tradition, pages 77–78 above.

4

POPULAR CATHOLICISM
Alienation or Hope?

Popular Catholicism is one of the most distinctive and pervasive elements in all of the country's Latino cultures.[1] It is arguably one of their most fundamental matrices, and historically it seems to have acted as bearer of some crucial dimensions of the Latino worldview.

For as long as U.S. Latinos remained a mostly rural or small-town population, popular Catholicism's universe could be plausibly maintained by the people and pastorally ignored by the Anglophone Church authorities. However, this century—and more particularly the second half of this century—has witnessed a vigorous challenge to the cultural assumptions of reality behind Latino popular Catholicism. Though still very much alive and important in all Latino communities, this religious universe has begun to face the modern, urban world as never before. And yet, given popular Catholicism's past role as crucial bearer of identity and values, the current challenge involves and implies more than just the possible transformation of religious forms or styles, or even the demise of a centuries-old type of Christianity.

This chapter assumes as correct the view that *religion is the socialization of the experience of the divine*,[2] thus necessitating a two-sided approach to the study of religion: one that concentrates on the sociohistorical dimensions; and another that focuses on the experience(s) of the divine claimed by the believers, which ultimately explain(s) *why* people believe. A multidisciplinary approach, therefore, where the social sciences and theology take each other seriously, is here assumed as the best course to follow.[3]

Originally published in *Aliens in Jerusalem,* eds. F.F. Segovia and A.M. Isasi-Díaz (Minneapolis: Fortress Press, 1995).

Latino popular Catholicism is a religion.[4] More concretely, it is the religion of those treated as subaltern by both society and Church in the United States. By its centuries-old history, Latino popular Catholicism *can be characterized as an effort by the subaltern to explain, justify, and somehow control a social reality that appears too dangerous to confront in terms and through means other than the mainly symbolic.*[5] However, this popular religion is *founded on the claim that the divine (identified by the people as the Christian divine) has been and is encountered by them in and through the symbols (ritual, ethical, and doctrinal) of popular Catholicism.*

This chapter will modestly attempt, within its limited nature and space, to interdisciplinarily point to the main roles played by U.S. Latino popular Catholicism as religion. Many other important themes, otherwise needed for a thorough analysis of popular Catholicism, can only be hinted at or indicated in passing. At the end it should become clear that the alternative answers implied in the chapter's title are, of themselves, insufficient.

To speak of religious phenomena, experiences, and practices presumes an understanding of "religion." However, the term "religion" has been defined in theology and the social sciences in so many and often contradictory ways that one may wonder if there has been or ever will be a commonly accepted definition.

There is no question that many of these efforts at defining religion have indeed contributed to a better understanding of the religious universe. Stripped of the occasional pretensions of being absolutely correct, much of what theology and the social sciences have contributed has withstood the test of history. And yet, there is no question that all attempts at defining religion have always demonstrated the ideological interests of the researcher. This chapter is no exception.

THE "EXPERIENCE OF THE DIVINE"

By "experience of the divine" I understand an encounter between a human being (or group) and some One that is strongly felt, undoubtedly experienced as near and as good, and which (however briefly) grants complete meaning and fulfillment to that human being's (or group's) life. It seems that this type of experience is available to many and not just to a few specially sensitive people.

It appears that studies of religion do uncover very frequent testimonies of this kind of experience among religious subjects. The social sciences will and should observe and study the consequences of and the manners through which religious people live and organize their religions in society. But what social scientists will not be able to do is judge as true or false human participation in the experience of the divine. In other words, the experience of the divine is beyond the observation of the nonparticipant. The effects of the experience are indeed observable, but not the experience itself or its meaning for the believer(s). Of the experience and its meaning we only have the witness of those who claim to have shared in it.

The experience of the divine always occurs in human culture, as we shall see. But without a prior, explicit acknowledgment that religion is born out of an experience that is perceived by the believers as an encounter with the divine (however the latter is explained), we would not do justice to the faith of the believers nor would we understand that very core which their witness claims as *the most fundamental reason for their belief*. In no way does this acknowledgment impose on the researcher the need to accept the existence of "the divine" or "God," or anything concerning "God" either. What it does is respect the most basic starting point: any religion exists *because* those who believe in it claim to have encountered the divine. And it is this claim—whose experiential core is unavailable to nonparticipants—that makes a believer out of a human being.

"THE SOCIALIZATION OF THE EXPERIENCE OF THE DIVINE"

Experience and Culture

Even after emphasizing that the experience of the divine lies at the core of all religion, and that without this one element there would be no religion, we must also recall the evident: no experience of the divine occurs in a vacuum. The same testimonies that point to the human encounter with "God" signal precisely that it is an *encounter*. One of the two involved is, by definition, contextualized in a concrete culture, in a concrete society, and in a concrete history. From the perspective of the human partner, the experience of the divine is only possible through cultural, social, and historical means.

Thus, when a human being believes him/herself to be encountering the divine, he/she is in fact encountering that which culture allows him/her to understand precisely as "divine." This fact does not refer primarily to questions about the existence or nonexistence of God. It does refer to the "inculturation" of all religious experience, if it is human and understandable for humans. All possibility of a "pure," acultural encounter with the divine is, therefore, excluded. The One met in any religious experience is only the humanly "comprehensible" One. To pretend to have a "pure" encounter with God would be, in theological terms, equivalent to "possessing" God (even if for a fleeting instant). This pretension is idolatrous, theologically speaking. No religion, regardless of its type or history, has ever believed that what it affirms of the divine is all that can be affirmed of or about it.

If the human partner in the experience did not have the means of understanding and interpreting it, he/she would not have had it. The culture within which the experience happens offers the human subject the hermeneutic tools needed: symbols, language, patterns of imagination, etc. Cultural diversity makes possible the diverse interpretations of the religious experiences of humankind. And therefore, the cultural "idiom" of an individual or group will shape the language, symbols, etc., used (by that individual or group) in the process of interpreting religious experience, thereby shaping the experience itself as "religious" and the image(s) of the divine therein.

Society and Conflict

Culture does not exist in a historical vacuum. In a dialectical process, it is born in and of society. Every human society creates culture, and every culture in turn enters the process that creates society.

So, if the experience of the divine can only happen in culture this also means that it can only occur in society. And just as culture imposes its epistemological, hermeneutic limits on the religious experience, so does society. The "place" of a religious individual or group in society will also shape the language, symbols, etc., used (by that individual or group) in the process of interpreting religious experience, thereby also shaping the experience itself as "religious" and the image(s) of the One encountered as "divine." Therefore, not only culture but "social place" makes possible the diverse interpretations of the religious experiences of humankind.

The above remarks might not seem important until we recall that in today's urban societies the "social place" of individuals and groups, and the cultures and subcultures born in and from them, bear the mark of conflict. Whether we wish to consciously identify or name the conflict, or not, in contemporary U.S. society, it is not possible to believe in good conscience that millions of Latinos "chose" to become part of the subaltern in society. It is simply impossible to argue that there is something "genetic" or deliberately chosen in the subaltern social place of U.S. Latinos. The fact (and it is unfortunately a fact) that most Latinos are at society's bottom has a great deal to do with ongoing conflict. The experiences of the divine culturally and societally available to them bear this mark.

The hegemonic[6] epistemology in American society has managed to keep Latinos, and their popular type of Catholicism, "in their place." And it is from this place that they claim to have experienced the divine. So, if our preceding observations are correct, the "God" experienced by U.S. Latinos is (necessarily) culturally and socially contextualized in ways possible only to them, and expressive of the language, symbols, understandings, and image(s) of the divine shaped by *their* culture, by *their* "social place," and by the *conflict* underlying much of American society. Thus, their religion cannot be like the religion of other Christians whose "social place" is different, who might not be at the bottom of society's ladder, and/or who benefit from the current configuration of American society.[7]

The Socialization of the Experience of the Divine within a Society in Conflict

Any individual or group in society may experience the divine.[8] Important differences among people and groups will not be found in any claim to having encountered the divine but on how the divine is imaged, on how the experience is undergone and interpreted, and so on. And just as it is impossible to conceive of the existence of an event without some prior understanding that would allow it to be labeled as "existing," it is equally impossible to speak or conceive of an experience of the divine without the prior understandings provided by culture and "social place." Therefore, the most important difference among individuals and groups in reference to experiences of the divine will be on which interpretations and images of it are presented to the rest of society and how they are received.

In other words, even if it may be true that the divine can be experienced by anyone or any group, the very instant an experience is perceived as "of the divine" the culture and social place of the individual or group utilize hermeneutic tools made available by that person's or group's standing in society, thereby making any subsequent testimony or report of the experience acceptable and "respectable" in society *in the same manner and degree as are given to the culture and social place of that individual or group.*[9]

The religious subject will him/herself interpret and attempt to remember, symbolize, and live by that which he/she experienced in the encounter with the divine. When this interpretation and these attempts are shared by others who also claim to have met "God," there a religion is born. When an individual or group "pours" the experience of the divine into meaningful symbols, images, memories (ethical or doctrinal), explanations, and guidelines for living, that can be shared by others in society, there the experience becomes socialized. This socialization, obviously, is not the result of detached calculation.

In theological terms, there is religion only where the experience of God has become truly incarnate in the culture, history, and life of the believing people. And, among other consequences, this implies (for example) that the Catholicism of the hegemonic group and their allies in a society will express itself through the symbols, the images, and the lifestyles of hegemony, which are not those of the Catholic subaltern groups in that same society.[10] To the degree that the hegemonic religious symbols, images, and lifestyles have penetrated the subaltern, and to the degree that the memory of Christianity's subaltern origins have remained among the hegemonic groups, then can people on both sides of society claim to participate in the same Catholic religion.[11]

Society and culture exist prior to religion. And if it is true that Catholicism, of its very nature, must incarnate in and symbolize the social and historical realities of the believers, then there cannot be one single way of being Catholic.[12] The different ways will reflect the conflicts, the social places, the classes, and everything else that are common part and parcel of human societies.[13]

If in the United States the Latino communities are by and large discriminated against, the object of racism and bigotry, and the victims of injustice, then their Catholicism cannot possibly be understood without further prejudice unless the conflicts and suffering of these communities are admitted as truly *shaping* their experience of God and their socialization of that experience. But by the same token, to the degree that other American Catholics (including some Latino Catholics) have benefited by their access to the hegemonic groups and ideologies (whose by-product has been the marginalization of most Latinos), to that degree their Catholicism is *shaped* in the likeness of society's victors, and as religion participates in the hegemonic power and culture that legitimize the marginalization of others.

The Roles of American Catholicisms in Society

Any religion may exhibit several roles in any given society, depending on the social place of the believers. Any religion may play, at any one time, more than one role or may change roles in the course of its history. America's Catholicisms (Latino, Euro-American, African-American, etc.) are no exception.

The Legitimizing Role

If hegemony in society is dependent on a given group's ability to persuade other groups within that society that it is the best qualified to lead, then this persuasion requires the creation and distribution of explanations, of symbols, of justifications, and of a "reading" of reality that legitimize the leading group's pretensions. To the degree that the other groups in society (especially the subaltern) accept the validity of the explanations and justifications, and to the degree that they assume the symbols of the leaders, the hegemony of the latter is secured. Given the conflict inherent in modern societies, the creation and dissemination of a leading group's reasons for hegemony do not happen without some form of coercion. And yet, no acceptance of the reasons for hegemony is ever complete or without some doubt.

The dominant group will attempt to present its leadership role and its explanations as necessary, and, when expressed through religious categories, it will affirm that its role is divinely sanctioned and willed, and that its explanations are either "revealed" as truth or as close to truth as possible. There is no better argument in favor of a particular group's hegemony (and hence, in favor of a particular social formation) than to spread the belief that it is divinely established or sanctioned. Obviously, there can be no possible appeal beyond God's decision. The sad story of Christianity's role in the justification of American slave-holding society and its complicity in legitimizing the doctrine of Manifest Destiny are clear examples of this. And these are also examples of how the reasons in favor of a group's hegemony are created and disseminated not only in the direction of the subaltern groups but also toward the very interior of the leading group. The rulers eventually become convinced of their "right" to rule and of other groups' "inferiority."[14]

There is no question that religion has played and still plays this legitimizing role in American society. And large segments of Euro-American Catholics, in their attempt to become acceptable to the hegemonic group, seem to have paid (for their admission into "respectability" and mainstream, middle-class status) the price of joining the latter's legitimizing effort. Euro-American Catholicism has very often lent its religious categories, symbols, and institutions to the hegemonic group's efforts at spreading its reasons for social dominance. One consequence of this price has been the internalization (by those "mainstreamed" Catholic segments) of hegemonic explanations concerning Latino social "inferiority" and lack of leadership capabilities. This in turn justified the frequent treatment (doctrinal and pastoral) of Latino popular Catholicism as religiously and ecclesially "inferior," defective, or of insufficient quality.[15]

I am in no way implying that every individual Euro-American Catholic is consciously or culpably aware of the legitimizing function that his/her religion has in society. However, her/his "reading" of the meaning of the experience of God, the doctrinal and pastoral shape of his/her religion, and her/his understanding of Catholicism's role in our society is very often in harmony with the legitimizing explanations and symbols of the country's hegemonic ideology. The private intentions of the individual believer do not cancel, unfortunately, the social consequences of his/her religion's public role.[16]

Latino popular Catholicism, because it too participates in American society, plays the many roles of any American religion, and thus it can also favor the legitimizing efforts of the hegemonic group. This Catholicism too has functioned as a dissemination channel for the explanations and justifications that, through religious categories, are directed at the subaltern in our society. Therefore, to the degree that popular Catholicism has been a successful tool in the internalization of their subaltern status by Latinos, so has their religion played the role of legitimizing contemporary America's social formation and dominant ideology. And because of this, popular Catholicism might have become, in many instances, a weapon for the alienation of and the social (and thereby ecclesiastical) control over U.S. Latinos.

The Rebellious Role

As I said earlier, the process of creating and disseminating the explanations, justifications, and symbols that legitimize the hegemony of a group in society is never completely successful. Those who benefit from hegemony as well as those who (as subalterns) internalize its reasons are always left with some margin of doubt. In theological terms we might speak of hegemony as incapable of completely erasing a "hermeneutic of suspicion." It also seems that the legitimizing process suggests to both groups that doubt is not desirable and that guilt should be felt in response to it.[17]

This doubt is all too frequently sensed and not reflected upon. It is symbolized rather than explained. It can externalize itself through ecclesiastically and socially "uncomfortable" or unsettling actions and rites, or it can be sensed through the quiet disregard of ecclesiastical or social norms, orthodoxy, and decisions. It is a refusal to yield to legitimation, often without knowing what or why. And it is always the proof that the legitimation of one group's hegemony in society has not fully succeeded.

And yet, when the doubt is allowed to become conscious, and when inescapable suspicion results from a confrontation with reality that profoundly and unequivocally calls into question the explanations and justifications of hegemony, then the same religion that acted as accomplice in the legitimating process can become the source and channel of serious, explicit challenge to the hegemonic group and to its explanations, justifications, and symbols. In other words, a popular religion can be either liberating or alienating in American society. It will play these roles to the degree that it is either confronted by true human, social reality or allowed to escape into a self-created, self-deluding, and therefore false world. The experience of doubt will lead to one role or the other only insofar as the perceived needs and interests of Catholics are served by and through either role. In contemporary American society there does not seem to be room for really credible, intermediate options that appeal to some sort of social neutrality.

The rebellious role is possible for both Euro-American and Latino Catholicisms.[18] But this possibility might not be likely among those who have the most to lose in symbolic, ecclesiastical, or social terms by a more prophetic (and in some sense, rebellious) stance on the part of their faith community.

The more frequent outcome, at least on the part of Latino popular Catholicism, has been a mixture of roles in the subaltern attempt to survive within an adverse context, while somehow hoping for and promoting a favorable change in that context.

LATINO POPULAR CATHOLICISM: ITS ROLES IN AMERICAN SOCIETY AND CHURCH

The subaltern in society are so because they do not have the means of creating and, more specifically, disseminating the explanations, justifications, and symbols needed to convince the rest of society that they —and not the current socially dominant group—should be entrusted with the leadership (or partnership in the leadership) of that society. In other words, they do not have the means to vie for hegemony. Hence, the subaltern groups have no decisive control, for example, over education or mass media. They have no important role in creating, disseminating, and sustaining the symbols and myths through which the society understands, organizes, and justifies itself. Their arguments in favor of change are not distributed by them to the rest of society, but only by the dissemination vehicles in the hands of the current hegemonic group. Consequently, the subaltern arguments are very seldom allowed to appear as actually capable of "convincing" supposedly "reasonable" members of the society. "Reason," after all, is purveyed (by the current socially dominant group) as the domain of the hegemonic sectors.[19]

U.S. Latinos, as a consequence of the occupation or purchase of their lands in the nineteenth century, became the recipients of the dissemination of justifications, symbols, and explanations of the dominant, victorious group and their social allies. Education, mass media, local ordinances, execution of justice, etc., all communicated to Latinos that their social place in the country they were being forced to join was to be inferior to the social place of the victors.[20] They were told, through the dissemination vehicles of hegemony (symbolic and coercive), that they were to remain secondary and ancillary, and that it was either historically inevitable that they be inferior, or it was probably the will of God.

As we saw earlier, the process of legitimizing hegemony always involves the internalization of the reasons of the victors by the vanquished, though always leaving a margin of doubt. Latinos did not and have not proven to be the exception to this process. The Anglophone Catholic Church, probably seeking to escape Protestant prejudice against it, as well as desiring to reap the benefits of joining the American mainstream, became an active participant in the process of legitimation and became an important vehicle for the explanations, symbols, and justifications of the victors to penetrate Latinos, and for keeping the latter "in their place."[21] In siding with the hegemonic group, the

Euro-American Catholic Church chose to marginalize most Latino Catholics while concurrently blaming them for the officially sanctioned pastoral and social neglect.

Legitimation

Latino popular Catholicism has also contributed to this marginalization. As I said at the beginning of the chapter, Latino popular Catholicism can be characterized as an effort by the subaltern to explain, justify, and somehow control a social reality that appears too dangerous to confront in terms and through means other than the mainly symbolic. However, this popular religion is founded on the claim that the divine (identified by the people as the Christian divine) has been and is encountered by them in and through the symbols (ritual, ethical, and doctrinal) of popular Catholicism.

Popular religion can and does legitimize the current American social formation by, in the first place, offering Latinos what appear and claim to be plausible symbolic and ritual means of explaining adverse reality and advancing in it. These means, however, seem to have minimally sufficient sociohistorical efficacy in them.

Popular Catholicism's foundational worldview posits as evident certain premises that do not coincide with those of contemporary, technological society's own worldview.[22] It is impossible in this chapter to thoroughly discuss the modern clash between worldviews witnessed within U.S. Latino popular religion. Nevertheless, let me indicate some of the premises.

The operative worldview apparently foundational to Latino Catholicism seems to posit as evident that the divine intervenes constantly, daily in human reality.[23] Evident also seems to be the premise that God's decisions are the ultimate reason and cause for all that exists. What exists can really change only as the result of God's will or by God's permission. Otherwise change is merely temporary and apparent. Therefore, human efforts at transforming what exists are doomed to failure if they do not correspond to the divine will. This will, unfortunately, is not easily known, and its unveiling is probably the most important (although not the most frequent) role of the Church's ministers.[24]

This foundational, operative worldview also assumes that human existence, from its beginnings, has always included the conflict between good and evil, between good persons and evil persons.[25] It is assumed as self-evident that God established humankind as divided between the rich and powerful on one side, and the poor and weak on the other; that the latter are very frequently being tested for their patience and humility; and, if not found lacking, they will be rewarded with eternal life. The rich and powerful, if they are generous and fair in their use of wealth and power, can also be granted the eternal reward.

Finally, this operative worldview considers as evident that people can leave their divinely appointed state in life only by two means: a divine decision that will allow them to change places in society as the prize for successfully completing a series of tests or challenges, or as the result of another divine decision caused or encouraged by the people's fervent, sincere prayer and penance.

Needless to say, today's American society does not seem to base its operative worldview on these premises. Though it is clear that some non-Latino segments of society share some of these important elements of the Latino worldview, it is also obvious that a more technological, secular set of assumptions seems to be operative in the larger society (even when verbally confessing to believe, perhaps sincerely, in the more traditional premises).[26] Among the "churched" population these traditional assumptions do not appear as operatively self-evident either. The hegemonic ideology is secular indeed, founded on a set of well-known secular worldview-building premises.

Thus, Latino popular Catholicism (which is still the majority religion among U.S. Latinos) is based on a very different set of assumptions about reality and its transformation, their common result being either a symbolic quest (through prayer, rite, and penance) to convince the divine to act, or a self-restraining attitude that leads to social quiescence.

As I mentioned earlier, the will of God is considered to be the final justification and explanation of reality. Unveiling this will and making it known is an important task of the Church's ministers (as representatives of God), according to popular Catholicism. It thus seems that the Anglophone Church, which trains and controls the ordained ministers, has had in its hands (not always successfully, for reasons explained earlier) a powerful means of control and suppression of Latino hopes for justice and change. And thereby a powerful means of enforcing compliance with the current hegemonic social formation and ideology in the country.

Latino popular Catholicism, by its own worldview's assumptions and by the means made possible by these assumptions, has contributed to legitimizing the hegemonic pretensions and claims of society's dominant group. An important traditional channel for change (i.e., the unveiling of the divine will by the clergy), which could have plausibly served as a bridge between cultures and worldviews, has been compromised by the double circumstances of the Anglophone Church's historical need for acceptability in mainstream American society, and the Anglophone hierarchy's canonical control over the training and pastoral work of the clergy (often resulting in the "deculturation" of and feelings of shame in Latino seminarians and priests). Thus, popular Catholicism has been left to its traditional worldview and means, thereby impeded from entering a process of adaptation that could lead it to empower the people in American society.

This popular religion in the United States has all too frequently been left to serve at best as a compassionate sedative to injustice or as an inefficacious palliative to change.[27]

Rebellious Hope

Are U.S. Latinos so naive that they cannot see how their popular religion can be an obstacle to their quest for justice? How does the doubt left by the dissemination of the reasons for hegemony relate to Latino religion in this country? These and other questions must be asked when seeking to understand the roles of Latino popular Catholicism in the United States. We have already pointed to the legitimizing function it plays. Let us now look at other possibilities.

Latinos are certainly not naive. It takes a great deal of courage and intelligence to survive and preserve significant portions of one's cultural identity in an inimical social context that is founded on very different assumptions about existence. Weakened and "sufficiently convinced" by the reasons for hegemony disseminated by society's dominant group and its ecclesiastical allies, Latinos have managed to keep alive (and share among themselves) the doubt about the legitimacy and finality of the current American social formation and the hegemonic ideology that sustains it.

Popular Catholicism, as weakened and "sufficiently convinced" as the people themselves, has nevertheless acted as a very important preserver of their dignity and identity, and as a guarantor of their hope that the transformation of reality is still possible. Thus, in ways that are far from idyllic and are quite expressive of the subaltern condition, popular religion also has the role of keeping a rebellious hope alive. How?

Latinos have not (usually) produced, disseminated, or controlled what is said about them in American society. This is part and consequence of their subaltern condition. Therefore, the contents of self-definition and self-identity (and thus of the resulting sense of dignity and self-worth) are received by Latinos, in the "public" realm, as filtered through and shaped by the holders of hegemony. The family and immediate neighborhood's interpersonal network (i.e., the "private" realm) are often no match for the hegemonic avalanche of symbols and justifications, in spite of their opposite message. The presence of the mass media within the Latino home has penetrated and often broken down the thin barrier between the ("public") symbols of the dominant and the people's ("private") self-definition.

Popular Catholicism stands out as one of the very few social (public and private) spaces that have been able to preserve some high degree of protagonism for Latinos, albeit oftentimes symbolic.

The all-too-frequent pastoral indifference of so many in the Anglophone Church toward Latinos turned out to be an opportunity for

Latino popular Catholicism to reaffirm its historical roots as laity-run and -oriented, and as parallel to the institutions and ordained ministries of the Church. Though explicitly self-identifying as Catholic, popular religion has had a long tradition of autonomy (and at times defiance) vis-à-vis the institutions and ministers of the Church and, occasionally, of prophetic opposition to them.[28]

Contemporary popular Catholicism cannot be misread as a bastardized, insufficient, or superstitious version of so-called normative Catholicism. The observations offered earlier in this chapter concerning the socialization of the experience of the divine should make us suspect that much of what passes for religiously "normative" or "orthodox" is so because it was also (or became) hegemonic.

But more importantly, Latino popular Catholicism sinks its roots in a specific patristic and post-patristic understanding and practice of Christianity, and is thus evidently older than the Tridentine and post-Tridentine "norm" put forth by the Anglophone Church. Though not in necessary opposition to Trent, it preceded it to the Americas by several generations, becoming the established mode of Catholicism (the one in which native and slave populations were evangelized).[29] It cannot be simply dismissed as a decayed form of Christianity without some implicit (or explicit!) complicity with the current hegemonic ideology, and without twisting post-Tridentine Roman Catholicism's claims of continuity with its earlier, patristic, and medieval counterparts.[30]

Today's Latino popular Catholicism still bears the marks of its history, of its Iberian roots, and of the traumatic conquest of Amerindians and African slaves by Christians.[31] It still displays, often through powerful symbols, the expressions of the despair of the vanquished and of their hope for justice.[32] This religion's survival, in spite of five hundred years of efforts to suppress, "educate," or "convert" it, portrays it as the enduring language of a subaltern people. *Religious in expression, content, and experience, this language has long been the code through which hope and courage have been shared and maintained as plausible by generations of Latinos.* Fundamental cultural values have found their place in and their medium of dissemination through popular religion.[33]

Lastly, and perhaps ultimately more importantly, *popular Catholicism embodies a rebellious hope by its very existence as religion.*[34] If, as we saw earlier, religion is the socialization of the experience of the divine, and if in Latino Catholicism the divine is identified with the Christian divine, then this religion of the subaltern claims that the *Christian* God is to be found in and through the culture and experiences of those considered insignificant by American society and Church.[35]

Even admitting the effects of the explanations, justifications, and symbols of hegemony on the subaltern, Latino popular Catholicism (because of its implied claims as socialization of the experience of the divine) may be understood in theological terms as potentially a prophetic sign of rebellion against many attempts to equate the ecclesiastically "normative," "orthodox," or "canonical" with the hegemonic. And in social terms, it may still be comprehended as containing a powerful suspicion (vis-à-vis current American social formation) that has in the past and could in the future translate into social protagonism.

It is needless to say that Latino Catholicism in the United States, though preserving its "hermeneutic of suspicion," has not very often gone beyond its hope into concrete action. The suspicion or doubt it carries seems to convey that today's social and ecclesiastical realities are not final. The doubt points to the possibility of another future, since it suspects that the present (including popular religion's own present) does not express all that can and should be.

IN CONCLUSION

Contemporary popular Catholicism among U.S. Latinos can be judged as alienating the people by assisting in the dissemination of the "reasons" of hegemony (that maintain Latino subaltern status in society). But popular Catholicism can also be judged as offering some of the most powerful and culturally authentic arguments and motives for social protagonism. It too can be (and is) the bearer of a rebellious, prophetic hope that the present is not the last word in history.

Consequently, the dismissal of the religion of Latinos as only (or mainly) a shackle vis-à-vis the necessary struggles for a better future, might be in itself a disguised contribution to the dominant ideology that purveys the people's Catholicism as ignorant and magical. On the other hand, the attempt to preserve popular religion as if it were a folkloric curiosity, a piece of the Latino past, or a tool for "better evangelization," might be as dismissive of the people (or ultimately more) as all the past attempts to destroy their religion. This apparent "preservation" can be a powerful ally of the hegemonic ideology.

Ultimately, the better judgment seems to conclude that popular Catholicism has been and is still important in Latino life. It is too complex in its genesis and history, contents, and sociocultural roles to be summarily dismissed or superficially examined. It has defied all efforts to destroy it, and it has shown extraordinary adaptability. No one academic discipline could ever hope to understand and explain it with sufficient adequacy.

Is this religion promoting a sedating alienation or a hopeful social protagonism? Both. And much more.

Notes

1. There are other, non-Christian "popular religions" in several of the U.S. Latino communities (e.g., *Santería* or *Regla de Osha*, *Vodún*, *Abakuá*, *Palo*

Mayombe or *de Angola*, Spiritism, etc.). Within Latino Protestantism a number of churches can be described as part of the "popular religion" universe (e.g. the church of Mita, and a number of other small and not-too-orthodox churches). I have argued elsewhere that some types of Latino Pentecostalism may be classified as "popular religion" as well (see "Pentecostalism and Popular Catholicism: Preservers of Hispanic Catholic Tradition?", in *ACHTUS Newsletter*, 4:1 [1993], 8-15). I will not be discussing any of these religions in this chapter, however, limiting myself to popular Catholicism as certainly the most widespread and culturally important of all of them.

2. I have surveyed much of the literature on the diverse definitions of religion (in theology and the social sciences), given the reasons for my own definition of religion, and the bibliographical support for it, in my *Evangelización y religiones negras* (Rio de Janeiro: PUC, 1984, 4 vols.), especially in vol. 2.

3. It will become evident that this chapter—as well as most of my work on popular religion—is dependent on the thought of Italian social philosopher Antonio Gramsci and Brazilian sociologist of religion Pedro Ribeiro de Oliveira. From their extensive bibliographies: by A. Gramsci, *Gli intelletuali e l'organizzazione della cultura* (Braz. trans., *Os intelectuais e a organização da cultura* [Rio de Janeiro: Ed. Civilização Brasileira, 1979]); idem, *Note sul Machiavelli, sulla politica e sullo stato moderno* (Braz. trans., *Maquivel, a política e o estado moderno* [Rio de Janeiro: Ed. Civilização Brasileira, 1980]); idem, *Lettere dal carcere* (Braz. trans., *Cartas do cárcere* [Rio de Janeiro: Ed. Civilização Brasileira, 1978]); idem, *Letteratura e vita nazionale* (Braz. trans., *Literatura e vida nacional* [Rio de Janeiro: Ed. Civilização Brasileira, 1978]); idem, *Il materialismo storico e la filosofia di Benedetto Croce* (Braz. trans., *Concepção dialética da história* [Rio de Janeiro: Ed. Civilização Brasileira, 1981]); idem, *Quaderni dei carceri* (Turin: Ed. Einaudi, 1975). And by P.R. de Oliveira, *Religião e dominação de classe* (Petrópolis: Ed. Vozes, 1985); idem, *Evangelização e comportamento religioso popular* (Petrópolis: Ed. Vozes, 1978); idem, *Éléments pour une étude sociologique de la magie* (Louvain: Institut des Sciences Politiques et Sociales/UCL, 1967); idem, *Catequese e socialização da fé* (Rio de Janeiro: CERIS, 1974); idem, *Catolicismo popular na América Latina* (Rio de Janeiro: FERES-AL, 1971); idem, "Catholicisme populaire et hégémonie bourgeoise au Brésil," in *Archives des Sciences Sociales des Religions*, 47:1 (1979), 53-79; idem, "Catolicismo popular como base religiosa," in *CEI-Suplemento*, 12 (1975), 3-11. The influence of these two thinkers is so evident in this chapter that I will refrain from referring to them constantly and repetitiously. The titles mentioned in this note are the ones I have used here.

4. The use of the term "popular" does not merely or mainly imply "widespread," although this is also meant. "Popular" wants to convey the origin and social location of the religion and of those who participate in it. Furthermore, I avoid the use of the term "religiosity," often applied to this symbolic system, because of the implied ideological (and dismissive) judgment on the people's religion.

5. See O. Espín, "Religión popular: un aporte para su definición y hermenéutica," in *Estudios Sociales*, 58 (1984), 41-57.

6. I am using "hegemony" in the Gramscian sense. See, L. Gruppi, *O conceito de hegemonia em Gramsci* (Rio de Janeiro: Ed. Graal, 1978, 2nd. ed.);

and also, H. Portelli, *Gramsci et le bloc historique* (Paris: Presses Universitaires de France, 1972).

7. Although I will be referring exclusively to the American Roman Catholic Church in this chapter, I believe that *mutatis mutandi* my remarks are applicable to (mainline) American Protestant churches as well.

8. Max Weber seemed inclined to think that religious "virtuosi" were the most apt to experience the divine. It appears that Weber assumed that the creation of religious symbols, etc. (i.e., the sphere of the "virtuosi"), was the identifying measure of those capable of the experience. Obviously, this assumption is not self-evident. See M. Weber, *The Sociology of Religion* (London: Methuen, 1966).

9. On this, see my "A 'Multicultural' Church?: Theological Reflections from 'Below'," in *Multicultural Experience in Church and Theology*, ed. W. Cenkner (Mahwah: NJ: Paulist Press, 1995).

10. See H. Portelli, *Gramsci y la cuestión religiosa* (Barcelona: Ed. Laia, 1977; Span. trans. of *Gramsci et la question religieuse* [Paris: Éd. Anthropos, 1974]), 141-162.

11. Ibid., 43-94.

12. I found stimulating, on this point of Catholicism's "sacramental ethos" and the "catholicity" it entails, the sequential reading of D. Tracy, *The Analogical Imagination* (New York: Crossroad, 1986); of A.M. Greely, *The Catholic Myth* (New York: Charles Scribner's Sons, 1990); and of W.G. Jeanrond and J.L. Rike, eds., *Radical Pluralism and Truth: David Tracy and the Hermeneutics of Religion* (New York: Crossroad, 1991).

13. See F. Houtart, "Religion et champ politique: cadre théorique pour l'étude des sociétés capitalistes périphériques," in *Social Compass*, 24:2-3 (1977), 265-272; and idem, "Weberian Theory and the Ideological Function of Religion," in *Social Compass*, 23:4 (1976), 345-354.

14. What might be *sincerely* and ultimately perceived as "real" and "true," therefore, become socially constructed products at the service of the hegemonic group, and a successful result of the arguments of hegemony even within the dominant sectors of society. It should be clear by now that social hegemony and dominance, in my view, are not causally linked to or mainly the consequence of control over the means of production (as in classic Marxist thought). On the contrary, it seems to me that the opposite is more correct; that is, that cultural and symbolic (ideological) hegemony is established before any economic "success" can befall a given group. History seems to point to cases in which those who did not control a society's means of production nevertheless ended up influencing its symbol-making processes and thereby provoked a transformation of the society's social configuration. For the traditional Marxist views on the relationship between culture (and religion), dominance, and the control over means of production, see the fine collection of texts edited by H. Assmann and R. Mate, *Sobre la religión* (Salamanca: Ed. Sígueme, 1974-75, 2 vols.). For the classic study on the "construction" of reality, see, P.L. Berger and T. Luckmann, *The Social Construction of Reality: A Treatise on the Sociology of Knowledge* (New York: Doubleday/Anchor, 1967).

15. The most complete history of Latino Catholicism in the United States is the one edited by J. Dolan, A.F. Deck and J. Vidal, (Notre Dame: University of Notre Dame Press, 1994, 3 vols.). For the particular history of Latino *popular*

Catholicism in the United States, see my text "Popular Catholicism among Latinos" which appears as chapter 5 below and in the third volume of this collective work. To the best of my knowledge, this is the only comprehensive history written on the subject.

16. See P. R. de Oliveira, *Religião e dominação de classe*, 205-346; J.M. Tavares de Andrade, *Religiosité et système symbolique* (Paris: Institut des Hautes Études d'Amérique Latine, 1976).

17. This guilt, as response to doubt in the process of establishing hegemony, is not the same as the theological concept of sin. Nevertheless, it often occurs that the dominant ideology utilizes the category of sin, torn out of its theological mooring, in order to reinforce its effort to stamp out the margin of doubt I am referring to here. A solid analysis of the Catholic, theological meaning and dynamics of sin might, probably, be a way of augmenting this doubt.

18. Since most U.S. Latinos share cultural roots with the peoples of Mexico and the Antilles, it might be useful to recall the role(s) that the *Virgen de Guadalupe* and the *Virgen de la Caridad* played in the development of the national conscience and independence of Mexico and Cuba, respectively. See, for example, J. Lafaye, *Quetzalcóatl and Guadalupe: The Formation of Mexican National Consciousness, 1531-1813* (Chicago: University of Chicago Press, 1976); and the very telling "Petición de los veteranos del ejército de liberación cubano al papa Benedicto XV para que declare como 'Patrona de la República de Cuba' a la Virgen de la Caridad del Cobre," in *La Virgen de la Caridad, patrona de Cuba*, ed. M. Vizcaíno (Miami: SEPI, 1981), 28-29.

19. On this point, see two excellent articles by R.S. Goizueta, "U.S. Hispanic Theology and the Challenge of Pluralism," in *Frontiers of Hispanic Theology in the United States*, ed. A.F. Deck (Maryknoll, New York: Orbis Books, 1992), 1-22; and "Rediscovering Praxis: The Significance of U.S. Hispanic Experience for Theological Method," in *We Are a People! Initiatives in Hispanic American Theology*, ed. R.S. Goizueta (Minneapolis: Fortress Press, 1992), 51-78.

20. From among the very vast (and growing) bibliography on this point, see, for example, R. Horsman, *Race and Manifest Destiny: The Origins of American Racial Anglo-Saxonism* (Cambridge: Harvard University Press, 1981); R. Acuña, *Occupied America: A History of Chicanos* (New York: Harper & Row, 1981, 2nd. ed.); D. Montejano, *Anglos and Mexicans in the Making of Texas, 1836-1986* (Austin: University of Texas Press, 1987); M. Barrera, *Race and Class in the Southwest: A Theory of Racial Inequality* (Notre Dame: University of Notre Dame Press, 1979); and L. Pitt, *The Decline of the Californios: A Social History of the Spanish-Speaking Californians, 1846-1890* (Berkeley: University of California Press, 1966).

21. See M. Sandoval, *On the Move: A History of the Hispanic Church in the United States* (Maryknoll, New York: Orbis Books, 1990); idem, ed., *Fronteras: A History of the Latin American Church in the U.S. since 1513* (San Antonio: Mexican American Cultural Center/CEHILA, 1983); D.F. Gómez, *Somos Chicanos: Strangers in Our Own Land* (Boston: Beacon Press, 1973); J. Hurtado, *Social Distance Between the Mexican American and the Church* (San Antonio: Mexican American Cultural Center, 1975); L.J. Mosqueda, *Chicanos, Catholicism and Political Ideology* (New York: University Press of America, 1986); D.J. Weber, ed., *Foreigners in Their Native Land: Historical Roots of*

the Mexican Americans (Albuquerque: University of New Mexico Press, 1973); R.F. Heizer and A.F. Almquist, *The Other Californians* (Berkeley: University of California Press, 1971); T.E. Sheridan, *Los Tucsoneros: The Mexican Community in Tucson, 1854-1942* (Tucson: University of Arizona Press, 1986); A. Chávez, *The Old Faith and Old Glory: The Story of the Church in New Mexico since the American Occupation* (Santa Fe: The Santa Fe Press, 1946); A.M. Stevens-Arroyo, ed., *Prophets Denied Honor: An Anthology of the Hispanic Church in the United States* (Maryknoll, New York: Orbis Books, 1980); J.P. Dolan, *The American Catholic Experience: A History from Colonial Times to the Present* (New York: Doubleday, 1985); M.J. McNally, *Catholicism in South Florida, 1868-1968* (Gainesville: University Presses of Florida, 1984); and especially the three volumes of the history of Hispanic Catholics (Notre Dame: University of Notre Dame Press, ed. by J. Dolan, A.F. Deck and J. Vidal).

22. I am in no way implying or suggesting that the worldview of the modern, technological society is superior to the Latino popular worldview. In fact, I could argue that the latter contains and expresses some fundamental humanizing and liberating elements altogether missing or lost in so-called modern American society. However, the fact remains that U.S. Latinos must live in and adapt to a technologically and symbolically "modern" context, and so must their popular religion. The alternative to adaptation is either nonviable cultural *anomie* (which cannot be sustained for long without disastrous social and cultural consequences), or a maddening and doomed attempt to keep modernity at bay (as in the case of some Protestant pentecostal and Catholic charismatic or traditionalist groups, and even the case of those who—in the name of the people's struggles—want to establish an inverse form of apartheid). Adaptation to modern society does not, on the other hand, imply "buying into it" uncritically, nor does it involve an assimilationist tendency at all. Perhaps the concept and dynamics of *mestizaje*, as suggested by Virgilio Elizondo and others, might illumine the preferred outcome (on the part of U.S. Latinos) to the challenge posed by modernity. See V. Elizondo, *Mestizaje: The Dialectic of Cultural Birth and the Gospel* (San Antonio: Mexican-American Cultural Center, 1978, 3 vols.); idem, *Christianity and Culture* (San Antonio: Mexican-American Cultural Center, 1975); idem, *Galilean Journey: The Mexican-American Promise* (Maryknoll, New York: Orbis Books, 1983); idem, *The Future Is Mestizo: Life Where Cultures Meet* (Bloomington: Meyer-Stone Books, 1988). Suggestive and useful, on this point, also are J.C. Scannone, ed., *Sabiduría popular, símbolo y filosofía* (Buenos Aires: Ed. Guadalupe, 1984); A. Mirandé, *The Chicano Experience: An Alternative Experience* (Notre Dame: University of Notre Dame Press, 1985); M. de França Miranda, *Um homem perplexo. O cristão na sociedade* (São Paulo: ed. Loyola, 1989); N. García Canclini, *Las culturas populares en el capitalismo* (Mexico: Ed. Nueva Imagen, 1982); R. Rosaldo, *Culture and Truth: The Remaking of Social Analysis* (Boston: Beacon Press, 1993, 2nd. ed.); F. Taborda, *Cristianismo e ideologia* (São Paulo: Ed. Loyola, 1984); A. Parra, *Dar razón de nuestra esperanza. Teología fundamental de la praxis latinoamericana* (Bogota: Publicaciones de la Universidad Javeriana, 1988); and F. Hinkelammert, *Las armas ideológicas de la muerte* (Salamanca: Ed. Sígueme, 1978).

23. See my "The Vanquished, Faithful Solidarity and the Marian Symbol: A Hispanic Perspective on Providence," in *On Keeping Providence,* eds. B.

Doherty and J. Coultas (Terre Haute: St. Mary of the Woods College Press, 1991), 84-101; and, with S. García, "Lilies of the Field: A Hispanic Theology of Providence and Human Responsibility," in *Proceedings of the Catholic Theological Society of America*, 44 (1989), 70-90.

24. The "daily, ordinary ministers" of Latino popular Catholicism are not those ordained by the Church. The ordinary ministers are usually the grandmothers and other older women. Occasionally older men also exercise leadership roles. The *sine qua non* conditions for this "daily, ordinary ministry" seem to be wisdom, a compassionate life, and the gift of counsel (thereby allowing for some exceptions on the age requirement). The laity, and not the Church's ordained ministers, are the real leaders in popular Catholicism. The ordained clergy's sphere seems to be the strictly ritual and "sacramental," as well as socially legitimizing activities. They are perceived, however, as the *probable* final arbitrers of the divine will, although only in cases of substantial disagreement or indecision on the part of the "daily ministers." But even here, the role and advice of the ordained are judged in popular Catholicism under the scrutiny of wisdom, compassion, and their proven gift of counsel. See my "Popular Catholicism among Latinos," in cit.

25. This is clearly seen (as well as the other premises), for example, in Victor Villaseñor's remarkable cultural and family saga *Rain of Gold* (Houston: Arte Público Press, 1991). Much of U.S. Latino literature also expresses the same fundamental worldview.

26. See R. Bellah, R. Madsen, W. Sullivan, A. Swidler and S. Tipton, *Habits of the Heart* (Berkeley: University of California Press, 1985).

27. See National Conference of Catholic Bishops, *The Hispanic Presence: Challenge and Commitment* (Washington: United States Catholic Conference, 1983), 26-27. The more recent (1987) *National Pastoral Plan for Hispanic Ministry*, of the Roman Catholic Church, merely repeats the 1983 official views on popular Catholicism. In Latin America (and, therefore, applicable to the U.S. context only after cautious and critical appraisal) there is at least one suggestive and thorough study on the different approaches that Church authorities, theologians, social scientists, and even political activists have taken in reference to the people's Catholicism; see C. Johansson Friedemann, *Religiosidad popular entre Medellín y Puebla. Antecedentes y desarrollo* (Santiago de Chile: Publicaciones de la Universidad Católica, 1990). I know of no equivalent published work in reference to U.S. Latino popular religion.

28. See my "Popular Catholicism among Latinos," in cit.

29. Ibid. See also my "Tradition and Popular Religion: An Understanding of the *Sensus Fidelium*," chapter 3 above and in *Frontiers of Hispanic Theology in the United States,* ed. A.F. Deck (Maryknoll, New York: Orbis Books, 1992), 62-87.

30. Important on this point are the powerful remarks of Prof. Gary Macy: "People speak of the history of the Roman Catholic Church, or of the Anglican Church, or of one of the Protestant churches as if somehow that particular group (and only that group) started with the apostles. They forget that none of these groups existed before the reformation. Before the reformation, Christians were simply Christians—eastern and western Christians sometimes, but mostly simply Christians. . . . The different Christian groups have a single, common past that reaches from the time of the apostles to the time of the reformation.

Each of the different groups emerging from that past can find its roots there because the past which Christians have inherited is a pluralistic past. What was lost in the reformation was not just Christian unity, but toleration of pluralism" (G. Macy, *The Banquet's Wisdom* [Mahwah: Paulist Press, 1992], 10, 14).

31. See L. Rivera Pagán, *Evangelización y violencia. La conquista de América* (San Juan: Ed. Cemí, 1991).

32. See my "Trinitarian Monotheism and the Birth of Popular Catholicism: The Case of Sixteenth-Century Mexico," chapter 2 above and in *Missiology*, 20:2 (1992), 177-204; and also "Grace and Humanness," in *We Are a People! Initiatives in Hispanic American Theology*, ed. R.S. Goizueta, 133-164.

33. Without suggesting that R. Luxemburg was in fact thinking of popular Catholicism, her few writings on the social role of religion seem akin to my point. It is a shame that this European thinker's work (1870-1919) is not well known in the American academic context. See selected writings on religion by R. Luxemburg, in *Sobre la religión*, vol. 2, ed. H. Assmann and R. Mate, 190-232.

34. This same point, on a broader context, is convincingly argued by V. Lanternari in his classic work, *The Religions of the Oppressed* (London: Macgibbon & Kee, 1963).

35. See my "The God of the Vanquished: Foundations for a U.S. Latino Spirituality," chapter 1 above and in *Listening: Journal of Religion and Culture*, 27:1 (1992), 70-83.

5

POPULAR CATHOLICISM
AMONG LATINOS

Popular religion seems to be an omnipresent phenomenon among U.S. Latinos.[1] It is difficult to understand any of the Hispanic cultural communities without somehow explaining and dealing with popular beliefs and rites.[2]

In this chapter I will attempt to introduce the reader to U.S. Hispanic popular Catholicism.[3] The brevity of these pages should make clear that no complete introduction can or will be attempted. My intent is solely to point to the salient features of popular Catholicism among Latinos, particularly emphasizing the history of this religious universe, while offering some suggestions for an adequate interpretation of this very complex religion. I hope that the bibliography included in the notes (necessarily selective) will lead the reader to further study.

Some clarifications are necessary at the start of this chapter. Hispanics in the United States are very diverse, and their diversity must be taken seriously. However, they also share some basic cultural elements that allow for their common study. The fundamental structures and roles of popular religion stand out as very important in all Latino cultures.

Our study refers only to *U.S.* Hispanics. Although many of them came to this country as immigrants, many others were born here. The nineteenth-century annexations of Florida and the Southwest included not just land but also populations, and the borders have since remained very porous. This evident fact should also explain why a study of U.S. Latino popular Catholicism cannot start with the Mexican-American

---

Originally published in *Hispanic Catholic Culture in the U.S.*, ed. J. Dolan and A.F. Deck (Notre Dame: University of Notre Dame Press, 1994.)

war or the Florida purchase. To disregard the Spanish and Latin American past of the people's religion would deprive the reader (and the people themselves) of some very important elements for an adequate interpretation of this religion. *Hispanic popular Catholicism in the United States, as it now exists, cannot explain itself without its earlier history.*

One final clarification. Although I will be insisting on the importance of popular religion for understanding Latinos, the reader should realize that not all Hispanic Catholics participate in the rites or hold the beliefs of this religious universe. However, an argument can be made on the enduring cultural importance of the symbols of popular Catholicism for all Latinos (including Protestant and agnostic ones).

POPULAR RELIGION

To understand popular Catholicism one should first set it within the more general context of popular religion.

"Popular" and "Official" Religion

Every major religion, to the degree that it has a well-defined normative core of beliefs and liturgy, has aided in the development of a popular version of itself.

Groups of "religious virtuosi"[4] seem to have developed in most religions, thereby becoming responsible for defining what is and what is not normative within the religions. Most believers, however, either do not or cannot have access to the training required for or the doctrinal arguments proposed by the "virtuosi," and hence the majority are placed in the role of following the symbolic production and doctrinal decisions of the specialists.

History shows, nevertheless, that among the majority of believers alternative paths are created to circumvent the exclusive defining power of the "virtuosi." These paths can and do lead to the formation of what could be called a "popular" version of the religion, parallel to the pretended "official" doctrinal and liturgical norm set up and controlled by the specialists, but somehow still connected to the normative version of the religion.[5]

This connection appears to be one of selectively shared symbols and ethos and an appeal to common foundational figures or events. Similarly, there is a re-reading of the doctrines and rites of the "official" religion whereby a set of different emphases is given to them. Furthermore, this re-reading can interpret the religion to the point of altogether disregarding some elements that the "virtuosi" might consider essential, while inversely considering fundamental certain beliefs, rites, or behaviors that the specialists would not emphasize at all.

Let us take Catholicism as an example. It is evident that its "virtuosi" are the theologians and the clergy (especially bishops and popes). It is the role of these specialists to define and set the limits as to what is or is not acceptable and normative in the Church. For most people, however, theological work and episcopal/papal ministry are not the common ways of participating in the religion. Most Catholics play the role of recipients of the doctrinal and liturgical production of the specialists. Nevertheless, the long history of Catholicism (in many culturally shaped ways) has witnessed the birth of parallel paths that attempt to bring the religion close to the people's needs and circumstances. Often enough these paths have re-read "official" Catholicism in the ways indicated above, and thereby produced the people's own version of the religion. This is "popular" Catholicism. It claims to be authentically Catholic, and yet it has re-interpreted the normative as set forth by the Church's "virtuosi."[6]

Apparently, popular Catholicism came into being very early in the history of the religion.[7] The reactions to it, on the part of the specialists, have historically run the gamut from co-optation to outright persecution. The wide variety of official reactions throughout the centuries seems to have depended on how far the popular re-reading of the normative had gone and on how the "virtuosi" perceived the importance of maintaining the links to popular religion in each historical context. All too often, political and other social reasons were more determining of the official reactions to popular Catholicism than strictly doctrinal considerations.

Other Popular Religions among Hispanics

We will devote most of this chapter to the study of popular Catholicism. So at this point I will not enter into the discussion of its origins, development, and contents. However, I do want to point out that the Latino popular version of Catholicism is not the only popular religion present among U.S. Hispanics, nor the only one with some links to it.[8]

Any acquaintance with the Latino communities of Florida and the Northeast (and of some areas of the Midwest and southern California) will indicate the presence of *Santería* and probably *Palo*, for example. It would be highly inaccurate to claim that either one of these religions is a type of popular Catholicism. It would also be unacceptable, given the solid research to the contrary, to view either of them as mainly (or solely) the result of mixing Antillean Catholicism with African religions.

These two Afro-Latino religions have indeed included some symbols of colonial Antillean Catholicism, but only peripherally and almost exclusively for self-preservation purposes. The great syncretic process did not fundamentally occur with Catholicism but among the several African religions (mainly Yoruba, Fon, and Kongo) that came to the Spanish Antilles during the slave trade. It was among these religions that doctrinal and ritual sharing occurred, resulting in *Santería* and *Palo* in this century. To some degree the same can be said of both the Haitian and Dominican forms of *Vodou*.

Many Hispanics, mostly of Cuban ancestry, brought *Santería* and *Palo* to the United States. But today these two religions have spread (and continue to spread) well beyond the Cuban-American communities, reaching into other Latino groups (for example, Puerto Ricans) as well as African-Americans and even Anglos.

Can these religions be called "popular," in the sense expressed earlier? I think so, and for several reasons. First of all, when studied vis-à-vis their African roots, the Antillean versions display the same processes and adaptation that I have pointed out in reference to popular religions in general. They have certainly re-read the religions of origin (whether Yoruba, Kongo, or Fon) and did create other paths in order to bring the older African specialists' normative core close to a people now enslaved in the Caribbean. These resulting paths, interestingly enough, in turn became the new norm in the Antilles.[9] New "virtuosi" came to define the religion in Cuba, simplifying it and adapting it to the new circumstances. With immigration, new parallel paths (now in the United States) have begun to appear, further separating present-day *Santería* and *Palo* from their original counterparts as the former "popularly" adapt and re-read (in the American context) the norms handed down by their "virtuosi."

· Another reason for believing that these two religions are indeed "popular" is the content resulting from their re-reading of the norm of the root religions. As I said above, they simplified and adapted to new circumstances. However, the way they have gone about it and, especially, some of the doctrines and rituals that have resulted from these processes are not quite in agreement with what a present-day Yoruba (or Fon, or Kongo) religious specialist would hold as "fully orthodox," if the latter category were used.[10]

Besides *Santería* and *Palo*, which are the most widespread of the other Hispanic popular religions, there are others. For example, among U.S. Latinos with roots in the Dominican Republic there are varieties of beliefs and rituals that can be identified as popular adaptations of the Dominican strand of *Vodou*. Among Dominican-Americans other religious forms of lesser importance appear as well.[11]

Puerto Ricans have created an interesting version of Kardecian Spiritism, with strong and lasting appeal among many. There is a growing bibliography on this type of spiritism, showing it in turn to be a popular adaptation of the Kardec canon.[12] In some quarters Puerto

Rican spiritism has begun a process of mixing with *Santería*, the results of which are still unpredictable.

Among the Mexican and Mexican-American populations there does not seem to be (as compared with Hispanics of Antillean ancestry) a wealth of popular religions, apart from popular Catholicism. However, some vestiges of ancient native religious practices and beliefs are discernable, though more frequently at the hermeneutic level, and well mixed with current popular Catholicism. I will return to this later.

Distinct popular religions, apart from popular Catholicism, do not seem to be in evidence among Mexicans or Mexican-Americans in the United States. I wonder, however, if research were done on some types of southwestern rural *curanderismo* whether we might not indeed discover more than just traces of ancient religions. Nevertheless, as far as the data presently allows us to conclude, non-Christian popular religions appear mostly in the U.S. Latino contexts of marked Antillean influence.

THE STUDY OF POPULAR CATHOLICISM

There is no doubt that the most frequent religion among U.S. Hispanics is popular Catholicism. This is the case among all the different cultural communities (Mexican and Mexican-American, Puerto Rican, Cuban-American, etc.). Certainly, many Latinos participate in the "official" type of Catholicism, but both numerically and culturally the symbolic universe of the popular version of the religion is by far the more widespread and commanding of the two.

It might seem, after only a superficial glance, that the different Hispanic cultural communities have their own style of popular Catholicism. And that is indeed the case. The influences that came together to forge this religious universe were quite distinct. Though the Spaniards imposed the same Iberian religion on their American colonies, here it was received and *interpreted* by diverse groups of native Amerindians or Africans. Hence, the resulting Catholicism of the Mexican-American is not, for example, identical to that of the Cuban-American or of the Puerto Rican. However, a closer look at these would clearly indicate a basic similarity in the fundamental structures and functions of the popular religious universe in all three communities.[13]

It can be argued that, first of all, popular Catholicism is the manner in and through which most U.S. Latinos are Catholic; and secondly, that this popular Catholicism is a key matrix of all Hispanic cultures. If this is the case, and I believe it is, then the importance of the study of this religion is crucial for an adequate understanding of all Hispanics, whether they currently participate in this type of Catholicism or not. I need not point out the obvious consequences for historical, pastoral, and theological studies.[14]

There is a growing body of literature on Hispanic religion, both in Latin America and in this country. However, the approaches taken in studies of this religious universe are extraordinarily diverse.[15] One can find works that run from the merely descriptive and panoramic to those that attempt a most detailed analysis of very minute pieces of the religious puzzle. There are studies that concentrate on the social implications while others look at the symbolics. Some have emphasized the political consequences without regard to the faith contents of the religion, and yet others have done the exact opposite.

The methodologies used vary from the Marxist (orthodox, humanist, etc.) to the naively pious, with every other possible interpretive school represented in between. The motives for studying popular Catholicism are as diverse as the methods employed, running the gamut from entrenched defense to utter disdain. And although most serious works have left their contribution to the field, it has become evident that the days are past when a single author, alone, could dream of understanding or explaining Hispanic popular Catholicism in a sufficiently adequate and complete way. Indeed, no single discipline could ever accomplish this feat.

I bring this up because it is important for the reader to realize that I am not claiming, nor could I claim, that what follows is that single, definitive presentation or interpretation of popular Catholicism among Latinos in the United States. This chapter is much more modest and realistic. It is a quick synthesis of my own and other people's research, requiring further study, nuancing, and contextualization.

POPULAR CATHOLICISM: A BRIEF HISTORY

Latino popular Catholicism is "popular" in the sense described earlier in this chapter. It is the religious universe that Hispanics created in order to bring closer to them what they interpreted to be the foundational and other key elements of normative Catholicism.

This creation occurred through a centuries-long process of re-reading and adapting what the Church's "virtuosi" presented as normative. It happened within the specific contexts of vanquishment and depredation resulting from the Spanish conquest of the Americas, and later the second-class status imposed on Latinos after the Euro-American annexations. In other words, there are very strong components of suffering and abuse that have acted as historical matrix for the religious universe of Hispanics and which still show themselves, for example, in iconography and ritual.[16]

How did contemporary U.S. Latino popular Catholicism come about? To answer this question adequately, no matter how synthetically, one must first turn to medieval Spain, then to its religious encounter with the native Amerindian and African worlds during the early and the late colonial periods. This section will summarily cover the history of popular religion, from Iberia to the dawn of the nineteenth century.

Without the story of the formation and development of *popular* Catholicism, no matter how briefly it is told, we cannot expect to understand the religious present of Latinos.

Medieval Spanish Catholicism

There is no need here to describe the beliefs, rituals, and other religious practices of the Spanish Middle Ages. However, some general understanding of the religious world of the *conquistadores* is necessary because, after all, it was their religion that was brought to, imposed on, and ultimately interpreted by Amerindians and Africans in this hemisphere—and unfortunately used to justify the conquest of these lands. Hispanic Catholicism, normative or popular, cannot be understood without recourse to the Iberian world.

Roman Catholicism, as we know and describe it today, did not exist before the Council of Trent (1545-63). What existed before Trent and the Reformation was simply Western Christianity.[17] Now, that distinction might seem surprising or meaningless to some readers, but I think it is very important because the religion brought to the Americas by the Spaniards was not *Roman* Catholicism, but Western Christianity in its *Iberian* form. It was not the Church of anti-Protestant polemics but the religion that had sustained the seven centuries of the Spanish *Reconquista*.[18] This Christianity, therefore, was medieval and pre-Tridentine, and it was planted in the Americas approximately two generations before Trent's opening session.

It might not appear obvious, at first reading, what I am implying by these distinctions. So let me explain.

The *Reconquista* Period

Iberian Christianity had a long history prior to 1492.[19] It was one of the oldest organized Churches in the West, its roots firmly planted in the patristic period. Leander and Isidore had been two of its great theological stars, profoundly influencing the later Middle Ages in the rest of Europe. Some of its regional councils and synods contributed decisively to settling doctrinal and disciplinary questions, with ramifications felt even today. The Iberian Visigothic Church, however, was to be tested by the crises begun in 711 C.E.

That year saw the start of the Muslim conquest and occupation of most of the Iberian peninsula. While the rest of Europe was confronting the so-called Dark Ages and then attempting to grow beyond them, in Muslim Spain a major civilization was being created, the synthesis of Islamic, Christian, and Jewish contributions. Arguably, the most advanced and sophisticated society in the medieval West was to be found in Spain during this period. Geography and historical circumstance had forced Muslims and Christians to live next to each other. Jointly they created great centers of learning, the envy of the rest of the continent. Through medieval Spain, for example, the wisdom and writings of the ancient Greeks were preserved, copied, and shared with Europe. In Spain, as opposed to the rest of the continent, Christians had to deal with the "infidel" for centuries, not merely or mainly in battle, but in everyday trade, family ties, and in religious dialogue.

For a number of political, economic, ethnic, and religious reasons, the sole remaining Christian land in the Iberian peninsula (the kingdom of Asturias) began the long process called the *Reconquista*. It took more than seven hundred years, and in 1492 it brought final victory to the Christians, by then led by the crowns of Aragon and Castille.

During this entire period, in the lands held by the Muslims as well as in those controlled by Christian kings, the new Spanish national character was being forged.

A unique mixture (perhaps difficult to comprehend in modern "either/ or" categories), the Spanish character that resulted from the seven centuries of Muslim occupation and Christian *Reconquista* became notorious for outstanding feats of heroism, for profound religious commitment and reflection, for sincere love and promotion of the arts and of learning, and for great cooperation with and tolerance of those who were different. And yet, somehow, this same resulting Spanish character was equally capable of incredible acts of cruelty, of militant religious bigotry, of great intolerance, and of sometimes despising even simple gestures of human compassion. Apparently the *Reconquista*, with its multisecular demands of cooperation with the enemy even while engaged in war against him, forged these contradictory national traits. Two powerful churchmen, both of the same fifteenth-century Spanish Church, stand out as telling symbols of this double-sided national character: Jiménez de Cisneros (the great reformer and humanist) and Torquemada (of inquisitorial fame).

As can be expected, this entire period had its impact on Iberian Christianity.[20] The increasingly victorious Spanish monarchies justified their military successes through religious categories. It was evident, as far as they were concerned, that the God of Christians was the only true God, and therefore they—defenders of the true faith against the errors of the Muslim "infidels"—were being blessed by God with victory over the enemies of true religion. In typical medieval fashion, religion was called upon to legitimize the spoils of the victors. So in 1492, after the defeat of the last Islamic ruler, the attention of the monarchy and the Church was turned to cleansing Spain of all who might otherwise "contaminate" the faith and land of Christians.

But just as this view of victorious Christianity was being promoted, another and quite different thread was also being woven into the

Spanish religious fabric. There was, during the same period, a renaissance of piety and devotion, of monasticism, and of theological learning. Both at the universities and in the villages, religious interests and fervor seem to have shown a marked increase. In the rural areas of Spain, especially in the south, the numbers of hermits and *penitentes* swelled considerably. The period of the *Reconquista* had indeed shaped Iberian Christianity in ways that paralleled the national character.

The year 1492 saw the final consolidation of Christian control over the Iberian peninsula. That same year brought to the Spaniards the news of a vast and very different world on the other side of the ocean. With this news the Spanish character engaged in the task of conquering that other world, therein displaying its dual capacity for heroic generosity and for brutal bigotry.

The Medieval and Pre-Tridentine Periods

I said earlier that it was important to distinguish between modern Roman Catholicism, the fruit of Trent and the polemics since the Reformation, and the Christianity that came to the Americas in the fifteenth and sixteenth centuries.

Iberian Christianity was medieval and pre-Tridentine. In that religious world, every dimension of daily life participated (or could participate) in the transmission and sustenance of Christianity. To some degree, the patristic notion of *traditio* remained very much the norm.

Traditio cannot be simply translated today as "tradition."[21] *Traditio*, during the Iberian Middle Ages, included the beliefs held by Christians as part of revelation and as part of the ancient creedal definitions. It involved the liturgical and sacramental practices of one's local and regional Church. But *traditio* also implied the behavior that was expected of Christians, the pious devotions of one's community, many other religious beliefs and demands held to be important for Christian living, the (canonical and consuetudinal) discipline of the local and Western Church, and just about every customary facet of daily life in which religion was involved. As can be deduced from this description, the medieval Iberian concept of *traditio* was practically coextensive with what Christians believed, how they worshipped, and how they lived.

With this view of *traditio* in mind, we can understand why pre-Tridentine Spaniards communicated their faith through symbol and rite, through devotions and liturgical practices, and why the *autos sacramentales*[22] became so popular and important. We can see that the cycles and components of village life became fundamental transmitters of the Christian message. The teaching of the gospel did not usually occur through the spoken, magisterial word, but through the symbolic, "performative" word. Even the great preaching crusades caused great celebrations and indeed took place as part of local communal celebration.

There were synods and great universities where bishops and theologians would explain and theorize, but the vast majority of people did not participate in this official, doctrinal world. For "common folk" (and for much of the clergy), essential doctrine was embedded in the ordinary.[23]

It would be naive to think that distinctions were not made in medieval Spain between what was essential to Christianity and what was not.[24] The people did have, after all, the Bible and the creeds. But their religious world, in spite of all the distinctions, did not divorce doctrine from the other aspects of Christian living, and did not teach doctrine except *through* all other dimensions of Christian living. One was a Christian not by merely or mainly holding to correct doctrine (though this too was necessary), but by also living accordingly. Medieval *traditio*, for all its evident shortcomings and abuses, was not as naive or farfetched a notion as today's Catholics might think. Within the Iberian sacral worldview, all of reality could "sacramentally" speak the message of religion.

At this point in our study I want to recall one crucial moment in the history of Western Christian theology.[25] During one of the sessions of the Council of Trent (in 1546), Jesuit theologian Claude LeJay made a distinction between *traditiones quae ad fidem pertinent* ("traditions that pertain to the faith") and the *traditiones ecclesiae* ("traditions of the church," which closely resemble what Luther had called "human sentences"). LeJay was probably not aware of the consequences his contribution was going to have. Incorporated into post-Tridentine theology, the separation between received, unchanging doctrine (*Traditio*, now with capital "T") and other (equally received) reformable traditions (*traditiones*, now with small-case "t") was to have an enormous impact on modern Roman Catholicism. As the decades progressed, revelation came to be viewed as "doctrinal," and the rest of Christian living (spirituality, worship, the ethical life of communities and individuals) became dangerously demoted to "reformable traditions." LeJay, Trent, and their successors in Catholicism seem to have responded to the reformers' arguments by assuming as valid many of the latter's premises. This was certainly not medieval Western Christianity.

The Colonial (Re)birth of Popular Catholicism

Most of the Spaniards that came to the Americas in the fifteenth and sixteenth centuries were people from the villages. They were often enough from southern Spain (especially Andalucia and Extremadura). Even the "official" missionaries, though trained in theology, were sent to the newly conquered lands not because of their profound theological expertise but because of their ability to communicate with "common folk." In other words, the Christianity brought to the Americas had to be—given the people who did the evangelizing—the "village" *traditio* and not the highly doctrinal and elaborate "university" or "magisterial" version. Later attempts at implanting a more doctrinally oriented and sophisticated, post-Tridentine Catholicism tended to remain largely at the level of the colonial elites.

There is no question that the majority of friars and other religious that came to the Americas did so with the sincere intention of proclaiming the gospel to the native and slave populations.[26] Most missionaries worked very hard and were very creative in developing catechetical methods for the conversion of the Amerindians and Africans. But they were children of their time and culture, thereby transposing to the new lands the national traits and religious universe of fifteenth- and sixteenth-century Spain.

The colonial evangelization of the Americas did not happen as the result of the religious dialogue between equals. The interlocutors engaged in this evangelistic process *because* they were definitively *not* equal.[27] The Christian missionaries arrived on this continent and had the possibility of making themselves heard only because other Christians had *first* violently conquered lands and peoples, forcing them to submit to the new religion. Evangelization was made possible by conquest, that is, by first vanquishing the potential hearers of the gospel. This irrefutable historical fact has colored and shaped Latino popular Catholicism.

It is of no lesser importance that the original justification offered to the native populations (and later to the African slaves) for their conquest and vanquishment was, precisely, that the Christian God had sent the Spaniards to them. It was argued by many of the missionaries that Christianity showed its superiority over the native religions in that victory had been given to the Spanish *conquistadores* over the Amerindians and Africans. It was evident, they claimed, that the Christian God had proven to have far greater power than all the native divinities. The consequence of this line of argument was clear to the conquered peoples—they had to submit to the new God and accept this divine power and will, as expressed by the missionaries and the Spanish colonial authorities.

Much has been said, and rightly so, on the frequent brutality that the Spaniards displayed against Amerindians and Africans. Even during the early colonial period a number of powerful Spanish voices were raised (very often without much success) against the atrocities being committed. One of the worst and bloodiest genocides in human history was perpetrated against the native populations of the Americas by the Spanish. And though many missionaries attempted to defend the victims, their defense proved quite insufficient.[28] In regard to the African slaves, the historical reality was even worse because there were no great voices ever raised on their behalf, and their slavery lasted well into the nineteenth century.[29]

It was in this context of conquest, brutality and vanquishment that the Christian gospel was first announced in the Americas. Unfortunately, the subsequent colonial and postcolonial history did not substantially change the structures of domination planted by the original conquest. Many of the blatant atrocities were either stopped or covered up in the later period, but violence and depredation continued in and through the new institutions (often well into the present).

Conversions and Sacral Worldviews

When confronted with the colonial history of the Americas, one might well ask why didn't the Amerindian and African populations rebel against the Spaniards and, more to our point, why did they accept Christianity? There were, indeed, many well-documented cases of rebellion on the part of natives and slaves.[30] There were also instances of refusal to accept the religion of the conquerors. But these attempts, remarkable as some were, ended in failure. Why?

In the specific area of our study (i.e., the religion of the people), it seems at least misleading or naive to claim that natives and slaves did not really accept Christianity but had it forced onto them. Although there is some truth to that claim, historical facts nevertheless point to a widespread acceptance of the new religion.[31] Even though some African religions have survived and are still very much alive among Latinos, they do not erase the great success of colonial Catholicism's evangelizing efforts. Once again, why was Christianity accepted?

I would argue that, in a horrible twist of coincidences, Spanish Christianity had in its favor the very religious arguments used to justify the conquest, and that Amerindian and African religions had against them their own sacral worldviews. Let me explain.

We have already seen that the Spanish believed theirs to be the only true religion and the only true God. Furthermore, they sincerely thought that this God had given them victory over the Iberian Muslim kingdoms precisely because they (the Spanish Christians) were defending truth against the errors of the infidels. We have also seen how these Christians held that it was their God who had made them overcome all odds and conquer the vast American lands. In their mind this divine favor only indicated that they were right, and consequently it was their privilege to subjugate the conquered ("infidel") peoples and impose Christianity on them.

What we often forget nowadays is that the Amerindian and African sacral worldviews assumed as basically true the same premises also held by the Spanish.

The Nahuatl-speaking peoples of Mesoamerica and the native Arawak (Taínos and Caribs) of the Antilles,[32] as well as the later African slaves (especially Yorubas, Fon, and Kongos), had inherited worldviews that explained human success and failure in explicitly religious terms. These peoples assumed that divine favor rested upon the victors and not upon the vanquished. They further believed that it was important to take on the worship (and the accompanying beliefs associated with this worship) of the gods of the victorious. Within their sacral worldviews, the refusal to adopt the new divinities was an invitation to more cosmic calamities and earthly punishment.

Evidently, these assumptions did not necessarily imply the abandonment of their religion on the part of the conquered, but they certainly can help us understand today why those who lost in fifteenth- and sixteenth-century America could accept the beliefs and worship of the winners, without our having to appeal to arguments of religious imposition, as if these were the only or best possible explanation. Nevertheless, one must also keep in mind that this acceptance of the victorious God happened in Mexico and the Antilles from the cultural perspective of Amerindians and Africans. Therefore, one can wonder if the "conversions" were so in fact (in the common Western sense of the term), or whether they were only part of the process of re-reading and interpreting normative Christianity. This process would eventually lead to today's popular Catholicism.

Public Ritual as Religious Communication

One interesting cultural detail is very germane to our discussion. It is well known that Amerindians (in Mesoamerica especially, but also in the Antilles) and Africans (particularly the Yoruba) engaged in religious "pageantry" at key moments in their ritual cycle.[33] Sacred spaces— often in front of temples or shrines—were reserved, at least at some point in the yearly calendar, for these elaborate public (and popular) ceremonies. It is no insignificant fact, for example, that the great Tenochtitlan included the great ceremonial avenues and causeways that led to its impressive temple complex.

These ceremonies appear to have been highly complex, involving the participation of large numbers of people. Preparation for the rite was almost as important as the ritual action itself. And through it all the holy stories of divinities and ancestors, the doctrinal contents of the religion and its ethical demands, were communicated to the participants. These elaborate ceremonies, therefore, acted as an indispensable "catechetical" moment in the religious life of the people.

Everyday life, however, was not as religiously elaborate. Nevertheless, there were small family and clan shrines, and frequent rites celebrated in them (on a daily basis in some places). And here again we seem to find ritual action used as a main channel for religious instruction. It is not insignificant that all ritual celebration, massive or familial, is necessarily symbolic.

The reader might recall the importance of the Iberian *autos sacramentales*, their popularity and use in catechesis. Religious rituals (symbolic, massive ceremonies or familial rites) were well known and liked in medieval Christianity. The coincidental similarity with the Amerindian and African liturgical universes proved to be indispensable when the missionaries attempted to communicate Catholicism to natives and slaves.[34]

Colonial "Normative" Christianity

In their culturally possible (and probably culturally expected) acceptance of Christianity, and in their subsequent interpretation of the latter, Amerindians and Africans had no way of knowing that *what they were assuming to be normative, "official" Catholicism was in fact Iberian and pre-Tridentine Christianity*. This fact is of utmost importance and consequence. The religion presented to natives and slaves by the Spaniards and their missionaries was the medieval *traditio*, the "village"-type of Catholicism that I mentioned earlier. Furthermore, the religion that the new colonial Christians passed on to their *mestizo*[35] (and native and Afro) descendants was this pre-Tridentine Christianity —it was, after all, the only Christianity that was preached to them for centuries.

When, almost a century later, the theology and reforms of Trent finally arrived in the Americas,[36] they were often used (by royal and church authorities) to keep Lutheran and Calvinist ideas out of the continent, thereby preserving pre-Tridentine Christianity on this side of the Atlantic (since no urgent reason other than anti-Protestant polemics was then found to systematically carry out what the council had mandated). Even though seminaries were established and other disciplinary reforms implemented, these benefited the Spanish and *criollo*[37] elites and seldom affected the vast majority of people. Perhaps the reformed liturgy, celebrated in a language (Latin) and through symbols doubly foreign to Amerindians and Africans, was the only popularly accessible Tridentine innovation—when and if priests were available. Furthermore, given that for quite a long period of time, during the colonial centuries, only Spaniards and their *criollo* sons could be admitted to the ordained ministry, even priests and bishops were not often inclined to work for any implementation or spread of Trent's teaching among Amerindians, Africans, and the new *mestizos*. In the clergy's view, this would at best be unnecessary for the people's religious well-being. Thus the medieval *traditio* remained, by and large, "normative" Christianity for the majority.

Interpretations of the "Normative" during the Colony

There are not many studies on colonial Amerindian and African inter-pretations of pre-Tridentine Catholicism in Mesoamerica and the Antilles.[38] One important reason for this dearth of material is that natives and slaves were not allowed to preserve in writing much of what they thought of Christianity. After all, they confronted almost certain danger if they dared to express (especially in writing) any "unautho-rized" understanding of or misgivings about the new religion. However, a few priceless pieces of evidence have survived. Other "texts"—written, visual, or performed—have also been preserved and through them we can surmise what the conquered thought of the new religion.

The evidence (written or otherwise) from the late colonial period is more plentiful, because by then some of the legal prescriptions against *mestizos* had been removed or had become obsolete. For most of the three to four centuries of colonial rule, however, the *mestizos* shared (both as actors and as victims) in most of the prejudice against natives and slaves. Although a number of these mixed-race people were able in time to move up the social ladder, both bigotry and law kept the vast majority of them (and not a few of those who seemed to have "suc-ceeded" in life) in second-class status vis-à-vis the Spaniards and white *criollos*. Much of today's popular Catholicism survived the late colonial period thanks in part to the *mestizos* who appropriated it in their search for a distinct national, ethnic, and cultural identity.

Evidence Available Today

Let me very briefly summarize the main types of evidence we have available to us today and through which we can surmise the people's re-reading of colonial, "normative" Christianity.

Some of the early pictographic catechisms used in evangelization have been preserved.[39] Their particular importance in tracing what the native populations understood is based on the fact that most of these cate-chisms were drawn by *tlacuilos*,[40] interpreting what the missionaries taught. The contents of these catechisms, though basically orthodox in doctrine, do evidence an emphasis on the devotional and the symbolic as the proper means of evangelizing. Needless to say, in this they closely resemble the methods of medieval *traditio*. But more importantly, these catechisms include some explanations of Christian beliefs and practices that could not possibly have come from the missionaries' preaching. Some of these pictographs re-interpreted terms and meanings, turning them into critiques (albeit mild) of the new religion, while other draw-ings indicate the beginnings of a re-reading of colonial Christianity in ways easily identifiable with today's popular Catholicism.[41]

Parallel to these pictographic catechisms drawn by natives are a number of other religious education texts directly written (seldom painted) by the Spanish missionaries themselves.[42] These other catechisms can indicate to us what, in the intended native listeners' or readers' understanding, was considered—in Spanish eyes—inadequate, unacceptable, or in need of further catechesis. As the colonial period progressed, fewer specialized catechisms appeared and more imitations (or outright copies) of imported Spanish models became common. Needless to say, this latter approach reinforced the perceived and actual distance between "official" Catholicism and the people's religion.

Other texts written by missionaries and other colonial authors also contribute to our contemporary understanding of the natives' and slaves' interpretation of and reaction to Christianity. These writings run the gamut from very detailed and descriptive chronicles to private letters sent to superiors or friends.[43]

In some rural areas of Mexico and of the Antilles today, one can still find interpretations of Christianity "performed" in popular liturgical rites, in songs, and in annual religious plays that date back to the colonial period. Many U.S. Latino communities have preserved (and somewhat modified) a number of these songs, rites, and dramas, and thus they can still be witnessed and heard.[44] The emphases and the explanations communicated through these "performed texts" of popular Catholicism often coincide with the normative Christianity of the colonial Church; but, once again, there are enough variations that indicate the presence of popular interpretations of the religion. And evidently, the very existence of these liturgical and catechetical "performances" recalls the evangelizing methods of pre-Tridentine Catholicism.

The pious, artistic styles of religious imagery (crucifixes, *santos de palo*, etc.) that originated in the Spanish period and that have been actively preserved till today, repeat the same pattern of substantial agreement with what was considered to be the Catholic norm, while at the same time displaying emphases that would point to an interpretive effort on the part of the popular artists.[45] The symbolic catechetical vehicle, so typical of medieval Spain, continues to be successfully used and displayed in the present.

Also preserved for us are a few writings, by early Amerindian and later Afro-Antillean authors, that clearly show the painful recognition of their peoples' plight and, with decreasing vehemence, incisively critique the religion of Spaniards and *criollos*.[46] As the colonial period progressed into the eighteenth and early nineteenth centuries, more of these writings appeared and often fueled the aspirations for independence of later *criollo* and *mestizo* generations. These texts are not necessarily attempts at religious interpretation, but what they assume to be integral parts of Catholicism (whether to accept them, ignore them, or critique them) does indicate the manner and content of the popular re-reading of Christianity at the time of their writing.

Interpretation of the "Normative"

What do these pieces of evidence taken together seem to say about what natives, slaves, and *mestizos* thought was "normative" in Christianity, as it was presented to them during the colonial period? What reinterpretation(s) of this religion does the evidence indicate?

Since later in this study I will present an overview of the religious contents of contemporary Hispanic popular Catholicism in the United States, at this point it seems best to limit the presentation of the re-reading to the Spanish colonial period (which ended early in the nineteenth century in Mexico, the American Southwest, and Florida, or very late in the same century in Cuba and Puerto Rico).[47]

Native, slave, and *mestizo* religious interpretation during the colonial age—a veritable "popular re-interpretation" of what was considered to be "normative" Catholicism—is very important. *Postindependence and postannexation developments in popular Hispanic Catholicism, which are with us today, occurred from the doctrinal, ethical, and liturgical premises assumed as true and normative in Christianity by the colony's conquered peoples and their descendants.*

It is equally important to keep in mind that the medieval Iberian village, which was the socio-economic and political microcontext for the shaping of Spanish Catholicism and of Spain's daily life, was sufficiently transplanted to and inculturated in Mesoamerica and the Antilles. It survives today (and not just architecturally).[48] The sacral worldview of the village was very much alive in the shaping of colonial popular Catholicism and its more contemporary descendant.

For the sake of brevity, I will point to one key area (the doctrines on the trinitarian nature of the one God) in which a "popular re-interpretation" of religion took place.[49] Obviously, the ideal introduction to Hispanic popular Catholicism would include sections on the ecclesiology, ethics, liturgy, etc., implicit in colonial popular religion. Unfortunately, we do not live or write in an ideal world.

What did natives and slaves hear and understand about the Trinity? The question is not irrelevant, and it certainly does not refer to some obscure or esoteric fine point of Christian theology. In mainstream, orthodox Catholicism, belief in the one and triune God is absolutely indispensable. Hence, no evangelization could possibly claim to be acceptable without clearly communicating the trinitarian doctrines. Trying to communicate is one thing, however; being successful in the attempt is another. Though other elements of Catholicism might seem more interesting, it can be argued that no other teaching has deeper consequences than the one on the Trinity.

Iberian Christians of the fifteenth century and later believed in the traditional trinitarian doctrines. They were familiar with the creedal formulations of Christian antiquity. After all, these doctrinal statements were repeated every Sunday at the Eucharist, included in the baptismal rite, and repeated often enough in other devotional and liturgical contexts. Every prayer and every major activity of the day began with the *En el nombre del Padre, y del Hijo, y del Espíritu Santo* ("In the name of the Father, and of the Son, and of the Holy Spirit").

Familiar with the doctrines and terms they were. But what did the people in the villages of Spain understand and believe about the Trinity? I am afraid that one can only guess (based on the few medieval indications we have) that most Christians in rural Spain simply did not worry about understanding or explaining trinitarian doctrines. They believed, or so they liturgically repeated and claimed, that there was only one God, and that there were three Persons in that one God: Father, Son, and Holy Spirit. In this the Iberian villagers were in agreement with doctrinally orthodox Christianity. But I would argue that this coincidence with orthodoxy was mostly at the terminological level. It seems that what they in fact held to be true was a strict monotheism that would leave little or no room for the trinitarian relations. And given this type of monotheism, their christology had to run the gamut from Arian to Docetist.[50]

The mendicant friars who were first responsible for the evangelization of the Americas, the Spanish villagers who came as the original conquerors, and all those who followed them were convinced of their doctrinal orthodoxy. The missionary effort that ultimately succeeded in "converting" first the natives and then the Africans was based on this conviction.

What did natives and slaves hear and understand about the Trinity? What *could* they! I have shown elsewhere why the probable doctrinal outcome of colonial evangelization on the Trinity was either strict monotheism (with concomitant Arian or Docetist christologies), or practical tritheism (frequently disguised by using the trinitarian language of the liturgy).[51] Clearly, the theological terms I am employing here would never have been accessible to the natives or the slaves, but the doctrinal contents expressed through these terms seem to have been there.

It is my belief, given the Hellenic background and European cultural settings of mainstream Christian doctrines and terms on the Trinity, that no evangelization on the one and triune God could have been successful in the fifteenth, sixteenth, or even later centuries. It is only today, with our growing awareness of the depth of culture's impact on human thought and on perceptions of truth, that new possibilities are slowly opening for authentically inculturated mediations of the Christian trinitarian doctrines among the non-European or non-"Europeanized."

There can be little doubt that the very idea of monotheism would have been extraordinarily foreign to natives and slaves.[52] Culturally, historically, religiously, all of Mesoamerican and Antillean reality defied the monotheistic doctrine of Christianity. Though it might be possible to theoretically argue that natives and slaves were somehow capable of understanding what the missionaries were teaching on the Trinity, in real life this understanding was not very likely—not because of lack of intelligence but because of the sheer alien and culturally outlandish nature of the concepts. More importantly, the massive "conversions" of peoples could not possibly have facilitated any kind of real native understanding of or reflection on what Christian monotheism was all about.

Monotheism, however, was being preached by people who must have culturally and religiously confused the natives and the slaves. Most of the Christians with whom Amerindians and Africans came in contact—during the foundational period of the colonial Church—were pre-Tridentine Christians. And we already saw how nominal (even if sincere) was the trinitarian belief of these Iberian Christians of the fifteenth and sixteenth centuries.

These Christians were claiming that there was only one God, in three "Persons." Native and African mythologies had also claimed that the one high god was capable of being in more than one form.[53] But the divine form, in these mythologies, had always been masculine, feminine, or both. So it was only a matter of time before these ancient and culturally reasonable categories came to the aid of natives and slaves as they attempted to make sense of Christian teaching on God.

It is well known that the missionaries did try to explain as best they could something about the three Persons of the Trinity, especially what each meant and did in a Christian's life. The missionaries, however, could not have prevented (or perhaps foreseen) their listeners' understanding these explanations from a dramatically different cultural perspective. A strong argument can be made to show that the trinitarian doctrine was probably heard and interpreted through the categories of the masculine/feminine forms of the one supreme god. The results of this highly plausible interpretation of Christianity are impressive, indeed.

Briefly presented, the early native interpretation seems to have concluded that the Christian high god, in his masculine form, was the so-called "Father," or just plain "God." This was the conquering, majestic, and frequently authoritarian divinity that had handed victory to the Spaniards. This God was to be feared, placated, and obeyed. He could be capricious, but could be convinced (through prayer and sacrifice) to be fair and just.

On the other hand, another early native interpretation of the Christian God seems to have occurred. The Mexican case is the most notable (but not the only) example. Catholic missionaries would have been shocked to know that their listeners had also interpreted the Christian high god in a feminine form. The Iberian devotion to Mary does not seem to have come across to the newly converted with all the important doctrinal explanations and nuances that the missionaries presented. What was heard by the natives (I would argue) was the feminine form of the Christian high god.[54]

This culturally acceptable, feminine form of the supreme divinity, however, was not to be called "divine" by the vanquished peoples. They soon learned the *ortholalia*[55] necessary for survival in an adverse environment. Nevertheless, the symbols employed and the manner of the devotion do indicate a link with the ancient forms of the divine. The short period of time that elapsed from first evangelization to "apparitions" (1523 to 1531 in the case of Guadalupe) could not have allowed for the thorough reshaping of cultural religious categories among the Amerindian populations. This reshaping of deeply held categories would have been required for a strictly orthodox Christian understanding of Mary or of Guadalupe.

The Virgin of Guadalupe cannot be simply identified with Tonant-zin[56]—not even at the very beginning. But I do not see either how the natives could have simply identified Guadalupe with the Catholic Mary. From the start it seems that there was an effort (on the part of the Amerindians) to speak a religious language, through culturally understandable religious categories, that would interpret for them the Christian message about God. And just as there had been much said to the natives about the conquering might of God, much had also been said to them about the compassionate mercy and care of that same God. These latter attributes or dimensions of the divine are the ones that were interpreted as the feminine form of the Christian high god, symbolized through the acceptable Catholic imagery of Mary.

Perhaps modern theologies of the Holy Spirit can explain, as indeed they have begun to, that Marian symbols have been used in the past to speak of the Holy Spirit.[57] After all, the symbols of a dove or a flame do not seem to have any more claim to doctrinal accuracy than the feminine symbols connected with Mary.

One difficulty remains as one attempts to understand the early Amerindian and African interpretations of the Christian doctrines on God: what of the "Son," in European Trinitarian terms? It seems that the overall message of the missionaries was profoundly christocentric. The emphasis was placed on Jesus as the crucified, innocent, eternal Son of God. The missionaries presented Jesus both as fully human (and his suffering was the most important sign of humanness) and as fully divine (his power to work miracles—his own resurrection included—was the great sign).[58]

The native and slave populations seem to have accepted the message but, once again, only as they were able to understand it through their cultural and religious categories. Their own sacred stories reminded them of divinities who were in solidarity with the victimized, and who were willing to share in human suffering as a sign of their sincere concern and care for humans. Some myths recalled the tragic end or the punishment endured by innocent gods. Indeed, some of the most popular and sincerely venerated divinities of both the Mesoamerican and Yoruba mythologies had experienced this kind of treatment or defeat.[59]

It was, therefore, very possible for natives and slaves to interpret Jesus and his story through the prism of their own traditional sacred stories. He could be accepted as both fully human and fully divine. And his power and caring solidarity could indeed move the newly converted to sincere commitment and devotion. This does not solve, however, the trinitarian doctrinal question.

The traditional high god had been responsible, according to the mythologies, for the birth of other deities. What could the Amerindians and Africans of the early colonial period have understood, from a doctrinal perspective, when they were also told that this "crucified God" had also been born of a woman thanks to the activity of the high god? I think that an argument can be made to the effect that the humanity and divinity of Jesus were accepted and believed in by the conquered peoples, but that they did so only in the manner that their traditional religious categories would have made possible. These religious categories could not have interpreted Jesus as "Son" in a trinitarian, orthodox way.

It soon became apparent, after the initial period of colonial evangelization, that the missionary task was far from complete. New lands were still being opened to the new religion by the advancing Spanish occupation forces. More importantly, however, there grew an awareness—as the colonial centuries progressed—that the Catholicism of the natives, slaves, and *mestizos* was not quite like the religion of Spaniards and *criollos*. The differences were not merely in emphases, devotional or liturgical. There were, from the "official" point of view, serious doctrinal shortcomings (if not blatant error) in the Catholicism of the people. A new effort at re-evangelization seems to have been started.[60]

Notice, however, that this new missionary effort was directed not mainly at "pagans" (as in the early colonial period) but at baptized Christians. Secondly, this re-evangelization was more explicitly for the correction of error (potential or otherwise) and for the more proper religious education of natives, slaves, and *mestizos*. It assumed that the religious worldview that had to be addressed now was the one born from the original evangelization of the fifteenth and sixteenth centuries. The original Amerindian and African interpretation of the Christian message became the focus of concern during the later part of the colonial centuries.[61]

But there was more. If I could continue using the doctrines on the Trinity as illustrative example, it could be shown that as the decades of Spanish rule continued, other influences came to play a part on the people's doctrinal understanding. The most important of these influences was the family.

The family structures had begun to shift. New family roles and relationships, by now profoundly influenced by colonial legislation and mores, came to be projected onto the popular interpretation of the Trinity. God as father, Mary as mother, Jesus as older brother, and the many saints as members of the extended family and community networks—a sufficiently elaborate (and seldom explicit) ecclesiology was put forth, founded on and reflective of earlier trinitarian interpretations.

The revived missionary effort of the late colonial period also saw the publication of new catechisms and the creation of new approaches; and even new devotions were introduced in order to catechize the baptized masses. Whenever inevitable, colonial authorities relaxed legislation against *mestizo* participation in the ordained ministries, thereby establishing a more responsive link between popular and official Catholicisms. As a result, some success at re-evangelization began to appear and consolidate itself.

The most important result of this late colonial catechetical process, in my estimation, was (and still is) the slowly growing identification of the Virgin of Guadalupe with Mary. However, the connection seems to have happened between the Mary of Catholic popular devotions and the Virgin of Guadalupe, and not between the latter and the historical person Mary of Nazareth.[62]

Another very important outcome of late colonial re-evangelization was the increased religious influence of the *mestizo*. Both in the cities and in the villages, in lay and clerical contexts, the *mestizos* frequently managed to bridge the worlds of the victorious and the vanquished. Later generations owe the definitions of nationhood and, to a great degree, of cultural identity to the *mestizos*. Much of contemporary popular Christianity, in Latin America and among U.S. Hispanics, is the *mestizos'* Catholicism.

The *mestizos* were, in the late colonial period, mainly responsible for the (often grudging and only partial) acceptance of many popular religious symbols by the ecclesiastical elites. Although through the *mestizos* bits of the re-evangelizing effort reached natives and slaves, most of it was addressed directly at them. In a strange twist of circumstances, mixed-race people were the most frequent vehicles of late colonial catechesis, thereby (and inevitably, in cultural terms) filtering the intentions, symbols, and doctrines of the ecclesiastical authorities through *mestizo* prisms.

The mixed-race *mestizos* were fast becoming the majority population. Aware of the Spanish and white *criollo* civil and ecclesiastical world, and to some degree its heirs too, the *mestizo* population soon began to have national and religious importance, still denied the Amerindians and Africans.

The re-evangelization of the late colonial period, so briefly described here, set the stage for today's U.S. Latino popular Catholicism. It is important to note that *mestizos*, who were mainly responsible for that catechetical process, were building their religious interpretations and symbolic syntheses on premises—considered "normative"—that were (still) pre-Tridentine. The doctrines and worldview born of Trent were only peripherally present in late colonial Catholicism, even when the ecclesiastical elites made themselves believe that the Tridentine decrees were being implemented.[63]

POPULAR CATHOLICISM IN THE NINETEENTH CENTURY

The early nineteenth century saw the flowering of a new nationalism all over Spanish America. Most countries in Latin America won their independence at that time. This century was also cataclysmic for the Hispanic populations already present on the lands that were annexed by the United States.[64]

I will not attempt to give a history of Hispanic Catholicism since the annexations. I will instead very briefly focus on the main outline of *how* Latino *popular* Catholicism seems to have developed and reacted to the history immediately after independence in Mexico and during the last colonial century in Cuba and Puerto Rico.[65] The approach I have chosen will stress the responses of Hispanic popular Christianity and the different elements that forced it to confront the modern world. The influences on the current status of this religious universe will become evident through this brief discussion.

The First Confrontation with the Modern World: Nationalism

We have seen that the religion taken to be "normative" Christianity, in the early colonial period, was Catholicism as *traditio* (in its medieval, Iberian, pre-Tridentine version). It was this religion that was interpreted by the native and slave populations in their attempt to make cultural and religious sense out of their conquest and vanquishment.

We have also seen how this interpreted Catholicism was perceived, late in colonial times, to be in need of re-evangelization. *Mestizos* were by then fast becoming the majority of the population, and it was through and to them that the new catechetical efforts were channeled. This allowed for some elements of re-evangelization to reach Amerindians and Africans, but the latter groups' religion remained basically as it had been.

The late colonial re-evangelization mainly reached the *mestizos*. This allowed them to interpret the new messages being presented through the prism of their inherited popular Catholicism (which was still seen by them as "normative"). This latest interpretation slowly became the Catholic norm for the mixed-race majority. It was this religion, for all

practical purposes, which was the only Catholicism acceptable by most
people during the independence movement.

A split can be clearly detected at the start of the nineteenth century,
bound to widen since. The "official" Christianity of the bishops and of
the social elites, presenting itself as the sole valid norm, was quite distinct from the Christianity of the vast majority of the population. This
"popular" religion also claimed to be the valid norm, though acknowl-
edging the existence of the "clerical" version.[66]

By the time pro-independence movements broke out, the bearers of
"official" Catholicism had usually become the main pillars of Spain's
colonial rule (and therefore, inimical to the anticolonial forces). The
other strand of Catholicism, the "popular" version that the ecclesiastical and social elites so deplored, was the religion of the independentists
(or at least openly allied with them).[67]

It became commonplace to find the symbols of popular Catholicism
used as gathering banners for the people against Spain. The eccles-
iastics that collaborated with the colonial rulers invoked all sorts of
religious arguments to condemn the independentists as enemies of
Christianity and of legitimate authority. On the other hand, the people
and other lesser clergy fighting Spain appealed to God, to the Virgin, to
the faith, and to religious symbols of the majority in order to demonstrate that God was indeed on their side.

The *mestizos* and *criollos* created the independence movements.
What had been official colonial Catholicism soon identified itself with
criollo interests (after independence in the case of Mexico and Cuba,
and after American occupation in the case of Puerto Rico), while most
mestizos still claimed popular religion as theirs. Therefore, even after
Spain's defeat, the "dual-level" Catholicism of the late colonial period
was preserved. And the link between the two versions of the religion
was maintained thanks to the *mestizos'* gift for cultural re-interpretation. Some *mestizos* had finally entered the clergy and risen through its
ranks, allowing popular Catholicism to receive partial acceptability
from the postindependence ecclesiastical hierarchy. This belated acceptability, however, had its price.

Nineteenth-Century "Uses" of Popular Catholicism

During most of the postindependence period in Mexico, and during
the colonial nineteenth century in Puerto Rico and in Cuba, the Church
hierarchy started participating in some key rites of popular Catholicism. Whether the bishops (and other clergy) suspected these rites of
syncretic, superstitious, or other elements did not seem as important as
the fact that these rituals were, indeed, Catholic. They were a sacred,
public link between the hierarchy and the people, recognized as such
by all.

The maintenance of this sacred and public link became very important during the nineteenth century. The institutions of the Church came increasingly under attack by a growing intellectual elite, *criolla* and *mestiza*, that was influenced by the European currents of modern thought. The Enlightenment had arrived in the Americas with an anti-Church zeal. The ecclesiastical hierarchy, apparently sensing the danger, saw in popular Catholicism an ally and tool in the Church's defense strategy. The natives, slaves, and *mestizos*, for centuries marginalized from the official institutions of Catholicism, were now courted and their religion blessed.

On the other hand, the intellectual elites—in typical nineteenth-century rationalist style—had no use for the Church and its economic and political power, while also condemning popular Catholicism as obscurantist ignorance. They thought that popular religion prevented the people from achieving higher levels of educational and material development. Intellectuals of the last century, in Mexico and the Antilles, in their disdain for Church and ignorance, actually fomented a strategic alliance (necessarily clothed in acceptable theological and pastoral language) between the ecclesiastical hierarchy and the masses of people.

Nineteenth-century official and popular Catholicisms confronted the same enemy in Mexico and the Antilles, and they joined forces. But by then the official brand was itself far too imbued with the mentality of the post-Reformation era and the Enlightenment. It was only a matter of time before the rationalist intellectuals and the Church establishment would discover a sufficiently comfortable dialogue, and then turn their sights and disdain onto popular Catholicism.

The intellectual elites of the nineteenth century have—one hundred years later—either lost their influence or have (most probably) transformed themselves into other ideological or political shapes and adopted new names. Modern-day education, business, and politics in Mexico and in the Antilles depend on the new versions of the rationalist mentality. Curiously enough, the powerful elites of the Right as well as many of the revolutionaries of the Left share the same basic worldview, one that sees the people's religion as an unfortunate (or at best, folkloric) vestige of the past. In their common view, the best use of popular religious symbol is its instrumentalization.[68]

For the ecclesiastical hierarchy, still dialoguing with but not fully trusting the modern world represented by the rationalism of either Right or Left, popular Catholicism remains a necessary buffer in cases of crisis and confrontation. The Church, since the nineteenth century, seems to have learned to tolerate popular religion as at best an ill-catechized form of pious devotionalism. This tolerance, it is hoped, will not lose the masses of people that justify (and potentially defend) the Church's institutional importance in the larger society. This instrumentalization of popular Catholicism has produced mixed results.

Popular Catholicism in the Annexed Lands

I have been discussing popular religion mainly in Mexico and in the Antilles during the nineteenth century. I have done so because of the great influence that events in both geographic areas have had on present-day U.S. Hispanic popular Catholicism. Immigrants from Cuba and Mexico, clearly, did not leave their religious history behind.

But the nineteenth century is also the time of the American purchase of Florida and of the U.S. military conquest and annexation of Mexico's northern half.

Florida's Hispanic Catholics,[69] mostly gathered in the cities of St. Augustine and Pensacola, chose either of two paths when their purchase from Spain occurred—a few decided to stay in the new American territory,[70] but most elected to leave Florida and settle in Spanish Cuba. It would not be until several decades later (in the mid-nineteenth century) that large communities of Hispanic Catholics settled again in the peninsula, fleeing the increasingly repressive Spanish colonial authorities in Cuba. The new settlers, however, this time established themselves in Tampa and Key West. Smaller groups of Cubans went to Philadelphia and New York.

Did these Cubans bring their popular Catholicism to the United States last century? There are some indications that Tampa and Key West, where few of the independentist elites settled, did see forms of popular religion. But one must be very careful on this point, because of the religious apathy that accompanied much of the Cuban nineteenth century.[71]

The Southwest, however, had a different story than Florida. The lands from Texas to California were annexed by the United States after military intervention, and with the lands came towns and villages. Many of these had been founded at least two centuries before, and the presence of Catholicism in them was as old.[72]

The "dual-level" Christianity of Mexico had also become part of the religious life of the Southwest (these lands were still, after all, part of Mexico). Here, however, popular Catholicism seems to have had so heavy an influence that even the local ecclesiastical establishment—too weak to claim power on its own—had to actively promote it, thereby publicly linking it to the clergy. The same fundamental reasons of defense and buffer, evident in the rest of Mexico at the time, were operative in the northern frontier as the clergy allied itself here with the symbols of popular religion.

The new American Southwest had been Mexico's remote northern border outposts. Not many of the Mexican "enlightened" elites of the period would have chosen to leave the big cities in the south and come to settle in the frontier. Even the few residents that pretended to belong to these elites were numerically insignificant and ultimately powerless.

Popular Catholicism remained the de facto religion of the vast majority of the population. Its shape, functions, and sociodoctrinal developmental process parallel the ones we have indicated for the rest of Mexico. In other words, the popular Christianity that preceded the American annexations was at its core the pre-Tridentine *traditio*.[73] It was *mestizo*, but in this case because *mestizos* were the ones who mainly settled here. This religion assumed as normative the Catholicism that had been interpreted by earlier "popular" generations in southern Mexico. However, the re-evangelization efforts, so important during much of the late colonial period, had barely any effect in the lands from Texas to California.

But then came the American military conquest and subsequent annexations. For the first time Hispanic American Catholicism was going to confront the Reformation.

The confrontation was going to be between, on one side, a militant Protestant nation, increasingly aware of its military might and apparently convinced of its moral superiority (its "Manifest Destiny"). On the other side there was a conquered people, suddenly and violently deprived of right and land, whose religion had long roots in the medieval past that the new conquerors loathed as obscurantist. The Catholicism of the people was not the post-Tridentine version, by now common enough in Catholic Europe and in the eastern American states. It had assumed as self-evident that the truth was "Catholic." It seemed to be no intellectual match for the Protestantism of the occupiers.

The religion of the people, however, was also going to face another confrontation—the arrival, with the annexation, of post-Tridentine Catholics.

THE CONFRONTATIONS WITH TRENT, THE REFORMATION, AND MODERNITY

I believe that Hispanic popular Catholicism in the United States is now, at the end of the twentieth century, displaying the effects and consequences of its first century of confrontation with post-Tridentine Roman Christianity, with the heirs of the Protestant Reformation, and with the modern world (initiated and disseminated mainly by the Calvinist and Roman theological traditions).

Confrontation with Post-Tridentine Catholicism after the Annexation

The implementation of the decrees and doctrines of Trent had been very selective in Spanish America. Tridentine Catholicism, arriving at least a century after the conquest, became identified mostly with the Spaniards and *criollos*. There were so few Protestants in Spain's colonies that the European urgency of reform seemed foreign here. The result, as we have seen, was the preservation of pre-Tridentine Christianity in the Western hemisphere.

The re-evangelization of the late colonial period attempted to bring Tridentine Catholicism to the people, but only with limited success. By then even the official religion was undergoing a profound change that would eventually lead to the centralizing Romanization started by Pius IX. Latin American Catholics first confronted Tridentine Catholicism, in an inescapable way, with the dawn of the twentieth century.[74]

However, U.S. Latinos were forced to deal with the Tridentine Church immediately after the American annexation. Their popular Catholicism, fundamentally untouched by the reforming council, suddenly confronted a new type of Church that seemed always on the defensive, that emphasized doctrinal knowledge (and guilt) over experience and affect, and that devalued lay participation. Worst of all, this new Church supported the American conquest of the Southwest.

Today we can understand why the Catholicism of the American eastern states appeared to be on the defensive. It was. And perhaps this in turn led to American Catholics' perceiving public, popular Hispanic Catholicism as superstition in need of correction and catechesis. Compounding this perception, however, was the growing influence and control of the Irish in the U.S. Church, especially when we know that many among the Irish became fierce opponents of the Mexicans in the annexed lands.[75] I am assuming that the American (specifically Irish) Catholics' need for acceptance and respect in the wider U.S. society led many to conceive of Hispanic religion as an added weight they did not want to carry, and as a source of embarrassment to their reformed, Tridentine Church.

Some of the public, social celebrations of popular Catholicism were soon transformed into more private, family expressions.[76] The new Church organized itself basically according to the ecclesiastical patterns developed in the eastern states. Although most Catholics in the Southwest were Hispanic, their participation and leadership in the institutions of religion were drastically diminished. The people's alternative seems to have been the withdrawal into the universe of popular Catholicism—it was *theirs*, and it made familiar sense of God and Christianity. By taking refuge in this religious world Latinos were also preserving one of the most important roots of their cultural identity.

However, for the new Euro-American ecclesiastical establishment in the Southwest, Hispanic flight into traditional religion implied that the new Catholic elites could ignore Latino Christianity and further emphasize, to the Protestant majority, that popular Hispanic Catholicism was not really "Catholic"—only a marginal anachronism from the past, in need of instruction. Euro-American Catholics had, thereby, assumed as true and valid the Protestant Reformation's premise that pre-Tridentine Christianity was deviant.

Confrontations with Contemporary Post-Tridentine Catholicism

As long as the Church in the Southwest doctrinally and pastorally ignored Latinos, and as long as the latter maintained the ritual link with the Roman clergy (thereby identifying themselves as Catholics), Hispanics could keep their popular Catholicism with only occasional hierarchical interference. Some local Latinos joined the ranks of the clergy, but their meager numbers and lack of real institutional influence did not alter the fundamentally ritual (i.e., "devotional") relationship that existed between priests and people since the colonial days.

But this uneasy truce between the official Euro-American (mostly Irish) Church and Hispanic popular Catholicism started to unravel in the middle of the twentieth century, and more specifically after Vatican II. Let us, therefore, look at the present situation.

The Contemporary Church's Approach and Alternatives

Several elements of the contemporary world came together to force the current confrontation.[77] There is, for example, the influence that decades of access to Euro-American mass media have had on the sacral worldview underlying and sustaining much of Hispanic popular Catholicism. There are also the efforts of public education (no matter how otherwise ineffectual and insufficient) in communicating the values and worldview of modernity. It is difficult to see how the long exposure to Euro-American society (heir to the Calvinist religious tradition, imbued with individualism, and increasingly secularized) could *not* have affected the very foundations and premises of the Hispanic religious and communal universe. The growth of urbanization and of a city-based job market after World War II began to deeply impact the stable, traditional family and community relationships so fundamental to Latino religion. Finally, the upsurge of immigration to American cities from Mexico and the Antilles added huge concentrations of Hispanics. This immigrant wave (which has not ended) brings to the United States people who are not accustomed to being treated as foreigners in their societies or Church.

Finally, and more importantly, the poverty and discrimination (and consequences thereof) suffered by so many Latinos seem to have socially justified, in the eyes of the larger society, the perpetuation of the "subaltern" role of the Hispanic populations.[78] The dominant ideology has long attempted to explain and "prove" the supposed reasons for this subaltern status. Needless to say, precisely as a symptom of their social vulnerability, many Latinos internalized the "proofs" put forth by the dominant ideology. Unfortunately, the Euro-American Catholic Church all too frequently uncritically assumed these ideological justifications, thereby reaffirming the "validity" of the arguments of prejudice within its ecclesiastical milieu. It also became an active accomplice in the Latino internalization of the dominant ideology.

Demographics (and probably not the long-standing pastoral need) finally made the Euro-American Church take notice. It is also true that many were moved to action by the new vision of Vatican II. But whatever the motive, the alternatives offered by official Catholicism—whether "progressive" or "conservative"—to U.S. Latinos seem clear and are certainly not new. Either leave the pre-Tridentine style of Catholicism behind by becoming religiously Euro-Americanized, or face the continued onslaught of accusations of ignorance and superstition, which would be followed by pastoral activity geared to "correctly" educate in "real" Roman Christianity. The American Church's attempts at understanding Hispanic popular Catholicism seem all too frequently motivated by the hope of the latter's early and definitive demise.[79]

The current trend at "multiculturalizing" the American Church seems to me to be concealing the obvious (and not surprising) fact that those who *really* set the pastoral agendas, determine the doctrinal parameters, and direct the implementation strategies for the multicultural dioceses and parishes of the future are still the Euro-American Catholics. Therefore, even this well-intentioned effort at cultural diversity does not question the unspoken premise that Hispanic popular Catholicism must be left behind.

Latino Catholic Responses to the Church's Alternatives

The U.S. Latino responses to the alternatives offered by the Euro-American Church are creative attempts at religious and cultural survival. There is still, for example, the learned pattern of flight into the traditional religious universe. Some Hispanics (perhaps the majority among a certain age group, or even many recent immigrants) do choose to perpetuate the forms and vision of pre-Tridentine Catholicism. They are probably not aware of its having been the "official" religion centuries ago, nor are they familiar with the long history of the Western Christianity that preceded the Reformation. For them this is *their* Catholicism, *their* way of being Christian, and that reason suffices.

But there are other responses to the official Church's alternatives. These alternatives have been, in different ways and to varying degrees, culturally optimizing paths for preserving traditional religion and its sustaining worldview vis-à-vis the always encroaching world of modernity and post-Tridentine Catholicism. These newer responses are compromises with a Euro-American reality perceived as (at best) overwhelming or (at worst) dangerously invasive.

I would argue that nonparochial lay movements and associations, such as the *Cursillos de Cristiandad* or even the more traditional *cofradías*, have allowed for the formation of an alternative Hispanic Church within the broader community of Catholicism. This Latino Church has acted, for all practical purposes, as parallel parish and diocese, permitting a high degree of participation and leadership to Hispanics otherwise marginalized from the Euro-American controlled parishes and dioceses. Through the acceptance of varying degrees of institutional links to the hierarchy, Latinos managed to preserve a considerable degree of autonomy within the lay movements.

A close examination of the latter would show how deep, indeed, is the influence of the symbols and the worldview of popular Catholicism on the movements. Acts of public piety, for example, are consistently encouraged, praised, and performed. Some of the associations have been specifically established for the purpose of preserving traditional forms of devotion and communal prayer. Through this lay-led, parallel Catholicism, Hispanics have managed to preserve and re-interpret significant elements of their shared worldview, together with their emphasis on family and community. The movements have also served as important vehicles for the dissemination of many of the doctrinal contents of popular Catholicism, though sufficiently adapted (*and* concealed) in forms acceptable to the modern ecclesiastical realities. It is important to also note how emphatically Christianity is presented by these movements and associations as a *traditio*, thereby affirming the very traditional foundation of pre-Tridentine Catholicism.

The Euro-American Church's reaction to the Hispanic lay movements and associations has been frequently adverse, demanding that local (Euro-American) parishes and dioceses exercise control over the people's alternative Catholic "spaces." Not perceived by most Latinos as the institution's sociological need to control, the Church's reactions have often been understood by the people as one more battle in the American clergy's continuing attempt to dismantle Hispanic religion. Of course, this religion could now only be the "popularly interpreted" pre-Tridentine version, since "official" Latino Catholicism either no longer exists in the United States or it has become an extension of the Euro-American, post-Tridentine Church's vision and interests.

Some Developments within Popular Catholicism

It is important to note that as Latino popular religion attempts to survive by (somewhat) adapting to post-Tridentine Roman Catholicism, it has begun to modify and re-interpret the doctrinal contents and symbols that have traditionally distinguished it. For example, the connection between the Virgin of Guadalupe and the Mary of Catholic devotion is (apparently) progressing. There is also a growing sense of social protagonism as part of the discerned will of God, thereby beginning the transformation of the mostly fatalistic past image of divine providence. Symbols of popular Catholicism have prominently appeared in and been associated with some important social and political movements among U.S. Hispanics.[80]

The most telling example of the contemporary re-interpretation of symbols and contents refers to the Bible. It seems highly inaccurate (indeed, arrogant) to think that Western Christianity did not know the Bible before Trent and the Reformation. In the Iberian villages, where people did not usually know how to read and where medieval culture was still very much alive, the Bible's contents were presented graphically through art, *autos sacramentales*, storytelling, and preaching. The same, as we saw, held true of pre-Tridentine colonial Christianity in the Americas. The Bible was known at the popular level, but through enacted or visual symbol and the spoken word, not through reading the printed page.

Currently, however, with the ever-increasing literacy rate, the direct reading of the text of the Bible has become widespread. There is no doubt that, after Vatican II, the official Roman Catholic insistence on biblical reading was heeded by Hispanics. The growing numbers of Latino Protestants have also been a strong influence. Whatever the reasons for this scriptural awakening, there is no question that the written text of the Bible has been taken out of the hands (and potential control) of the ecclesiastical institution and is now being interpreted by the people themselves. Interestingly, this increase in familiarity with the sacred texts of Christianity does not seem to have contributed in a significant way to the massive exodus of Hispanic Catholics from the Roman Church. It seems, in fact, to be strengthening the symbols and fundamental worldview of popular Catholicism through another process of re-interpretation, this time biblical.

Popular Catholicism, Pentecostalism, and the Reformation

There is another common Hispanic response to the either/or alternatives offered to popular Catholicism. This is pentecostalism. I have elsewhere argued that Latino pentecostalism has shown itself as an important, culturally acceptable vehicle for the preservation of the pre-Tridentine (and premodern) religious worldview.[81] Though obviously (and consciously) rejecting many medieval and colonial Catholic symbols and practices, pentecostalism has managed to hold on to the very "sacramental," symbolic ethos and worldview that made pre-Reformation Christianity possible. More importantly, it seems to view Christianity in the manner of *traditio*, so essential to pre-Tridentine religion. Many symbols have been "reformed," some modern ones added, but the fundamental structures and premises of the traditionally religious Hispanic worldview have basically remained.

I do not think that one can understand the current popularity of the Catholic charismatic movement among U.S. Latinos, or the ever-increasing number of Protestant pentecostal churches within the Hispanic religious universe, without realizing the seemingly crucial role of cultural (and religious) preservation that the pentecostal movement (in its Catholic or Protestant versions) is playing.

It is well documented that the growth of the charismatic, pentecostal communities is in direct relation to people's perceived sense of threat or invasion at the hands of modernity.[82] In these studies, the Christian Churches (of any denomination) that appear allied to the modern worldview and against the traditional religious and communal relations, will suffer considerable numerical losses. It is, therefore, highly ironic that the Roman Catholic Church, which engaged in the ideological battles that followed the Reformation on the side of tradition, should now be an uncritical bearer of the Reformation's own theological premises vis-à-vis pre-Tridentine Hispanic Catholicism.

The contemporary confrontation of Hispanic popular Catholicism with the Euro-American Roman Catholic Church, I would argue, is the modern version of the sixteenth-century Reformation that Latino religion never had to face. This time, however, it is official Roman Catholicism that has taken the side of the Protestant reformers, arguing through similar logic and with surprisingly similar doctrinal assumptions. Unfortunately, popular pre-Tridentine Catholicism had earlier been robbed (by the consequences of annexation, prejudice, and poverty) of most theological and institutional means of defense and self-affirmation needed in this new Reformation.

CONCLUSION

Popular Catholicism among U.S. Latinos has a long history and is the bearer of an old tradition. Its roots are planted in the medieval type of Christianity that preceded Trent and the Reformation, and in the Iberian *Reconquista* process that formed the Spanish character. However, it is not understandable without the sacral worldview and histories of the Amerindian, African, and *mestizo* peoples of Mesoamerica and the Antilles.

We have seen how this popular Christianity preserved the pre-Tridentine *traditio*, and how it has attempted to adapt itself to the realities of today's Euro-American Roman Catholic Church. Unfortunately, this Church has all too frequently been Hispanic popular Catholicism's worst foe.

I have tried to bring out the several strata of traditions, adaptation techniques, and historical moments of interpretation throughout the story of popular religion among U.S. Latino Catholics. The reader must realize by now that the full, complete history of this religious universe is extraordinarily complex and is yet to be written. No easy formula of understanding can be applied to this religion of millions. Perhaps that is very good.

What does the future hold for Hispanic popular Catholicism in this country? No one knows for sure. There are some indications from the past, however, that would question prophecies of its early demise at the hands of modernity and its religious messengers.

Popular Christianity has been around for too many centuries. It has proven to be very resilient and adaptable, and it has all too frequently frustrated the modern penchant for perfectly logical explanations. The Right and the Left, Protestant and Roman Catholic, have all thought at one point or another (and perhaps still think) that popular religion can be "educated" or properly "evangelized" into oblivion. Historical results, after centuries of attempts, have shown how resilient and adaptable Latino popular Catholicism is indeed.

Perhaps there are two important starting points that can lead to an adequate interpretation of the people's religion and to the keys to discovering how to respectfully relate to and work with it. These are, namely, to seriously rethink the crucial distinction between "Tradition" and "traditions" made by Claude LeJay in 1546 and shared by the Reformation[83]; and to challenge the fears and ideologies that fan Euro-American cultural and ecclesiastical assumptions of what is truth.

Popular Catholicism is not an interesting vestige of the Christian past, nor just a cultural symbol that can be instrumentalized for this or that agenda. It is a different way of relating to reality and of living the Christian gospel.

Notes

1. Throughout this article I will explicitly refer to, name, and discuss numerous rites, symbols, and beliefs commonly identified with popular Catholicism among U.S. Latinos. A descriptive list of "examples" of popular Catholicism is not really necessary and can even be misleading. From the many references and discussions, it will become apparent that the symbolic and doctrinal repertoire of the people's religion is broad and varied. However, two important interpretive keys to keep in mind are the historical, developmental nature of this repertoire, and the fact that it is not mainly ritual. Even when some symbols, rites, or beliefs might be important for one generation, they might not be important (or at least not in the same manner or for the same reason) for another generation. Nevertheless, the living fact of popular Catholicism and its crucial importance have remained constant throughout the centuries. It is my hope that this article will make this point perfectly clear.

2. In this paper the terms "Hispanic" and "Latino" will be used interchangeably. Both terms will only refer to U.S. populations of Latin American (or perhaps even Spanish) cultural roots. I will also use the term "Antilles" (and its adjective "Antillean") in reference to the Spanish-speaking islands of the Carib-

bean. The latter term ("Caribbean"), more generic, is avoided here because it also refers to other linguistic areas.

3. It will become evident that, in this chapter, I assume Mesoamerica and the Antilles to be the cultural and historical roots of U.S. Hispanics. This is certainly the case with the immense majority of all U.S. Latinos. There are other Hispanic communities in this country, however, that claim roots in other Latin American areas. Much of what will be said here, however, is probably applicable to these remaining populations too.

4. The expression and following insights are derived from Max Weber, with input from Renato Ortiz. See M. Weber, *Essays in Sociology* (Oxford: Oxford University Press, 1946); and R. Ortiz, *A consciência fragmentada. Ensaios de cultura popular e religião* (Rio de Janeiro: Ed. Paz e Terra, 1980).

5. See O. Espín, *Evangelización y religiones negras* (Rio de Janeiro: Ed. PUC, 1984), vol. II.

6. See Espín, *Evangelización*, II, 220-245; and also A. Gramsci, *Os intelectuais e a organização da cultura* (Rio de Janeiro: Ed. Civilização Brasileira, 1979); and P. Vrijhof and J. Waardenburg, eds., *Official and Popular Religion* (The Hague: Mouton, 1979).

7. See, for example, J. O'Callahan, *El cristianismo popular en el Egipto antiguo* (Madrid: Ed. Cristiandad, 1978).

8. For what follows see, for example, Espín, *Evangelización*, esp. vols. II and III; idem, "Religiosidad popular. Un aporte para su definición y hermenéutica," in *Estudios Sociales*, 58 (1984), 41-57; L. Cabrera, *El Monte* (Miami: Ed. Universal, 1969); J.M. Murphy, *Santería: An African Religion in America* (Boston: Beacon Press, 1988); M. Cros Sandoval, *La religión afrocubana* (Madrid: Ed. Playor, 1975). Toward the end of this chapter I will mention Pentecostalism and briefly discuss the possible relation between popular Catholicism and Hispanic Protestantism's own popular religion.

9. See O. Espín, "Irokó e Ará-Kolé: Comentário exegético a um mito iorubá-lucumí," in *Perspectiva Teológica*, 44 (1986), 29-61.

10. See E.B. Idowu, *Olódùmaré. God in Yoruba Belief* (London: Longmans Green, 1963); and J.O. Lucas, *The Religion of the Yorubas* (Lagos: CMS, 1946).

11. See O. Espín, *Evangelización*, III, 551-614; idem, "Ashé-Sê y lo fundamental en el Vodú," in *Estudios Sociales*, 59 (1985), 17-30.

12. See J.J. Santiago, *The Spiritistic Doctrine of Allan Kardec: A Phenomenological Study* (Rome: Gregorian University, 1983. Doctoral dissertation); and, V. Crapanzano and V. Garrison, eds., *Case Studies in Spirit Possession* (New York: John Wiley & Sons, 1977).

13. I think I have shown the fundamental religious similarities among the main communities in my paper, "The Vanquished, Faithful Solidarity, and the Marian Symbol," in *On Keeping Providence,* ed. J. Coultas and B. Doherty (Terre Haute: St. Mary of the Woods College Press, 1991), 84-101.

14. See R.S. Goizueta, "Rediscovering Praxis: The Significance of U.S. Hispanic Experience for Theological Method," in *We Are a People! Initiatives in Hispanic American Theology,* ed. R.S. Goizueta (Minneapolis: Fortress Press, 1992), 51-78; and O. Espín, "Grace and Humanness," in idem, 133-164.

15. See a summary presentation of the more common approaches in my article, "Religiosidad popular. Un aporte para su definición y hermenéutica."

16. See, for example, O. Espín, "The God of the Vanquished," chapter 1 above and in *Listening: Journal of Religion and Culture*, 27:1 (1992), 70-83. An interesting volume not exclusively (but mainly) on religious iconography is O. Debroise, E. Sussman, and M. Teitelbaum, eds., *El corazón sangrante. The Bleeding Heart* (Seattle: University of Washington Press/Boston: Institute of Contemporary Art, 1991).

17. See the very suggestive and well-founded explanation for these assertions in G. Macy, *The Banquet's Wisdom* (Mahwah: Paulist Press, 1992), 10-14. See also, L. Rothkrug, "Religious Practices and Collective Perceptions: Hidden Homologies in the Renaissance and Reformation," in *Historical Reflections/ Réflexions Historiques*, 7:1 (1980), 3-251; B. Hamilton, *Religion in the Medieval West* (London: Edward Arnold, 1986); K. Pennington and R. Somerville, eds., *Law, Church and Society* (Philadelphia: University of Pennsylvania Press, 1977).

18. *Reconquista* is the usual historical term for the long period of Christian "reconquest" of the Iberian peninsula from the Muslims.

19. For what follows on medieval Iberian history see, for example, L.P. Harvey, *Islamic Spain, 1250-1500* (Chicago: University of Chicago Press, 1990); R. García-Villoslada et al., *Historia de la Iglesia Católica. Edad Media*, vol. II (Madrid: Biblioteca de Autores Cristianos, 1976); F. Martín Hernández, *La Iglesia en la historia*, vol. II (Madrid: Atenas, 1984); J.C. Olin, *Catholic Reform: From Cardinal Ximenes to the Council of Trent, 1495-1563* (New York: Fordham University Press, 1990); A. Ballesteros Beretta, *Alfonso X el Sabio* (Barcelona: Ed. Laia, 1963); J. Boswell, *The Royal Treasure: Muslim Communities under the Crown of Aragon in the Fourteenth Century* (New Haven: Yale University Press, 1977); R.I. Burns, *The Crusader Kingdom of Valencia: Reconstruction on a Thirteenth-Century Frontier* (Cambridge: Harvard University Press, 1967); idem, *Moors and Crusaders in Mediterranean Spain: Collected Essays* (London: Longmans Green, 1978); idem, *The Worlds of Alfonso the Learned and James the Conqueror: Intellect and Force in the Middle Ages* (Princeton: Princeton University Press, 1985); J.N. Hillgarth, *The Spanish Kingdoms, 1250-1516* (Oxford: Oxford University Press, 1976-78, 2 vols.).

20. To the bibliography in the preceding note, add (for example) the following on medieval Iberian Christianity: J.M. Palomero Páramo, *La imaginería procesional sevillana. Misterios, nazarenos y cristos* (Seville: Publicaciones del Ayuntamiento, 1987); L. Melgar Reina and A. Marín Rújula, *Saetas, pregones y romances litúrgicos cordobeses* (Cordoba: Publicaciones del Monte de Piedad, 1987); A. Aroca Lara, *El Crucificado en la imaginería andaluza* (Cordoba: Publicaciones del Monte de Piedad, 1987); W.A. Christian, *Apparitions in Late Medieval and Renaissance Spain* (Princeton: Princeton University Press, 1981); idem, *Local Religion in Sixteenth-Century Spain* (Princeton: Princeton University Press, 1981).

21. For what follows on *traditio*, see O. Espín, "Tradition and Popular Religion: An Understanding of the *Sensus Fidelium*," chapter 3 above and in *Frontiers of Hispanic Theology in the United States*, ed. A.F. Deck (Maryknoll, New York: Orbis Books, 1992), 62-87, and the bibliography indicated there. See also my "Pentecostalism and Popular Catholicism: Preservers of Hispanic Catholic Tradition?" presidential address at the 1992 Colloquium of the Academy of Catholic Hispanic Theologians of the United States, published in *ACHTUS Newsletter*, 4 (1993).

22. *Autos sacramentales* were theatrical representations of biblical scenes or of Christian virtues that had to be taught to the people. Very frequently whole villages were involved in these religious plays. These dramatic representations were either complete theatrical creations (as in the case of plays on virtues and sins), or they were re-enactments of the biblical stories (used as the basic script). In the latter case, however, adaptations and interpretations were frequent. Most of the peasant actors were illiterate, and so their use of the biblical texts depended heavily on memory and on fidelity to the transmitted gestures and words. This use of memory, however, may not be construed as necessarily leading to misunderstandings of the biblical text. On the contrary, the relative freedom of adaptation often allowed for very informed and correct understandings and applications of the scriptures. The village clergy, usually not well educated (if educated at all), seems to have had little influence on the actual plays.

23. See the texts of the reports of one massive religious census, in W.A. Smith, *Local Religion in Sixteenth-Century Spain*. This census, though held under Philip II, unquestionably reflects as well the local, village-type religion common during the fifteenth century.

24. See E. Vilanova, *Historia de la teología cristiana* (Barcelona: Ed. Herder, 1987-92, I-III vols.), esp. I, 650-654, 856-943.

25. For what follows on LeJay, and on the theology of Trent and the reformers, see the bibliography in note 20, above. And also, E. Vilanova, *Historia de la teología cristiana*, II, 569-572; J. Delumeau, *Naissance et affirmation de la Reforme* (Paris: PUF, 1965); idem, *Le catholicisme entre Luther et Voltaire* (Paris: PUF, 1971); H. Jedin, *A History of the Council of Trent* (St. Louis: Herder Book Co., 1957, I-II vols.); J. Pelikan, *The Christian Tradition. Reformation of Church and Dogma, 1300-1700* (Chicago: University of Chicago Press, 1984).

26. On colonial evangelization and Church, see (from a vast bibliography), O. Espín, "Trinitarian Monotheism and the Birth of Popular Catholicism: The Case of Sixteenth-Century Mexico," chapter 2 above and in *Missiology*, 20:2 (1992), 177-204; L. Lopetegui and F. Zubillaga, *Historia de la Iglesia en la América española* (Madrid: Biblioteca de Autores Cristianos, 1965, I-II vols.); R. Ricard, *The Spiritual Conquest of Mexico* (Berkeley: University of California Press, 1966); E. Rull Fernández, *Autos sacramentales del Siglo de Oro* (Barcelona: Ed. Plaza y Janés, 1986); H. Goodpasture, ed., *Cross and Sword: An Eyewitness History of Christianity in Latin America* (Maryknoll, New York: Orbis Books, 1989); R. De Roux, *Dos mundos enfrentados* (Bogota: CINEP, 1990); J.M. de Paiva, *Colonização e catequese* (São Paulo: Cortez Editora, 1982); L. Rivera Pagán, *A Violent Evangelism: The Political and Religious Conquest of the Americas* (Louisville: Westminster/John Knox Press, 1992); J.F. Schwaller, *The Church and Clergy in Sixteenth-Century Mexico* (Albuquerque: University of New Mexico Press, 1987); E. Dussel, ed., *Materiales para una historia de la evangelización en América Latina* (Barcelona: Ed. Nova Terra/CEHILA, 1977).

27. This point of the inequality of the interlocutors is very well documented and explained by Luis Rivera Pagán in his *A Violent Evangelism*. This context of inequality as precondition for evangelization is of extraordinary importance, and it remains a concealed but operative reality in modern Euro-American (Catholic and Protestant) evangelizing attempts directed at U.S. Latinos.

28. One is reminded, of course, of Antonio de Montesinos, Bartolomé de

Las Casas, and many others. See, for example, B. de Las Casas, *Brevísima relación de la destrucción de las Indias* (Mexico: Fondo de Cultura Económica, 1965); idem, *En defensa de los indios. Colección de documentos*, A. Larios, ed. (Seville: Editoriales Andaluzas Unidas, 1985); G. Gutiérrez, *Dios o el oro de las Indias* (Salamanca: Ed. Sígueme, 1989).

29. See, for example, J.M. Mira, *A evangelização do negro no período colonial* (São Paulo: Ed. Loyola, 1983); and also Espín, *Evangelización y religiones negras*, esp. vol. III and the extensive bibliography mentioned there.

30. The literature on the slave and/or native rebellions is very vast. As examples, see C. Esteban Deive, *Los guerrilleros negros* (Santo Domingo: Fundación García Arévalo, 1989); R. Price, *Sociedades cimarronas* (Mexico: Siglo XXI Editores, 1981); K. Gosner, *Soldiers of the Virgin: The Moral Economy of a Colonial Maya Rebellion* (Tucson: University of Arizona Press, 1992). Luis Rivera Pagán, in *A Violent Evangelism*, documents a number of native and slave rebellions during the early stages of the conquest. I must add that the very existence today of non-Christian religions from colonial days, as well as popular Catholicism itself, underline the fact and degree of resistance of so many of the vanquished peoples.

31. See R. Ricard, *The Spiritual Conquest of Mexico*, 83-95; J. García Icazbalceta, *Don Fray Juan de Zumárraga, primer obispo y arzobispo de México* (Mexico: n.ed., 1881), 208-219. There are numerous references to native willingness to adopt Christianity in the writings of Bartolomé de Las Casas. See the collection of his writings, *En defensa de los indios*, and Antonio Larios's superb introductory essay.

32. For what follows on Amerindian and African peoples and religions, see (as examples from a very vast bibliography) I. Rouse, *The Tainos: Rise and Decline of the People Who Greeted Columbus* (New Haven: Yale University Press, 1992); J. Soustelle, *La vie quotidienne des aztèques à la veille de la conquête espagnole* (Paris: Ed. Hachette, 1955); M. León-Portilla, ed., *The Broken Spears: The Aztec Account of the Conquest of Mexico* (Boston: Beacon Press, 1962); idem, *Aztec Thought and Culture: A Study of the Ancient Nahuatl Mind* (Norman: University of Oklahoma Press, 1963); L. Burkhart, *The Slippery Earth: Nahua-Christian Moral Dialogue in Sixteenth-Century Mexico* (Tucson: University of Arizona Press, 1989); A. Demarest and G. Conrad, *Ideology and Pre-Columbian Civilizations* (Santa Fe: School of American Research Press, 1992); R. Markman and P. Markman, *The Flayed God: The Mesoamerican Mythological Tradition* (San Francisco: Harper Collins, 1992); D. Carrasco, ed., *To Change Place: Aztec Ceremonial Landscapes* (Niwor: University Press of Colorado, 1991); M. Moreno Fraginals, ed., *Africa en América Latina* (Mexico: Siglo XXI Editores, 1977); W. Bascom, *Sixteen Cowries: Yoruba Divination from Africa to the New World* (Bloomington: Indiana University Press, 1980).

33. See D. Carrasco, *To Change Place: Aztec Ceremonial Landscapes*; R. Ricard, *The Spiritual Conquest of Mexico*, 176-193; L. Cabrera, *El Monte*; R. Markman and P. Markman, *The Flayed God*, 29-62.

34. See R. Ricard, *The Spiritual Conquest of Mexico*, 194-206; B. de Las Casas, "Apologética historia sumaria," in *En defensa de los indios*, 63-98; J. García Icazbalceta, "Representaciones religiosas de México en el siglo XVI," in J. García Icazbalceta, *Opúsculos varios* (Mexico: n.ed., 1896), vol. II, 307-368.

35. *Mestizaje* is the racial and/or cultural mixing of Spanish and Amerindian. *Mulataje* is the mixing of Spanish and African. *Mestizo(-a)* or *mulato (-a)* is the person of mixed blood or culture. In this chapter I am using these terms mainly in their cultural connotations. I have chosen, for the sake of simplicity, to use *mestizaje* and *mestizo(-a)* only and include therein the people and processes of *mulataje*.

36. To understand the history of the implementation of Trent in the Spanish colonies, one must first understand the *patronato regio* (the royal "patronage," or almost complete control over the Church in the Americas). See E. Dussel, *Historia General de la Iglesia en América Latina* (Salamanca: Ed. Sígueme/ CEHILA, 1983), vol. I, 241-251; A. de Egaña, *La teoría del Regio Vicariato español en Indias* (Rome: Pontifical Gregorian University, 1958); J. García Gutiérrez, *Apuntes para la historia del origen y desenvolvimiento del regio patronato indiano* (Mexico: Fondo de Cultura Económica, 1941). On Trent's implementation, see J. Villegas, *Aplicación del concilio de Trento en Hispanoamérica* (Montevideo: Ed. Lozada, 1975); E. Dussel, *Historia General de la Iglesia en América Latina*, I, 372-396; P. de Leturia, *Perchè la nascente Chiesa ispano-americana non fu rappresentata a Trento* (Rome: Pontifical Gregorian University, 1959), 495-509; idem, *Felipe II y el Pontificado en un momento culminante de la historia hispanoamericana* (Rome: Pontifical Gregorian University, 1960), 59-100.

37. *Criollos* are the white descendants of the Spaniards, born in the colonies. The term can also be used in a broader sense to refer to cultural components typical of Latin America. In this chapter, however, the term refers to the descendants of the Spaniards as well as to those who are, in fact, their cultural and political (if not always racial) heirs. These often tend to be today's social elites.

38. Some bibliographical references in E. Dussel, *Historia General de la Iglesia en América Latina*, I, 358-365. See also M. León-Portilla, ed., *The Broken Spears*; and L. Burkhart, *The Slippery Earth*.

39. Texts are collected in J.G. Durán, ed., *Monumenta Catechetica Hispanoamericana. Siglo XVI* (Buenos Aires: Universidad Católica Argentina, 1984). See also, J.B. Glass, "A Census of Middle American Testerian Manuscripts," in *Handbook of Middle American Indians*, 14 (1975), 281-296.

40. *Tlacuilos* were Aztec scribes.

41. O. Espín, "Trinitarian Monotheism and the Birth of Popular Catholicism: The Case of Sixteenth-Century Mexico." above and in *Missiology*, 20:2 (1992).

42. See many of these also in J.G. Durán, *Monumenta Catechetica Hispanoamericana. Siglo XVI*. This series will eventually collect and publish colonial religious education texts from the sixteenth through the eighteenth centuries.

43. There are numerous examples of these other texts. For example, there are the (published) chronicles and collected writings of Bartolomé de Las Casas, Bernal Díaz del Castillo, Agustín Dávila Padilla, Toribio de Benavente (Motolinía), Bernardino de Sahagún, Ramón Pané, and many others.

44. See R. Ricard, *The Spiritual Conquest of Mexico*, 176-206; O. Espín and S. García, "Lilies of the Field: A Hispanic Theology of Providence and Human Responsibility," in *Proceedings of the Catholic Theological Society of America*, 44 (1989), 68-90; J.M. Kobayashi, *La educación como conquista. La empresa franciscana en México* (Mexico: El Colegio de México, 1974); S. Gudeman,

"The *Manda* and the Mass," in *Journal of Latin American Lore*, 14:1 (1988), 17-32; F. Lizardo, *Danzas y bailes folklóricos dominicanos* (Santo Domingo: Fundación García Arévalo, 1974).

45. See R.F. Dickey, *New Mexico Village Arts* (Albuquerque: University of New Mexico Press, 1990, 3rd ed.); E. Boyd, *Popular Arts of Spanish New Mexico* (Santa Fe: Museum of New Mexico Press, 1974); A. Cabrillo y Gariel, *Autógrafos de pintores coloniales* (Mexico: Universidad Nacional Autónoma de México, 1953); J. McAndrew, *The Open-Air Churches of Sixteenth-Century Mexico* (Cambridge: Harvard University Press, 1965); F.A. Schroeder, "Retablos mexicanos," in *Artes de México*, 106 (1968), 11-28; E.W. Weismann, *Mexico in Sculpture, 1521-1821* (Cambridge: Harvard University Press, 1950).

46. See J. Castellanos and I. Castellanos, *Cultura afrocubana* (Miami: Ediciones Universal, 1988-92), vols. I-III; M. León-Portilla, ed., *The Broken Spears*; idem, "Testimonios nahuas sobre la conquista espiritual," in *Estudios de Cultura Náhuatl*, 11 (1974), 11-36; L. Burkhart, *The Slippery Earth*; J. Klor de Alva, *Spiritual Warfare in Mexico* (Unpublished doctoral dissertation, University of California at Santa Cruz, Dept. of History, 1980).

47. Mexico (and hence, the present American Southwest) became independent from Spain in 1821, the same year of Florida's purchase. Cuba and Puerto Rico remained part of the diminished Spanish colonial empire until the Spanish-American War of 1898. That year both islands came under United States jurisdiction. Cuba became an independent republic in 1902, while Puerto Rico remains an American territory (technically an "associated state").

48. The last five years of the fifteenth century saw the establishment of the first *ayuntamientos* in the Americas, strictly following the Iberian model of local government. The organization of town and village life in the colonies was one of the earliest (and most urgent) political decisions of the Spanish crown. See, F. Moya Pons, *Historia colonial de Santo Domingo* (Santiago de los Caballeros: Publicaciones de la UCMM, 1976).

49. What follows on the popular hermeneutic of trinitarian doctrines is dependent on the research for my article, "Trinitarian Monotheism and the Birth of Popular Catholicism: The Case of Sixteenth-Century Mexico." The present chapter, however, further develops or specifies some items first discussed in that article.

50. Arianism and Docetism were heretical movements in Christian antiquity. Today they have become symbolic of two opposed points of view on Jesus of Nazareth—that he was only human (Arianism) or that he was only divine (Docetist). Historically, however, these two movements were not as doctrinally simplistic as might appear here. See, R.C. Gregg, "Arianism," in *Westminster Dictionary of Christian Theology*, A. Richardson and J. Bowden, eds. (Philadelphia: Westminster Press, 1983), 40-41; and F. Young, "Docetism," ibid., 160.

51. O. Espín, "Trinitarian Monotheism and the Birth of Popular Catholicism: The Case of Sixteenth-Century Mexico."

52. In the article cited in the preceding note I argue these points based, mostly but not exclusively, on the evidence from the pictographic catechisms of the sixteenth century. One important example is the Testerian text called the *Libro de Oraciones*, currently in Mexico's National Museum of Anthropology

(MNA 35-53), and published in limited edition by Zita Basich de Canessi (*Un catecismo del siglo XVI* [Mexico: Editorial Offset, 1963]).

53. See, for example, R. Markman and P. Markman, *The Flayed God: The Mythology of Mesoamerica*; P.F. Verger, *Orixás: Deuses iorubás na África e no Novo Mundo* (Rio de Janeiro: Corripio Editora, 1981).

54. See my article "Vanquishment, Faithful Solidarity, and the Marian Symbol." For research that allows me to conclude that there was an interpretation of the Christian God through feminine forms of the divine in Mesoamerica, see M. León-Portilla, *Aztec Thought and Culture: A Study of the Ancient Nahuatl Mind*; A.M. Garibay, *Llave del Náhuatl. Colección de trozos clásicos, con gramática y vocabulario, para utilidad de los principiantes* (Mexico: n.ed., 1940); E. Hunt, *The Transformation of the Hummingbird: Cultural Roots of a Zinacatecan Mythical Poem* (Ithaca: Cornell University Press, 1977); J.I. Dávila Garibi, *Breve estudio etimológico acerca del vocablo "Guadalupe"* (Mexico: Emilio Pardo e Hijos, 1936); C. Siller Acuña, *Para comprender el mensaje de Guadalupe* (Buenos Aires: Ed. Guadalupe, 1989, 2nd ed. This book includes the complete text of the *Nican Mopohua*, the Nahuatl-language account of the Guadalupe story). I am indebted to Juan Alvarez Cuauhtemoc for some very suggestive interpretations of the Nahuatl tradition, and for some bibliographical indications. I do not necessarily agree with his christological conclusions.

55. A neologism meaning "right speech" or "right words." It also points to the social defense mechanisms implied by the need for "right speech."

56. "Tonantzin" is a Nahuatl word that means "our true mother." It was one of the names of the goddess Cihuacóatl, the consort of Quetzalcóatl (the "plumed serpent" god who in turn was the symbol of wisdom, creation, etc.). Tonantzin was immensely popular and revered before the Spanish conquest. One of her sanctuaries had been on the hill called Tepeyac, right outside Mexico City. Much of the external appearance and demeanor referred by the visionary Juan Diego to Guadalupe had clear roots in the appearance and demeanor of Tonantzin.

57. For example, see L. Boff, *O rosto materno de Deus. Ensaio interdisciplinar sobre o feminino e suas formas religiosas* (Petropolis, Brazil: Ed. Vozes, 1979).

58. See my articles, "God of the Vanquished" and "Trinitarian Monotheism and the Birth of Popular Catholicism."

59. See J. Lafaye, *Quetzalcóatl and Guadalupe: The Formation of the Mexican National Consciousness, 1531-1813* (Chicago: University of Chicago Press, 1976); and O. Espín, "Irokó e Ará-Kolé: Comentário exegético a um mito iorubá-lucumí."

60. See the Acta and decrees of the many synods held in Spanish America during the colonial period. For example, J. García de Palacios, ed., *Sínodo de Santiago de Cuba de 1681* (Madrid/Salamanca: Instituto de Historia de la Teología, 1982); C. de Armellada, "Actas del concilio provincial de Santo Domingo (1622-23)," in *Missionalia Hispanica*, 27 (1970), 129-252; J.A. Soria Vasco, "Concilios hispanos y latinoamericanos," in *El concilio de Braga y la función de la legislación particular en la Iglesia*, ed. J.A. Soria Vasco (Salamanca: Pontificia Universidad de Salamanca, 1975); J.T. Sawicki, ed., *Biblio-*

graphia synodorum particularium, Monumenta Iuris Canonici, Series C, Subsidia vol. II (Vatican City: Apostolic Library, 1967); and J. Gutiérrez Casillas, "Concilios provinciales mexicanos," in *Historia General de la Iglesia en América Latina. V: México,* ed. A. Alcalá Alvarado (Salamanca: Ed. Sígueme/ CEHILA, 1984), 61-64.

61. On late colonial re-evangelization efforts, see (for example), J. de Martín Rivera, "La vida cotidiana en la cristiandad americana," in A. Alcalá Alvarado, ed., ibid., 95-164.

62. I suspect that this identification between the Virgin of Guadalupe and the Mary of Catholic devotion was never very solidly established among the people (by now mostly *mestizos*). Even today one can see significant lacunae in this identification. The Church's attempts at making Guadalupe into the historical Mary of Nazareth in Aztec garb have, at best, touched those already involved with the ecclesiastical institutions and few others beyond these circles. The same observation, I think, can be made in reference to the Cuban devotion to the Virgin of Charity. One should remember the mechanism of *ortholalia* before optimistically evaluating catechetical success at the popular level. Brazilian anthropologist Nina Rodrigues, describing the facts and results of the evangelization of African slaves and their descendants in Latin America, said that the Church deluded itself if it thought that these populations had ever been properly or even sufficiently evangelized (in *L'Animisme fétichiste des nègres de Bahia* [Salvador, Brazil: n.ed., 1900], 101).

63. On one side of the Church were the immense majority of Catholics, i.e., natives, African slaves, and *mestizos*. These still shared, substantially, in the religious worldview of the medieval *traditio*. Evidently, the *mestizo* population, by their very racial and culturally mixed reality, were the living link between the majority of Catholics and the dominant ecclesiastical (Spanish and *criollo*) elites. *Mestizo* Catholicism was, in itself, the result of "mixing," not in a simplistic syncretic sense, but in the same manner that the earlier Iberian Catholicism had been able to assimilate and integrate Roman, Visigothic, and Islamic elements within the Spaniards' experience of the *Reconquista*. *Mestizos*, within their experience of alienation and second-class status in colonial society, assimilated and integrated Spanish, pre- and post-Tridentine Catholicism, thereby bringing forth doctrinal, ecclesiological, and sacramental re-interpretations not possible in earlier centuries. These re-interpretations made sense of Catholicism in a new way (not "modern" while not merely "traditional") and from within a new sociohistorical context (different from the native and African ones, as well as from the Spanish and *criollo* milieux). The elites had begun, by the end of the colonial period, their march toward modernity and toward the worldview and cultural premises thereof. The nineteenth century would consolidate the *cultural* split within U.S. Hispanic (and Latin American) Catholicism—a "modern" minority that attempted to follow Trent (and, later, the first and second Vatican councils), and a majority that was still grounded in the worldview (and, consequently, the practices) of pre-Tridentine Catholicism, safe in the still traditional, rural context. The twentieth century has begun to force the confrontation between *traditio* and elite Catholicisms.

64. For this section, see (for example) L. Medina Ascensio, "La Iglesia ante los nuevos estados," in *Historia General de la Iglesia en América Latina. V:*

México, ed. A. Alcalá Alvarado, 165-230; A. Alcalá Alvarado, "La reorganización de la Iglesia ante el estado liberal," in ibid., 231-285; M. Figueroa Miranda, *Religión y política en la Cuba del siglo XIX* (Miami: Ed. Universal, 1975); M. Fernández Santelices, *Bibliografía del P. Félix Varela* (Miami: Saeta Ediciones, 1991); W. Moquin and C. Van Doren, *A Documentary History of the Mexican Americans* (New York: Praeger Publishers, 1971); M. Sandoval, ed., *Fronteras: A History of the Latin American Church in the U.S.A. since 1513* (San Antonio: MACC/CEHILA, 1983). Within this latter book, see especially the chapters on the nineteenth century by R. Santos ("The Age of Turmoil"), C. Tafolla ("The Church in Texas"), L. Hendren ("The Church in New Mexico"), M. Sandoval and S. Alvarez ("The Church in California"). See also L. Pitt, *The Decline of the Californios: A Social History of the Spanish-Speaking Californians, 1846-1890* (Berkeley: University of California Press, 1966); J. Castellanos and I. Castellanos, *Cultura Afro-Cubana*, vol. III; and the pertinent sections in A. Morales Carrión, ed., *Puerto Rico: A Political and Cultural History* (New York: W.W. Norton, 1983).

65. For the development of popular Catholicism in the Antilles (especially during the nineteenth century), I have yet to find a better synthetic exposition than the one by J. Vidal in his "Popular Religion among the Hispanics in the General Area of the Archdiocese of Newark," in *Presencia Nueva*, Office of Research and Planning, ed. (Newark: Archdiocese of Newark, 1988, limited edition), 235-352. Vidal includes an extensive bibliography.

66. See O. Espín, *Evangelización y religiones negras*, II, 220-245, and the extensive bibliography cited there.

67. See J. Lafaye, *Quetzalcóatl and Guadalupe*; and M. Vizcaíno, ed., *La Virgen de la Caridad, patrona de Cuba* (Miami: SEPI, 1981).

68. Compare these two points of view, that could not be more different, concerning popular Catholicism among Cubans: M. Rodríguez Ader, "Cuba y la Virgen de la Caridad," in *La Virgen de la Caridad*, ed. M. Vizcaíno, 40-44, and F. Castro, *Fidel y la religión. Conversaciones con Frei Betto* (Santo Domingo: Ed. Alfa y Omega, 1985). Instructive are M. Fernández, *Religión y revolución en Cuba* (Miami: Sacta Editores, 1984), and R. Gómez Treto, *La Iglesia durante la construcción del socialismo en Cuba* (San José: Ediciones del DEI, 1989).

69. For Hispanic Catholicism in Florida, see M.V. Gannon, *The Cross in the Sand: The Early Catholic Church in Florida, 1513-1870* (Gainesville: University Presses of Florida, 1983, 2nd ed.), and M.J. McNally, *Catholicism in South Florida, 1868-1968* (Gainesville: University Presses of Florida, 1982). Both works include extensive bibliographies.

70. In northern Florida (in and around St. Augustine), the only identifiable group of Hispanic Catholics from the colonial period have usually called themselves "Minorcans" (from the Balearic island off the Mediterranean coast of the Iberian peninsula). They have assimilated into mainstream American life, with only a few noticeable vestiges of their origins remaining. It would not surprise me if their refusal to be identified as "Hispanics" came from fear of Protestant persecutions and prejudice, or from suspicion that they might not be patriotic Southerners. Northern Florida, after all, is part of the American South.

71. See the bibliographical reference in note 64, above. I think that J. Vidal's understanding of Antillean religious apathy (at worst) or growing disconnection from and disenchantment with the Church (at best), during the nineteenth century, is fundamentally correct and merits further study.

72. See M. Sandoval, ed., *Fronteras*, and L. Pitt, *The Decline of the Californios*. For Hispanic Catholicism in the Southwest during the nineteenth century, see the pertinent sections in R. Alvarez, *Familia: Migration and Adaptation in Baja and Alta California, 1800-1975* (Berkeley: University of California Press, 1987); M. Barrera, *Race and Class in the Southwest: A Theory of Racial Inequality* (Notre Dame: University of Notre Dame Press, 1979); L.J. Mosqueda, *Chicanos, Catholicism and Political Ideology* (Lanham, MD: University Press of America, 1986); R. Acuña, *Occupied America: A History of Chicanos* (New York: Harper and Row, 1981, 2nd ed.); A. de León, *The Tejano Community, 1836-1900* (Albuquerque: University of New Mexico Press, 1982); A. Mirandé, *The Chicano Experience* (Notre Dame: University of Notre Dame Press, 1985).

73. There are many *surviving* examples of this. One important case is the *Hermandad de Nuestro Padre Jesús Nazareno*, the famous *penitentes* of New Mexico. See M. Weigle, *Brothers of Light, Brothers of Blood* (Albuquerque: University of New Mexico Press, 1976).

74. See P. Ribeiro de Oliveira, "Religião e dominação de classe: o caso da 'romanização,'" in *Religião e Sociedade*, 6 (1980), 167-188.

75. See, for example, L. Pitt, *The Decline of the Californios*, 55-61.

76. Although the home altars have older roots, their survival in the modern American Southwest seems to be due (at least in part) to the enforced transformation of public piety into private devotional expressions. See, for example, K.F. Turner, "Mexican-American Home Altars: Towards Their Interpretation," in *Aztlan*, 13:1-2 (1982), 318-60; T.J. Steele, *Santos and Saints: The Religious Folk Art of Hispanic New Mexico* (Santa Fe: Ancient City Press, 1982).

77. For this section, besides the vast literature from the social sciences on the impact of "modernity" on U.S. Latinos, see F. Bean and M. Tienda, *The Hispanic Population of the United States* (New York: Russell Sage Foundation, 1990); F. Schick and R. Schick, eds., *Statistical Handbook on U.S. Hispanics* (Phoenix: Oryx Press, 1991); and the pertinent sections in A. Figueroa Deck, *The Second Wave: Hispanic Ministry and the Evangelization of Cultures* (Mahwah: Paulist Press, 1989).

78. I have found Antonio Gramsci's social analysis, which takes popular Catholicism seriously into account, to be very useful when applied to U.S. Hispanic populations. The term "subaltern" is Gramscian. A good introduction to his thought on religion is H. Portelli, *Gramsci y la cuestión religiosa* (Barcelona: Ed. Laia, 1977). See also O. Maduro, *Religión y conflicto social* (Mexico: Ediciones del CRT, 1977).

79. The Euro-American Church seems to have also assumed that incorporation into the American middle-classes (and into the world of modernity and "progress," with all that these entail) will inevitably and automatically bring about the religious Euro-Americanization of Latinos. Middle-class status and overall success at joining the American economic and political mainstream can indeed play an important role in the possible religious Euro-Americanization of U.S. Latinos. However, the process of *religious* Euro-Americanization has limits

today, even among the successfully "mainstreamed" Latinos. There are at least three reasons for this. First, the Hispanic middle-classes have begun to find ways to "negotiate" the culturally cognitive and symbolic means necessary to remain *religiously* Latino (in varying degrees of authenticity) while justifying their successful participation in American society. Second, there are sufficiently exposed doubts as to the merits of modernity and "progress," and the latter's consequences on cultures such as the Hispanic ones. And third, it is theologically and pastorally absurd for the Euro-American Church to be promoting modernity among Latinos as the preferred cultural setting for Catholicism, considering the profoundly secularizing philosophical premises of modernity and its terribly high historical and social costs.

80. For example, the *Vírgenes* of Hispanic popular Catholicism appear prominently in gatherings, publications, and even on neighborhood walls, where cultural identity and pride are consciously emphasized. The United Farm Workers have proudly and frequently displayed images of the Virgin of Guadalupe and of the Virgin of San Juan de los Lagos. Cuban-Americans have been emphasizing the Virgin of Charity as a unifying cultural (and political) symbol since the 1960s. Although most of the time for laudable causes and motives, I suspect that popular Catholicism is, nevertheless, being instrumentalized in most of these cases.

81. For this section, I refer the reader once more to my paper, "Pentecostalism and Popular Catholicism: Preservers of Hispanic Catholic Tradition?"

82. See, for example, F.C. Rolim, *Religião e classes populares* (Petropolis, Brazil: Ed. Vozes, 1980); B. Leers, *Catolicismo popular e mundo rural* (Petropolis, Brazil: Ed. Vozes, 1977); P. Ribeiro de Oliveira, ed., *Renovação carismática católica* (Petropolis, Brazil: Ed. Vozes, 1978). See also the very suggestive article by R. Finke and R. Stark, "How the Upstart Sects Won America: 1776-1850," in *Journal for the Scientific Study of Religion*, 28:1 (1989), 27-44.

83. See note 24, above.

6

POPULAR RELIGION AS AN EPISTEMOLOGY (OF SUFFERING)

AN INTRODUCTION ON THE URGENCY OF EPISTEMOLOGICAL REFLECTION

I have become very convinced that popular religion is one of the most fundamental ways through which Latinos deal epistemologically with suffering, and indeed with all of reality. However, theology and the social sciences, even when done by Latinos, have all too frequently dismissed popular religion as insignificant, a mere "practical" problem, or, at best, as a vestige of a dying past. In other cases, popular religion has been co-opted, interpreted as folklore or simply as "widespread devotions," just a version, a subversion, or a partner of "official" religion. Theology and the social sciences, no matter what the ultimate intentions of their practitioners, have all too often *un*critically assumed the premises of the "mainstream" academy to be sufficient and correct in the interpretation of popular religion.

Unfortunately, many theologians and social scientists do not seem to realize that by assuming as sufficient and correct the methodological and epistemological premises[1] of the academy, they are thereby assuming as true the premises of the hegemonic groups in American society. Hegemony is indeed successful if it can produce and disseminate scientific and theological "evidence" to convince the rest of society (and, in boomerang fashion, the theologians and social scientists as well) of the validity and implied claims of truthfulness and "objectivity" of the socially dominant ideology.[2] The mainstream academy's theology and

Originally published in *Journal of Hispanic/Latino Theology*, 2: 2 (1994): 55-78.

social sciences have been masterfully used to purvey this ideology and its implied claims to the rest of American society. Consequently, popular religion—to the degree that it is, indeed, a marginalized people's own—is insistently judged by theology and the social sciences as insufficient, superstitious, etc. At best, it is folklore—ultimately insignificant in the real world and to mainstream society. It is socially declared to be like its creators—of marginal interest.

The significance of the fact that popular religion is the real and unquestioned mainstream religion of U.S. Latinos is lost on most theologians and social scientists, or is dismissed by them as unimportant. The equally crucial fact that most of our people have kept their popular religion alive, after all these centuries and in spite of so many efforts to take it from them, is also lost as significant on the academic specialists.[3] Most scholars have not even wondered why the massive transdenominational shift among Latinos is occurring between popular Catholicism and (popular!) Pentecostalism,[4] and not (as mainstream scholars would have us believe) between Roman Catholicism and mainline Protestantism (the latter two understood institutionally by the academicians, and, of course, made to fit the latter's post-Reformation definitions of the terms).

Furthermore, we need to wonder if self-conscious *Latino* scholarship, to the degree that it is done by academicians trained in the methods and epistemological assumptions of the "modern" world, might not be actually dismissing its own *Latinidad*, its very *razón de ser*. What makes Latino scholarship distinct from so-called mainstream scholarship is certainly not the ethnic background of its practitioners, nor the language of its printed texts, nor the frequent reference to Latino sources or even Latino experience. I am not discounting the contribution and crucial importance of these, but the *Latinidad* (i.e., the "Latino-ness") of our work cannot ultimately rest on them alone or even mainly. The very core of the distinctiveness must be, above all else, our work's epistemological claims and premises.

The *Latinidad* of our academic production rests ultimately and exclusively, I believe, *on the epistemological question* and, at a second and dependent moment, on the methods that may flow therefrom. Because if we produce theology and social sciences in ways that follow the established mainstream methods, we are implicitly (and necessarily) accepting as sufficient and correct not the epistemological and ideological assumptions of our peoples but those of the dominant, hegemonic groups in American society—the very groups and ideologies that created and/or inherited those assumptions, and who are at the source of our people's marginalization and suffering.

I needed to pose these questions as I start this paper.[5] The issue of the foundational role of epistemology must be addressed. Although I have been asked to reflect on suffering and popular religion, underlying these pages is the deeper question (which a number of Latino theologians have begun to investigate)[6] of the possibility, nature, and structure of a distinctly Latino epistemology. Do we as Latinos know "the real" *latinamente*, construct reality *latinamente*, think and know in ways that are specific to us? The spontaneous answers might all be affirmative, but the crucial questions remain until we can discover, describe, and justify our *Latinidad* epistemologically, and vice versa, until we can adequately discover, describe, and justify our epistemology as distinctly Latina.

My paper will address popular religion and suffering. But it is part of the growing effort to ask and answer these broader and more crucial epistemological questions. It will be my contention that popular religion is *a* Latino epistemology of suffering, but in order to point to how popular religion is an epistemology (and I do not think that at this stage of the reflection anyone can do more than "point to"), as well as indicate how it is specifically an epistemology of suffering, we must first face other issues.

AN EPISTEMOLOGY

Popular Religion as Epistemology . . . But Whose Epistemology?

So, how do Latinos know, explain, and make sense of suffering? As I said earlier, it is my contention that popular religion is one of the key elements in the answer to this question. I am not implying, and much less saying, that popular religion (in any of its many forms) is *the* epistemology of suffering within the Latino context. I have carefully tried to avoid that impossible statement. However, I do think that popular religion can be understood as *an* epistemology of suffering (and indeed, of all reality) among Latinos.

Notice, however, that as I just made that statement I also raised a most crucial, underlying, and prior set of questions. In saying that popular religion can be understood as an epistemology of suffering, and indeed of all reality among Latinos, I have assumed *another* point of departure for my own knowing, one that is not equal to the peoples' epistemological point of departure. In other words, if I can (if we as theologians or social scientists can) understand popular religion as *an* epistemology, then we are assuming that there is another epistemology operative in our own reflection, one that allows us to distinguish, evaluate, and prioritize. Indeed, one that allows us to "see" popular religion as a distinct field and component of study, fitting inside another (our) reality. These observations on assumed (and unconscious) epistemologies must also be made when we speak of our people's suffering.[7]

Now, it could be argued that since those speaking (i.e., we, the theologians and social scientists) are Latinos, and since we are reflecting on *our* peoples' suffering and religion, that we must therefore be *ipso facto* somehow qualified to understand and evaluate them as *Latino* suffering and religion. We might be qualified, I would say, *only* to the degree in which we do share and participate in our peoples' real suffering, and to the degree in which we experience and interpret it as they do. In other words, *we would be speaking and reflecting on Latino suffering as Latinos only when our assumed epistemology is, precisely, our peoples' own.*

Evidently, cries can and will be heard in academic quarters as many attempt to cover up their sense of discomfort at our peoples' epistemology of suffering. Indeed, arguments will be raised to disprove the need to see and construct reality as our peoples do, and/or from their perspective and social location. All sorts of "evidence" will be mustered to indicate that Latino scholarship can be and has been authentically Latino without assuming the Latino peoples' epistemology. And, obviously, definitions of *Latinidad* will be put forth that allow academicians, epistemologically (and not just epistemologically) outside of Latino socially constructed reality, to claim that there is an authentic *Latinidad* possible, without involving the Latino peoples in the definitions of "authenticity" and "*Latinidad*." Needless to say, it seems rather odd that what is authentically Latino could be defined without the people's indispensable and protagonistic role in the very process of (self-) definition.

Can I authentically speak of Latino suffering and of popular religion as an epistemology thereof when I am not socially or existentially situated within real-life contexts that allow me to claim and experience that suffering, that religious universe, and that epistemology *as my own*? And if I cannot so speak, then is my resulting theological (or social scientific) reflection authentically Latino?[8] The apparent, honest answer seems to disqualify most Latino scholars and debunk the hope (and the very concept) of a truly Latino scholarship. But is this apparent answer, for all its potentially sincere existential honesty, really addressing the issue?

I am not about to suggest one more creative but ultimately dissatisfying escape from the dilemma this line of questioning might have created. Such a creative way out would be blatantly inauthentic. I would propose, rather, that we begin to ask the real social creators of *Latinidad* how *they* would address and perhaps resolve the dilemmas and the issues involved in the epistemological inauthenticity so frequent in Latino scholarship.

Needless to say, this paper cannot address all the issues and possible avenues for an authentic reflection from within the Latino worldview. Nevertheless, I might be able to point toward some potentially rich paths when dealing with popular religion as an epistemology of suffering.

Popular Religion: Going Beyond the State of the Question

There are some issues, however, that must be confronted first and made explicit, if we are to deal with popular religion as an epistemology of Latino suffering. The very concept of what is popular religion, and the best approaches to it, might not be universally acceptable or epistemologically innocent.

Over a decade ago it was customary among most Latino social scientists to dismiss popular religion. Either because it was interpreted as an obstacle to our peoples' liberation and struggle for justice, or because it was understood as a vestige from the rural past, or for whatever reason, popular religion did not receive a sympathetic treatment among Latino social scientists. Given the very ambiguous and more than occasionally inimical role of the Roman Catholic Church vis-à-vis Latinos in American society, many social scientists felt compelled to vigorously critique what they perceived as the (negative) role of religion among our communities.[9] Their frequent use of Marxist or other positivist categories of social analysis did not help them see any other intellectually honest approach.

Theology, also, more than a decade ago, tended not to take Latino popular religion seriously. Perhaps because they did not see another scientific approach to it beyond the one proposed by the social scientists, theologians left the reflection on popular religion to the pastoralists. It did not merit real theological examination. This religious universe was an embarrassment to the Church and a superstitious legacy to be erased by good, reasoned catechesis. Both Roman Catholics and Protestants agreed on the need for Latino popular religion's early demise.

A shift in theological reflection then began to appear. A few Roman Catholics admitted the powerful grip that the symbol of the *Virgen* of Guadalupe had on Latinos of Mexican descent (and, after them, theologians from other Latino communities repeated the same process with their "*Vírgenes*").[10] These scholars started to theologically reflect upon the social and religious importance and function of popular Marian symbols. This style of theological approach, with varying and ever-increasing degrees of methodological sophistication, is still with us and is now quite acceptable and widespread in Latino theology.

However, too many crucial questions are not being faced by the theologians who engage in this type of reflection, not the least of which is the uncritical acceptance of the Marian symbols both as Marian and, indeed, as that which might positively and especially validate popular religion.

In the same vein, a significant body of literature has begun to emerge, assuming that the popular religious universe could be identified, defined, and best understood as the collection of the people's symbols and rituals (Marian or otherwise). In other words, *the (merely)*

*ritual determined and defined popular religion, thereby ultimately dis-
missing popular religion by labeling it "devotional," a custom, a pastoral problem, the traditional religious expression of people of "simple
and child-like" faith, or perhaps akin to religious folklore, or something along those lines.*

Unfortunately and unlike theology, the Latino social sciences still
seem rather deficient in their reflection on popular religion. Either they
are still within the mainstream academic trap of identifying popular
religion (even popular Catholicism) with Roman Catholicism, or they
are still reacting to the frequently inimical and colonizing role of the
European and/or Euro-American Roman Catholic Church in Latino
history. Perhaps a methodological attachment to and *añoranza* for the
certainties of one type of Marxist analysis still impede (among most
scholars, but with a few exceptions) a fresh social scientific approach to
popular religion.

Latino theologians have nowadays begun to accept popular religion
as a topic for their systematic reflection. Indeed, within the last ten
years it has become *de rigueur* to say something about the foundational
or even revelatory role of popular religion, whether discussing ecclesiology or the most difficult issues in trinitarian studies. But assumed as
valid by most authors is the still uncritical view that popular religion is
to be fundamentally understood and handled as a collection of rituals,
prayers, devotions, processions, and symbols.[11] Marian devotion continues to be presented and accepted as if evidently referred to the historical Mary of Nazareth, or at least as if essentially the same as the
Roman Catholic Church's officially sanctioned Marian devotions. Sympathetic and even adversarial theologians are uncritically assuming that
the Roman Catholic Mary is at the core of Latino popular religion—
indeed, I expect a few surprised reactions at my doubting this well-
intentioned Marian connection.[12]

Most theologians have (inaccurately) taken for granted, and their
social scientific colleagues have agreed, that Latino popular religion is
usually coextensive with popular Catholicism and, worse still, that the
latter is certainly a "popularized" version of *Roman* Catholicism.[13]
Furthermore, theologians (as social scientists had before them) have
also uncritically taken the post-Reformation and post-Enlightenment
operative definitions of "Church,"[14] of "Roman Catholicism,"[15] of
"Protestantism,"[16] of "religion,"[17] and of "western medieval Christianity," as sufficiently and substantially correct.

Within the relatively short history of the academic study of Latino
popular religion, I also find quite unacceptable the apparently innocent
attempt by some scholars to approach the people's religion from a definition of the category "popular" that is identified with "popularity"
("if it is widespread, then it must be popular" . . . or so they claim,
thereby conveniently co-opting, socially and ecclesiastically, the most

important religious creation of the Latino peoples).[18] By approaching the Latino religious universe in this fashion, these authors[19] not only choose to ignore decades of very serious research that directly contradicts their misuse of the category "popular," but more importantly, they deprive this term of its existential, socio-analytic and historical roots in the *pueblo* (the latter employed not as a demagogic or "politically correct" term but as a precise socio-analytic category). Popular religion is popular not because it is widespread but because its creators and practitioners are the people, and more concretely, the marginalized people in society (i.e., those social sectors *pushed* against their will to the dispensable or disposable margins of society). It is rather incomprehensible (or perhaps all too comprehensible) that the scholars who take this approach dismiss as unimportant the marginalized status of the creators and practitioners of popular religion in their academic definition of the popular religious universe. To attempt to impose the label "folk" on the religion of the marginalized of American society is, innocently or not, to dismiss them and their religious universe as ultimately insignificant for theology and society. The label "folk" bears no connotation of importance, under any definition or use of the term in current American usage. As a matter of fact, it is very frequently associated with groups, activities, or objects that are regarded as quaint, passed by history, and old-fashioned, their beauty or value being more nostalgic ("historical" in this myopic sense), and not even remotely empowering or liberating. I find this overall approach to the study of Latino popular religion quite unacceptable.

Needless to add, as summary, the short history of the social scientific *and* theological study of Latino popular religion has been rather naive in its uncritical acceptance of the *epistemological premises* of the mainstream academy, as the latter reflects and disseminates the legitimizing reasons for the current American hegemonic ideology. This alone would be enough, in my view, to make us wonder about the real genesis and (implied) beneficiaries of the limited and essentially flawed perspectives that Latino scholarship (theological and/or social scientific) has employed—unwittingly—in its approaches to popular religion.

I propose that we go beyond the current state of the question. I suggest that we attempt to view and study popular religion not only with greater critical rigor, but (especially!) *latinamente*.

In order to accomplish this shift, as I said earlier, we cannot remain imprisoned in the methods of the mainstream, European, and/or Euro-American academy (regardless of our particular disciplines). We must go beyond the current analyses, and approach the people's religion freshly from a set of epistemological premises that are authentically Latino.[20] The *Latinidad* and rigor of our methodologies and of the assumptions on which they are based are the only road to travel if we wish to avoid all the social and academic traps that make our peoples' religious universe an *object* for hegemonic study (with all the consequences that this reification historically implies and does to our peoples).

Popular Religion as Epistemology

How do Latinos understand? How do they grant meaning to reality? These and many more questions must be raised when discussing popular religion as epistemology (and not just of suffering). If popular religion is a fundamental Latino epistemology, then we must find the answers *latinamente* within that religious universe. But I must insist again that we *not* define popular religion as a collection (no matter how beautiful or important) of rituals and devotions. We must go beyond this ultimately superficial approach to a more substantial one. *I propose that we view Latino popular religion, provisionally, as an "epistemological network."*[21]

A network is a *communication relationship* among interconnected nodes[22] that have the capability of transferring data from one to another.[23] It is important to emphasize that it is the nodes that transfer data from one to another via their relationship/network. Hence, the relationship/network is constituted (*and* constantly *re*-constituted and *re*-configured) by the internodal communication, and not the other way around.[24]

In the case of popular religion, which are the nodes that become related in the network and that fashion the network? What data do these nodes communicate among themselves? And, more crucially for us, what is their *estatuto de/en realidad*?

The nodes of the popular religion network can be grouped, for the sake of clarity, under the following four categories: (1) *Beliefs*: about God and the sphere of the Sacred (e.g., *Vírgenes*, saints, etc.); about life (human and otherwise) and living; and about human social and familial roles. (2) *Ethical expectations*: from moral/immoral evaluation of individual and social behavior, to the manner(s) in which these evaluations are communicated in families and communities (e.g., popular wisdom, sayings, counsel, shame, etc.). (3) *Rites*: from *"mandas/promesas"* and other individual/familial rituals, to very public ceremonies. (4) *Experiences*: from encounters with the Sacred and the sphere of the Sacred, to trusting that one's prayers have been heard and one's life/family protected, to discovering deeper and more humanizing levels of social and familial relationship.

The four groups of nodes cannot be understood as more than assumed and plausible premises,[25] real and true for those who hold them, but probably not self-evident for those who do not. This in no way allows for the conclusion that, therefore, the nodes of the popular religion network are not real. The contemporary philosophy of science (among other disciplines) does not allow us such a naive rationalistic reaction.

Notice that these are the components that come together to configure the network, but they (by their mere coming together) do not suffice to explain and give shape to the network. The four groups of nodes (beliefs, ethical expectations, rites, experiences) are themselves the possible and plausible *results* of Latino living. But it is the social and historical *experiencia*[26] of the Latino communities that serves as the shaping matrix for the construction of these nodes, and for their mutual relating as plausible assumptions about the substance, nature, and configuration of all reality. And this reality, in turn, is perceived as real indeed only to the degree and extension that it is encountered as part of the Latino *experiencia*.

The grounding and founding character of *experiencia*, I think, cannot be underestimated in a Latino epistemology. Whatever exists is granted its status as existing only to the degree and extension that it becomes part of, or it flows from, the people's *experiencia*. Its existential importance is similarly granted.

This *experiencia*, however, does not appear as fundamentally individual. Rather, it presents itself as social, communal, familial, and historical. Consequently, the conditions and circumstances of society, the communities, the family, and history do have a crucial impact on the Latino *experiencia*. Poverty, vanquishment, and suffering, therefore, are not irrelevant elements in the Latino construction of plausible reality. Indeed, they have not simply been unfortunate consequences of historical events thrust upon our peoples. Rather, once these events occurred (unwanted and violent as they often were), they forcefully entered and imprinted our peoples' *experiencia de la vida* and have ever since been an undeniable and major part of the Latino perception of what is real and significant.[27]

I hasten to add and clarify that this does *not* necessitate, in my view, the conclusion that our people are condemned to be or be seen as poor, vanquished victims. Not at all! Poverty, vanquishment, and suffering do not by any stretch of the imagination define all that Latinos are.[28] Nevertheless, I do want to emphasize that to downplay our peoples' suffering (and vanquishment and poverty) is ethically and epistemologically unacceptable. It would be tantamount to dismissing their pain as ultimately insignificant and, thereby, somehow exonerate the oppressor from responsibility and guilt. And it would also make the people's construction and understanding of reality an ideological, senseless joke.

The nodes of the popular religion network, therefore, come from and are granted *estatuto de realidad* within the matrix of Latino historical, social, communal, and familial *experiencia*. In other words, the assumed beliefs, ethical expectations, rites, and experiences about/within plausible reality (i.e., the nodes that form the network) are themselves the results of actual, engaged living. And, therefore, the conditions and circumstances of this living, of *experiencia*, shape the reality status of the nodes *and* of the "data" (about reality) they communicate. These four groups of nodes are, consequently, not just assumed, plausible premises for Latinos. They are true and real, in the fuller sense of both terms. Whatever else might claim existence, reality, and truth, and does not fit within the worldview of these nodes (beliefs, ethical expectations, rites, and experiences), will be perceived by most Latino communities as either false or utterly insignificant, ultimately devoid of any *realidad*.[29]

The nodes of the popular religion network are not foundationally unrelated. From the ground and origin of their very plausibility, they are lived and reflected upon in relationship. Indeed, they are nodes in a network! And this network gains its shape, its configuration, and (thereby) its *meaning* precisely by the fact that—and the manner through which—these nodes intimately relate with and among each other.

The relationship between/among beliefs, ethical expectations, rites, and experiences, creates a certain configuration that is imprinted and shaped by the *experiencia* of the people who perceive the former as true and real. But once a plausible configuration is achieved (i.e., a network held to be true and real), it in turn becomes its own justification. The nodes communicate therein (and therefore) data that is also perceived as true and real, and equally justified. The manner of this internodal communication might perhaps be described through another expression borrowed from information technology, "multiplexing," and more specifically, "time-division multiplexing" (TDM).[30]

In the popular religion network, the messages shared by the nodes are "transmitted" according to need, thereby (for example) making the popular religion universe seem at times explicitly ritual while at other moments appear very ethically evaluative, and so on, depending on the "time" allotted the messages and the nodes that transmit them. The need that provokes this or that internodal message sharing, at its allotted time, is determined by the *experiencia* (including the *experiencia de vida*) in nonprioritized (i.e., "asynchronous") order of importance.

Considering the grounding, foundational character of the nodes of the Latino popular religion network, we can understand how the latter's configuration is a crucial (indeed, indispensable) lens for any reading of reality that is *latinamente* authentic. What justifies and grants *Latinidad* to the network seems to be the grounding of plausibility in Latino *experiencia*. Furthermore, *Latinidad* is also granted by the specifically familial and communal manner in and through which the nodes are related among themselves within/from within Latino *experi-*

encia. The result is a particular way of plausibly understanding the plausibly real and of knowing the plausibly true. In other words, a Latino epistemology.

The configuration that makes this network Latino-specific, rests in turn on the *experiencia*'s operative understandings (and network usages) of "God," "life," etc. These operative understandings are grounded on the prereflective moment of the *experiencia*, and are similarly imprinted and molded by the *experiencia*'s historical, social, communal, and familial circumstances and contexts (hence, by poverty, suffering, vanquishment, etc.). These operative understandings are the messages of/within internodal communication.

It is very important to note and recall, especially when mentioning the operative understandings of "God," "life," etc., that there is one *specifically* familial and communal manner in and through which the nodes of the network are related among themselves and understood within/from within Latino *experiencia*. This specific manner of relating and understanding the nodes has been inherited from (medieval and pre-"modernity") Catholic Christianity.

In summary, Latino popular religion is a network: a particular resulting configuration of relationships between/among beliefs, ethical expectations, rites, and experiences.[31] This configuration/network posits as plausible the operative, daily-life understandings of "God," "life," etc. It discovers in *experiencia* the grounds of plausibility of the Latino perception of the real and the true. Similarly, it treats as impossible or insignificant what might not be deduced from within this plausibility.

The rituals, devotions, and objects of popular religion are, therefore, not the issue, the defining factors, or much less the question in the study of Latino popular religion. The rituals, devotions, and objects, however, have been historically shown to be capable of acting as significant means of social empowerment, as well as challenges to previously plausible perceptions and understandings of reality and of *experiencia*.[32] In this view, the rituals, devotions, and objects cannot be easily dismissed or treated as epistemologically insignificant.

AN EPISTEMOLOGY OF SUFFERING

The "Reality" of Latino Suffering is not the Question (. . . for Latinos)

It is more than obvious that Latinos in the United States do suffer, and they suffer as the group at the bottom of this society's ladder. Statistics are there to abundantly prove these statements, and our own experience daily reminds us of this terrible fact.[33] Latinos have no doubt about the reality of suffering.

Obviously, not all individual Latinos are or become victims of poverty, of racism and public stereotyping, of woefully inadequate educational and health facilities, of chronic unemployment and underemployment, of deficient housing, or of brutality and officially sanctioned disregard and disdain. It is true that some in our communities are not poor, but they are clearly the exceptions when seen against the nation-wide picture. Poverty and marginalization still shape the more frequent context of Latino life in the United States. And this context is diversely experienced as and through suffering.

The problem is not whether Latinos suffer. That is terribly and cruelly evident! The problem (and a crucial question for this paper) is how they explain their suffering, know it as suffering, and make at least some sense of it. In other words, the problem is epistemological. My contention is that popular religion is one of the most fundamental ways through which Latinos deal with suffering epistemologically.

I hasten to add that I am in no way implying the morally obscene notion that to understand suffering and to somehow make sense of it is more important than eliminating it. I am certainly not saying that the struggle for justice and empowerment is not the most important and urgent task for our communities. Rather, it seems to me that unless we *also* deal with issues of meaning and knowing, there cannot be any substantive and justified hope for the emancipation of our peoples. Real-life struggles are sustained precisely *because* a set of meanings and certain types of knowing are in fact underlying, guiding, and critiquing the options and actions that are the struggle. It is very evident that one cannot naively separate critical reflection from daily life, pretending that the latter is self-sustaining. In fact, it has been carefully suggested that critical reflection upon and from within daily life is one constitutive element of an authentic Latino epistemology.[34]

A Latino Way of Suffering?

Do Latinos suffer *latinamente*? The answer must be affirmative, or suffering is dismissed as unimportant to our communities.[35] But then, what is there in the suffering of Latinos that would allow me to say that they do suffer *latinamente*? The suffering itself, in all its terrible variety, is certainly not our cultures' monopoly; and it would be obscene to set our pains and horrors in competition with other peoples' pains and horrors, as if poverty and discrimination in the United States had no victims other than Latinos. Although in some specific corners of the country our peoples might suffer in ways not imposed on other groups, this alone does not make them suffer *latinamente*.

The *Latinidad* of the pain is not to be found in the pain itself. This is important to remember because we might otherwise imprison ourselves in the role of victims—we deserve no suffering! Conversely, I am certainly not claiming that Latinos are incapable of committing moral evil.

Indeed, we are quite capable of sin. But our *Latinidad* is not the cause—and that is my point. To suffer *latinamente* does not imply that the suffering is somehow ours by nature. And yet, Latinos do suffer *latinamente* by the manner in and through which we confront suffering, attempt to understand it, and deal with it.

If we were to ask familial and communal Latino *experiencia* to expose the innermost source of our pain, that *experiencia* would probably (to the surprise of many scholars) point to sin as the ultimate source of suffering: not disincarnate sin, however, and probably not clothed in the theological terminology on sin.

The sin that the *experiencia* would refer to is quite real, sociohistorically visualized often enough in the actions, choices, and attitudes of individuals, as well as in events and social or familial conditions ("personal" and "structural" sin?). This sin is frequently described in popular wisdom through the oft-heard lamentation, "¡*no es justo!*" ("it isn't fair!"). In other words, the sin at the origin of Latino suffering seems to be sensed as real injustice or unfairness, profoundly felt or experienced within and through the suffering.[36]

In their suffering, our Latino communities also seem to assume that there is a divine decision ("the will of God") to allow this suffering while *at the same time* encourage our fight against it. In other words, God both chooses to permit evil and chooses to empower us to stand against it.[37] Furthermore, it seems that there is an explicit effort, on the part of Latinos, to not simply accept the will of God but to actively seek to change it when it appears to be unfair! Latino *experiencia*, and its gained wisdom, are not known for neatly explaining their intuitions, so we will not attempt to reconcile what the people themselves have not. It is important, however, that we notice (first) that God is active in Latino suffering, and *not* solely as responsible for that suffering, and (second) that the people feel themselves capable of changing the will of God.[38]

Perhaps it might be wise to recall Job's expression, "The Lord gives and the Lord takes away. Blessed be the name of the Lord!" The modern, academic need to fit this mentality within the rationalities of the professional theologians and social scientists is not our Latino communities' problem. Like Job, their suffering is understood religiously; therefore, if God has permitted suffering there will be no ultimately (logically) satisfying explanation as to how a good God can *also* be choosing to allow pain to strike the people. Like the book of Job before them, Latinos do not find an explanation, outside of the categories of sin and God's will. Contemporary theodicies might clothe themselves in more rigorous discourse, but usually arrive at their own (and similar?) logical dead ends.[39]

However, by contextualizing their understanding of the sources of suffering in the religious sphere, Latinos have thereby placed the possible responses in the same sphere. If evil occurs because of God and sin, then evil might be dealt with through appeal to God and through repentance from, or somehow dealing with, sin.[40] Popular religion has been most creative in the myriad ways it has promoted to accomplish these tasks.

We cannot, however, fall into the easy and dismissive temptation of considering the concrete rituals of delivery as popular religion's sole or main understanding of (human reaction to) sin. Popular religious imagery, rituals, and objects operate as symbolic means to confront sin and evil. But (as I pointed out earlier) the symbols of popular religion have historically proven themselves quite capable of promoting explicit and often socially effective responses to evil.[41] Popular religion allows its practitioners to discover power there where hegemonic ideology had veiled the possibilities for self-determination. Instead of utter powerlessness, through popular religion's symbols, the people can define themselves as empowered. In so doing, popular religion is thereby granting meaning and hope.

Latinos do suffer *latinamente* when they place their explanation of that suffering within the religious sphere, *and* when they attempt to confront and deal with suffering through the means offered them by popular religion (in accord with what their *experiencia* has taught them).[42]

In dealing with popular religion, often with the best of intentions, Latino theologians and social scientists (and pastoralists as well) should ask themselves if they really want to help their communities reflect upon their own religious universe and their own existential premises, *latinamente* and, hence, in a culturally authentic manner. Only in this way can academicians contribute without profaning or violating their own people. The Latino communities must be free to be Latinos *latinamente*, and to also choose so *latinamente*. Sometimes one wonders, however, if what scholars (and pastoral agents) really want is to get rid of a cultural embarrassment that does not seem to go away, or to bring the rest of our Latino communities (whom we assume to be less wise than our highly educated selves) to our type of "better catechized" (or "more biblical") Christianity, or to our type of living, or to our "more reasonable" type of knowing and thinking, even at the price of their (and our) *des-latinización*.

Popular religion seems to me to be an epistemology of suffering (and of living) for most Latinos. I am not blind to its numerous difficulties and shortcomings. I do believe, however, that too much of the Latino universe is understood and shared through the popular religious network to have it too easily dismissed (in Latino and Euro-American scholarship) as ultimately irrelevant.

Notes

1. *One* frequent example of these premises would define epistemology as a narrow propositional notion/explanation of knowledge and understanding. I am here taking epistemology to be broader and more inclusive: involving understanding, experiencing, and meaning-granting. It is dynamic and historical, with a past. And, as Jean-Pierre Ruíz rightly points out, it has to do with the root meaning of Tradition as the handing-on of experience (private communication to this author, 17 June 1994).

2. See R. Holub, *Antonio Gramsci: Beyond Marxism and Post-Modernism* (London: Routledge, 1992); L. Gruppi, *O Conceito de hegemonia em Gramsci* (Rio de Janeiro: Graal, 1978); and especially, O. Espín, "A 'Multicultural' Church?: Theological Reflections from 'Below'," in *Multicultural Experience in Church and Theology,* ed. W. Cenkner (New York: Paulist Press, 1995).

3. For a history of U.S. Latino popular Catholicism, see O. Espín, "Popular Religion among Latinos," in *Hispanic Catholic Culture in the United States: Issues and Concerns,* J. Dolan and A.F. Deck, ed. (Notre Dame: University of Notre Dame Press, 1994; vol. III of the "Notre Dame History of Hispanic Catholics in the U.S."); as well as my "Trinitarian Monotheism and the Birth of Popular Catholicism: The Case of Sixteenth-Century Mexico," chapter 2 above and in *Missiology,* 20:2 (1992), 177-204.

4. For a development of this question, see O. Espín, "Pentecostalism and Popular Catholicism: Preservers of Hispanic Catholic Tradition?" Presidential Address at ACHTUS's Fourth Annual Colloquium (San Diego, 1992). Text in *ACHTUS Newsletter,* 4 (1993).

5. I hasten to add that this paper should be read as part of an ongoing, broader project. Its arguments and conclusions are, therefore, *provisional.* I must also say that, although this paper is on popular religion as an epistemology of suffering, I intentionally placed in parentheses the "*of Suffering*" part of the title because it became evident to me that my interest was not mainly focused on the experience of suffering per se, but on the epistemological questions and dimensions underlying Latino popular religion in general. This does not imply an underestimation of the painful living conditions of most of our Latino communities. Not at all! Rather, the introduction of suffering into this paper (aside from having been part of the overall theme of the Seventh ACHTUS Colloquium) responds to its crucial role in the real life of Latinos and its function in the shaping of *experiencia* and *realidad,* as will be explained below.

6. I know of the ongoing work of María Pilar Aquino, Roberto S. Goizueta, Ada M. Isasi-Díaz, Ana M. Pineda, Jean-Pierre Ruíz, Justo L. González, and others, in the field of Latino theology. Outside of theology, in the behavioral/educational sciences, see for example (from a growing body of literature), the work of Manuel Ramírez and Alfredo Castañeda (examples: *Cultural Democracy, Bicognitive Development, and Education* [Orlando: Academic Press/Harcourt Brace Jovanovich, 1986]; and *Psychology of the Americas: Mestizo Perspectives on Personality and Mental Health* [New York: Pergamon, 1983]). And in sociology see, as an example, Otto A. Maduro, *Mapas para la fiesta. Reflexiones sobre la crisis y el conocimiento* (Buenos Aires: Centro Nueva Tierra, 1993). There seems to be an increasing awareness among Latino

theologians that there is much to be learned from and shared with African-American theological scholarship, especially as exemplified by Robert Gooding-Williams, ed., *Reading Rodney King: Reading Urban Uprising* (New York: Routledge, 1993). Euro-American feminist scholars have opened newer spaces for reflection on epistemology and, thereby, on Latino epistemology; see, for example, Mary McCanney Gergen, ed., *Feminist Thought and the Structure of Knowledge* (New York: New York University Press, 1988), and Victoria Lee Erickson, *Where Silence Speaks: Feminism, Social Theory, and Religion* (Minneapolis: Fortress, 1993). Latin American authors have also influenced our growing U.S. Latino (theological) reflection on epistemology; for example: Juan Carlos Scannone, *Evangelización, cultura y teología* (Buenos Aires: Guadalupe, 1990); Enrique Dussel, "The Ethnic, Peasant, and Popular in a Polycentric Christianity," in *The Future of Liberation Theology*, ed. Marc H. Ellis and Otto Maduro (Maryknoll, New York: Orbis, 1989), 240-249; Cristián Parker, *Otra lógica en América Latina: Religión popular y modernización capitalista* (Mexico: Fondo de Cultura Económica, 1993). The impressive work of Latin American philosophers Leopoldo Zea, Henrique de Lima Vaz, Enrique Dussel, and José Carlos Mariátegui (among others) has been foundational for many of us. Finally, it might be fruitful to *critically* revisit the writings and intuitions of an earlier generation of U.S. Latino scholars, especially Carlos E. Castañeda (1896-1958), George I. Sánchez (1906-1972), and Arthur L. Campa (1905-1978).

7. My views on these issues have been especially shaped by two authors, Peter L. Berger and Antonio Gramsci. In spite of their profound philosophical differences, Berger and Gramsci seem to me to share some foundational intuitions on the roles of conscience, epistemology, and reality-construction that can greatly affect and enrich the Latino theological enterprise. They are certainly not the only thinkers to address these and parallel issues, but they have seemed to me to better articulate them in a manner relevant to those socially "marginalized." This paper has clearly been influenced by Berger and Gramsci, but I do not claim to be simply repeating what they said. From Berger's long list of publications, see *The Social Construction of Reality*, with T. Luckmann (New York: Doubleday/Anchor, 1967); *The Sacred Canopy* (New York: Doubleday/Anchor, 1969); *A Rumor of Angels* (New York: Doubleday/Anchor, 1970); and *The Heretical Imperative* (New York: Doubleday/Anchor, 1980); *The Precarious Vision* (New York: Doubleday, 1961); "Marriage and the Construction of Reality," with H. Kellner, in *Diogenes*, 46:2 (1964), 1-24; and "Reification and the Sociological Critique of Consciousness," in *History and Theory*, 4:2 (1965), 196-211. A fine synthesis and analysis of Berger's thoughts on culture may be found in R. Wuthnow, et al., *Cultural Analysis: The Work of Peter L. Berger, Mary Douglas, Michel Foucault and Jürgen Habermas* (London: Routledge & Kegan Paul, 1984). For a strong reaction against Berger, see J.M. González García, *La sociología del conocimiento hoy* (Madrid: Ediciones Espejo, 1979). I have read Antonio Gramsci's complete works in Portuguese translations, and it is these that I use here. From Gramsci's bibliography, see *Os intelectuais e a organização da cultura* (Rio de Janeiro: Ed. Civilização Brasileira, 1979 [Trans. of *Gli intellettuali e l'organizzazione della cultura*]); *Cartas do cárcere* (Rio de Janeiro: Ed. Civilização Brasileira, 1978 [Trans. of *Lettere dal carcere*]); *Maquiavel, a política e o estado moderno* (Rio de Janeiro: Ed. Civilização Brasileira, 1980 [Trans. of *Note sul Machiavelli*,

sulla politica, e sullo stato moderno]); *Concepção dialética da história* (Rio de Janeiro: Ed. Civilização Brasileira, 1981 [Trans. of *Il Materialismo storico e la filosofia di Benedetto Croce*]); *Literatura e vida nacional* (Rio de Janeiro: Ed. Civilização Brasileira, 1978 [Trans. of *Letteratura e vita nazionale*]); *A Questão meridional* (Rio de Janeiro: Ed. Paz e Terra, 1987 [Trans. of *La questione meridionale*]). For fine syntheses and analyses of Gramsci's thought, see H. Portelli, *Gramsci y el bloque histórico* (Mexico: Siglo XXI Editores, 1980), and, idem, *Gramsci y la cuestión religiosa* (Barcelona: Editorial Laia, 1977); also, L. Gruppi, *O conceito de hegemonia em Gramsci* (Rio de Janeiro: Edições Graal, 1980); C.N. Coutinho, *Gramsci* (Porto Alegre: L&PM Editores, 1981); M.A. Manacorda, *El principio educativo en Gramsci* (Salamanca: Ediciones Sígueme, 1977); C. Buci-Glucksmann, *Gramsci e o estado* (Rio de Janeiro: Ed. Paz e Terra, 1980); R. Holub, *Antonio Gramsci: Beyond Marxism and Post-Modernism*, cit.; and R. Ortiz, *A Consciência fragmentada: Ensaios de cultura popular e religião* (Rio de Janeiro: Ed. Paz e Terra, 1980).

8. It is very much possible that Latino individuals could suffer (or construct reality) in non-Latino ways. But, then, one might question the cultural authenticity of these individuals. Our communities, increasingly confronted by Euro-American modernity's tempting calls for assimilation, are facing some of the most crucial cultural decisions in their long history. Individuals, at their level, also face the same decisions. Although the popular religious universe is certainly not static, and hence has no permanently (or even clearly) defined contours, participation in this universe's *epistemological* context seems to be an essential component of *Latinidad*.

9. For all the (assumed to be sincere) declarations of many bishops and priests in the American Roman Catholic Church, the historical fact remains that the American Church clearly perceives itself as non-Latino (in spite of its internal demographic realities), treats Latinos as "them" (i.e., the "objects" of the Church's charity and/or pastoral concern, but ultimately insignificant at any level of effective decision-making), and acts towards Latinos as a major medium of assimilationist and deculturalizing forces. The American Church seems to have fervently committed itself to the Anglo middle class and its ideology of modernity and has so far refused to think of itself and its mission in society in other terms or in other cultural categories (thereby effectively—and actively—denying, at the end of the twentieth century, its own self-perception as the Church historically shaped by the experience of immigrants and of the poor). In the experience of large numbers of Latino Catholics (and former Catholics), the American Church is not and has not been *really* interested in Latino culture, religion, effective ecclesial participation, or social well-being. The written or spoken declarations of the Church, in the view of most Latinos, are very seldom translated into real-life, effective decisions. This generalized perception of the often inimical role of the American Catholic Church's hierarchy and clergy vis-à-vis Latinos cannot be underestimated or dismissed as merely "gripes" of a few "malcontents" or of a handful of "anti-Catholic" social scientists. The motives of the increasing number of Latinos who leave the Catholic Church (who "vote with their feet," as the people sometimes explain) cannot be viewed simplistically, "blamed" on other Christians, or (much less!) on popular religion. On all of the above, of course, I readily and gladly admit that there have been and are some admirable individual exceptions.

10. Virgilio Elizondo is, without question, the most significant name in this category. See, for example, his *La Morenita, Evangelizer of the Americas* (San Antonio: Mexican American Cultural Center, 1980). And also: A.G. Guerrero, *A Chicano Theology* (Maryknoll, New York: Orbis Books, 1987); O. Espín, "The Vanquished, Faithful Solidarity, and the Marian Symbol," in *On Keeping Providence,* eds. B. Doherty and J. Coultas (Terre Haute: St. Mary of the Woods College Press, 1991), 84-101; A.M. Isasi-Díaz and Y. Tarango, *Hispanic Women, Prophetic Voice in the Church: Toward a Hispanic Women's Liberation Theology* (San Francisco: Harper and Row, 1988); J. Rodríguez, *Our Lady of Guadalupe: Faith and Empowerment among Mexican-American Women* (Austin: University of Texas Press, 1994). One must keep in mind, of course, that Latino theology *qua* theology does not have a very long history in the U.S. context.

11. Latino scholars have frequently understood popular religion in this way, whether to attempt a defense, to propose a better "pastoral answer," to analyze its liberating/alienating dimensions, to dismiss it as ultimately irrelevant, or to announce its desirable demise. One finds this overall approach to popular religion in such very diverse authors as C. Gilbert Romero, A. Figueroa Deck, R. Griswold del Castillo, R.A. Gutiérrez, M. Sandoval, A. de León, F.M. Padilla, and J.R. Vidal, among others. I also used this approach in the past, especially in the several texts (1988-1990) I co-authored with Sixto García.

12. I brought this subject up in a paper ("Our Lady of Charity and the Afro-Cuban World") presented at the first International Symposium on Our Lady of Charity, organized by and held in the Archdiocese of Miami, summer of 1988. But I am certainly not the first or only Latino theologian to suggest that the *Vírgenes* of our popular religion are not (simply) identifiable with Mary of Nazareth. The theological argument for the distinction (in the U.S. context) between the *Vírgenes* and Mary appeared first in Ada M. Isasi-Díaz and Yolanda Tarango, *Hispanic Women, Prophetic Voice in the Church*, esp. 17-18 and 118.

13. A thorough study of the bibliography and of the different approaches to the study of popular religion in Latin America (which, I would argue, have their clear parallels in our own U.S. context) is C.J. Friedemann, *Religiosidad popular entre Medellín y Puebla: Antecedentes y desarrollo* (Santiago de Chile: Pontificia Universidad Católica, 1990). See also O. Espín, "Religiosidad popular: un aporte para su definición y hermenéutica," in *Estudios Sociales*, 58 (1984), 41-56. For a summary description of the wider universe of Latino popular religion (not coextensive with popular Catholicism), see my "Popular Religion among Latinos," cit.

14. Gary Macy has brought to my attention the growing body of evidence that points to a very varied and rich experience of "Church" prior to the sixteenth-century (Protestant and Catholic) Reformations. It seems less and less possible to argue in favor of a univocal meaning of "Church" during the medieval period. Geographical and ethnic, theological and pastoral, political and local circumstances and contexts made the pre-Reformation ecclesial experience probably so diverse that the modern use of "Church" (as referred to a single, identifiably the same, institution in medieval Europe) is highly questionable when applied retrospectively to that historical period. See G. Macy's *The Banquet's Wisdom* (New York: Paulist, 1992), esp. 8-10. Macy is finishing a

paper precisely on this issue. See also, as examples, H. Fichtenau, *Living in the Tenth Century: Mentalities and Social Orders* (Chicago: University of Chicago Press, 1991); L. Rothkrug, "Religious Practices and Collective Perceptions: Hidden Homologies in the Renaissance and Reformation," in *Historical Reflections/Réflexions Historiques*, 7:1 (1980), 3-251; A. Vauchez, *The Laity in the Middle Ages: Religious Beliefs and Devotional Practices* (Notre Dame: University of Notre Dame Press, 1993); K. Pennington and R. Somerville, eds., *Law, Church, and Society* (Philadelphia: University of Pennsylvania Press, 1977); and, based on earlier data, W.A. Christian, *Local Religion in Sixteenth-Century Spain* (Princeton: Princeton University Press, 1981).

15. As a consequence of the preceding note, it also seems difficult to argue that the "Roman" Catholic Church was standard medieval, western Christianity. If by "Roman" Catholicism one means that institution which is recognizable in today's world (or even in the immediate post-Reformation period), then it is doubtful that we could be referring to any medieval western Church(es), except *perhaps* the one found mainly in and around central Italy during the Middle Ages. I am not implying that post-Reformation Roman Catholicism does not have its roots clearly planted in pre-Reformation western Christianity. It definitely does, but so do the Anglican and Lutheran communions! See, for example, D.V. Bagchi, *Luther's Earliest Opponents: Catholic Controversialists, 1518-1525* (Minneapolis: Fortress, 1991); the pertinent essays in K. Hagen, ed., *The Quadrilog: Tradition and the Future of Ecumenism* (Collegeville, MN: The Liturgical Press/Michael Glazier, 1994); and P. Avis, *Anglicanism and the Christian Church: Theological Resources in Historical Perspective* (Minneapolis: Fortress, 1989). I think that remarkable results can be had if the *sources* of Luther's *Small Catechism* and Kolde's *Mirror for Christians* were explicated and compared; for their complete texts, see D. Janz, *Three Reformation Catechisms: Catholic, Anabaptist, Lutheran* (New York: Edwin Mellen, 1982). Furthermore, I wonder if, within the heated controversies of the post-Reformation period, and perhaps for the sake of simplifying, focusing, and/or clarifying apologetic arguments, the operative definitions of "Roman Catholicism" and of "Protestantism" lost their real-life nuances (based on real-life diversity). One case to exemplify this might be Robert Bellarmine. He seems to have assumed (in his *Disputationes de controversiis christianae fidei adversus huius temporis haereticos* [1586-93]) that pre-Reformation, western Christianity was co-extensive with and substantially equal to his contemporary Tridentine Roman Catholic Church. Given the apologetic "popularity" of Bellarmine's work, I wonder if Roman Catholic, Lutheran, and Calvinist controversialists might not have found it more convenient to just assume as standard medieval Christianity, and, consequently, as standard "Roman" Catholicism what Bellarmine (and those who followed him) described. Lastly, the reforming role (and not just in matters of ecclesiastical discipline) of the Council of Trent (1545-63) cannot be ignored or downplayed. Trent argued and assumed that it was in continuity with medieval Christianity; but the results (if critically and nonapologetically analyzed) would show it to have been a deeply reforming Council, especially in matters not canonical or disciplinary. I have briefly indicated one case of Tridentine theological reform (and its consequences) in my "Pentecostalism and Popular Catholicism: Preservers of Hispanic Catholic Tradition?" cit.

16. Following the two preceding notes, can one naively accept and univocally use the term "Protestantism" today, given the immense diversity implied by the term? Would a Presbyterian feel at home in a Pentecostal context? Can we place the Protestant Episcopal Church in the United States (and that is its official denominational name) in the same category and under the same label as Jehovah's Witnesses? The enormous diversity that is covered by the term "Protestant" cannot be simply ignored or brushed aside as insignificant when it comes to the operative definitions of theology and the social sciences.

17. A further complication for the operative definitions employed by theologians and social scientists (but most especially, today, by the latter) is the term "religion." Latino theology has begun to question the very notion of "religion" that we have inherited from the post-Enlightenment and post-Reformation. Although still in use by us, *the term and its implications have become increasingly problematic given their hegemonic (as well as rationalist/modernist) origins and intent.* Do our Latino cultures ever perceive or construct reality nonreligiously, and remain identifiably Latino? Do we risk cultural inauthenticity or even unrestrained assimilation by proposing a nonreligious Latino construction of reality? Do we mean to say "ecclesiastical" or "institutional" when we, inaccurately, employ the term "religious" in our academic research and writing? Alejandro García Rivera raised some of the more serious questions on the term and its implications for Latino scholarship at the 1994 ACHTUS Colloquium in Baltimore. In this paper, given the incipient character of the discussion on "religion," I will continue to guardedly use "religion" (as in "popular religion") in its usual, modern, academic sense.

18. A tempting argument could be made to the effect that popular religion is the specific creation of the Latino *poor.* Indeed, the poor do seem to massively participate in this religious universe; therefore, a connection with the Christian preferential option for the poor can be promoted in the study of popular religion (as, for example, in the *Puebla Document,* 444ff.). But a serious question can also be raised against this argument's assumed accuracy: how do we explain the pervasive presence of popular religion in all social classes throughout the U.S. Latino cultures? Perhaps we might pay closer attention to the role that the "conscience of modernity" plays, within a loosely Gramscian understanding of hegemony's invasion of the (culturally) subaltern worldview. A possible approach, although from a Latin American context, is Cristián Parker's in his *Otra lógica en América Latina: Religión popular y modernización capitalista,* cit.

19. One recent example of this approach is R.E. Wright, "If It's Official, It Can't Be Popular? Reflections on Popular and Folk Religion," *Journal of Hispanic/Latino Theology,* 1:3 (1994), 47-67.

20. I admit, on the other side of my own argument, that I find great difficulty in selecting appropriate/adequate language when reflecting upon the field of Latino epistemological assumptions. There is even more difficulty when the reflection wants to occur *latinamente,* from within the very Latino experiential and living context of popular religion. Avoiding terminology that would further the hold of dominant ideology is quite complicated, because I *am* in fact writing in English (the language of dominance) and in a North American professional context (not always agreeable to Latino organic scholarship, in the Gramscian sense). Historically, technical academic terminology seems to be

intricately interwoven with hegemonic ideologies, and thus the use of the former could compromise the very intent and purpose of the reflection. Nevertheless, what other language do we have in order to contribute *effectively* to the North American scholarly dialogue (and ultimately to our people's liberation)? Should the legitimate fear for the negative side effects of dominant terminology preclude our use of the same terminology, especially if the latter is adopted (and sufficiently adapted) for liberating and culturally affirming ends? Is "terminological purity" a legitimate end or tool for Latino scholarship that wants to be socially effective and historically liberating? The remainder of this paper will inevitably evidence these terminological difficulties, which are only one part of the long-range Latino epistemological task.

21. Here is one example of the terminological difficulties I was referring to in the preceding note. I have chosen terms from the field of information science and technology in order to better describe and somehow understand the popular religious universe. However, this terminology is obviously linked to the dominant ideology and finds its source in the historical dynamics of modernity. On both counts this terminology could be deemed suspect, based on my own arguments throughout this paper. However, the terms (when adopted and adapted for purposes different from the intent of the information technologies) can yield a certain graphic, descriptive richness. Popular religion, in an earlier version of this paper, was described by me as a "constellation." However, Jean-Pierre Ruiz raised several questions regarding the apparently static nature of a stellar constellation and its applicability to popular religion. ("Constellations of stars tend to stay in the same place, with the relationship among the various stars remaining fixed," were his words.) Popular religion, on the other hand, is a living, dynamic, historical process, constantly changing and adapting. A static image (like "constellation") did not seem adequate. I think that can justify my option for terminology drawn from information technology because the terms have been *adapted* (and not merely adopted) for use within (I hope!) a culturally affirming and liberating Latino context. I also believe that the adaptation opened these terms to broader and richer semantic fields not available within their previous information technology moorings. Potentially harmful (socially, ideologically) terminology, I think, can be recuperated, reoriented, and empowered by self-conscious use in new (or at least different) liberating social/semantic contexts. My fundamental concern is that the terminology chosen actually express and unveil the epistemological premises of the Latino peoples—this, and this alone, justifies the terminological option as *latinamente* adequate.

22. A "node," in a communication network, is a processor unit with the memory and computing capacities necessary to provide communication from that node to other nodes in the network. A node must be able to receive and send messages, store messages, and provide routing information. See C. Watters, *Dictionary of Information Science and Technology* (Orlando: Academic Press/Harcourt, Brace Jovanovich, 1992), 152.

23. See C. Watters, *Dictionary of Information Science and Technology*, 149; and W. Stallings, *Data and Computer Communication* (New York: Macmillan, 1988). Useful for a reflection on the adoption/adaptation of information terminology to Latino theology, see H. Inose and J.R. Pierce, *Information Technology and Civilization* (New York: W.H. Freeman, 1984); and M. Tehranian,

Technologies of Power: Information Machines and Democratic Prospects (Norwood, NJ: Ablex Publishing, 1990).

24. Obviously (after note 21, supra), my use of the term "nodes" will not be (cannot be!) exactly that of information technology; but, it will closely parallel it (*mutatis mutandi*).

25. See Peter L. Berger's understanding of "plausibility" (in his *Social Construction of Reality* and in *The Sacred Canopy*), as well as Antonio Gramsci's frequent and multifaceted use of "conscience" and "ideology." See also Gramsci's discussion of southern Italian popular religion in (at least) his *A Questão Meridional*.

26. Jeanette Rodríguez brought to my attention the common meaning—at least in Latino popular usage—of the Spanish-language term *experiencia*. It is certainly *not* equivalent to or coextensive with the meaning and usage of the English term "experience," although it might include them. *Experiencia* is better approximated by an (awkward) expression such as "living and reflecting upon reality." In Latino usage, people gain *experiencia* as they live and reflect upon their lives and contextual reality. Wisdom, therefore, seems to be either a result or a constitutive moment of *experiencia*. Consequently, most Latinos consider that fuller and deeper *experiencia* usually (but not necessarily) comes with age. It seems evident to Latinos that older women are the wiser members of their communities, precisely because they have lived and reflected upon reality better and longer than most others. Given the crucial importance of *experiencia* for a Latino epistemology, it seems that further systematic reflection on it has become indispensable. Similarly important is the Spanish-language term *realidad*. Intimately connected to *experiencia*, it also deserves further systematic reflection. *Realidad*, besides meaning "reality" (in all its senses), is often equivalent to the English term "experience," more closely so than *experiencia*. See Rodríguez's article, "Experience as a Resource for Feminist Thought," in *Journal of Hispanic/Latino Theology*, 1:1 (1993), 68-76; and her recent book, *Our Lady of Guadalupe: Faith and Empowerment among Mexican-American Women* (Austin: University of Texas Press, 1994), 61-62, 114, 139.

27. See O. Espín, "The God of the Vanquished: Foundations for a U.S. Latino Spirituality," chapter 1 above and in *Listening: Journal of Religion and Culture*, 27:1 (1992), 70-83.

28. Ibid., 78-80. See also Justo L. González, *Mañana: Christian Theology from a Hispanic Perspective* (Nashville: Abingdon, 1990), esp. 38-41; and C.E. Gudorf, *Victimization: Examining Christian Complicity* (Philadelphia: Trinity Press, 1992).

29. This is no insignificant consideration when reflecting on potential pastoral approaches to popular religion, as well as on evaluations of existing approaches.

30. "Multiplexing" is the simultaneous sharing of a transmission medium by multiple signals, usually accomplished by frequency division, time division, or statistical division. "Time-division multiplexing" (TDM), specifically, is a technique that allows multiple signals to be transmitted by a single carrier (i.e., a "multiplexed line") by assigning each input a time slot for transmission. In asynchronous TDM, the input sources are allocated their time slots only when and as needed. See C. Watters, *Dictionary of Information Science and Technol-*

ogy, 143 and 229, as well as W. Stallings, *Data and Computer Communication*, cit.

31. Please recall how I earlier described these four categories of nodes.

32. The empowering role of the objects, rituals, and devotions of popular religion has been well documented and established across Latin America and among U.S. Latinos. But I am very much aware that they have also played an alienating, intoxicating role in both geographic/social contexts. I deal with this internal tension within the network (but without appeal to the language of information technology) in my article, "Popular Catholicism: Alienation or Hope?," chapter 4 above and in *Aliens in Jerusalem: Towards a Hispanic American Theology*, eds. A.M. Isasi-Díaz and F.F. Segovia (Minneapolis: Fortress, 1995). That article includes ample bibliography on the subject.

33. See, for example, F.D. Bean and M. Tienda, *The Hispanic Population of the United States* (New York: Russell Sage Foundation, 1987); and F.L. Schick and R. Schick, eds., *Statistical Handbook on U.S. Hispanics* (Phoenix: Oryx Press, 1991).

34. It seems to me that this is clearly suggested in Roberto Goizueta's writings. See, for example, his three programmatic articles, "*Nosotros*: Toward a U.S. Hispanic Anthropology," in *Listening. Journal of Religion and Culture*, 27:1 (1992), 55-69; "U.S. Hispanic Theology and the Challenge of Pluralism," in *Frontiers of Hispanic Theology in the United States*, ed. A.F. Deck (Maryknoll, New York: Orbis Books, 1992), 1-22; and "Rediscovering Praxis: The Significance of U.S. Hispanic Experience for Theological Method," in *We Are a People! Initiatives in Hispanic American Theology*, ed. R.S. Goizueta (Minneapolis: Fortress Press, 1992), 51-78.

35. I do not mean to imply the untenable notion that all Latino individuals suffer *latinamente* in identical ways. There is too much diversity in the Latino contexts! What I do want to stress, however, is that regardless of how *Latinidad* is expressed in each particular community, they *all* suffer *latinamente*. To a greater or lesser degree, modern elements have variously intertwined with premodern elements, in a process of cultural *mestizaje*, thereby producing diverse Latino responses to suffering . . . but they are still identifiable *Latino* responses. See note 8, supra.

36. I found the same intuitive description of sin in some of the interviews included by Ada María Isasi-Díaz and Yolanda Tarango in their first book, *Hispanic Women, Prophetic Voice in the Church*, cit. I suspect that the data from the same (and later) interviews are behind Isasi-Díaz's more recent elaboration of the category of sin in her latest book, *En la Lucha/In the Struggle: A Hispanic Women's Liberation Theology* (Minneapolis: Fortress, 1993), esp. 39-40, 149, 152-153, 158-59, 193. The forceful analysis and critique of patriarchy in María Pilar Aquino's last book is also, in my view, motivated by the intuition of sin experienced as *lo injusto*; see her *Our Cry for Life: Feminist Theology from Latin America* (Maryknoll, New York: Orbis, 1993), esp. 186-190.

37. See O. Espín and S. García, "Lilies of the Field: A Hispanic Theology of Providence and Human Responsibility," in *Proceedings of the Catholic Theological Society of America*, 44 (1989), 70-90.

38. A graphic (and perhaps sufficiently accurate) *description* of this double-sided approach to the divine will is the one conveyed by both Doña Margarita

and Doña Guadalupe in Victor Villaseñor's superb novel, *Rain of Gold* (Houston: Arte Público Press, 1991).

39. See G. Gutiérrez, *Hablar de Dios desde el sufrimiento del inocente. Una reflexión sobre el libro de Job* (Lima: CEP/Instituto Bartolomé de Las Casas, 1986). See also A. MacIntyre, *Whose Justice? Which Rationality?* (Notre Dame, IN: University of Notre Dame Press, 1988); T.W. Tilley, *The Evils of Theodicy* (Washington: Georgetown University Press, 1991).

40. Evidently, U.S. Latinos are not the first people to contextualize suffering in religious terms, with all the consequences. See, for example, M.C. Kirwen, *The Missionary and the Diviner* (Maryknoll, New York: Orbis Books, 1987); and L. Cabrera, *La medicina popular en Cuba* (Miami: Universal/Chicherekú, 1984). On U.S. Latinos, see the frequent references in P. Preciado Martin, *Songs My Mother Sang to Me: An Oral History of Mexican American Women* (Tucson: University of Arizona Press, 1992); also, see many of the short stories by Tomás Rivera, in *Tomás Rivera: The Complete Works*, ed. Julián Olivares (Houston: Arte Público Press, 1992); as well as L. Siems, ed., *Between the Lines: Letters Between Undocumented Mexican and Central American Immigrants and Their Families and Friends* (Hopewell, NJ: Ecco Press, 1992); R. Behar, *Translated Woman: Crossing the Border with Esperanza's Story* (Boston: Beacon Press, 1993); and J.E. Skansie, *Death Is for All: Death and Death-Related Beliefs of Rural Spanish-Americans* (New York: AMS Press, 1985).

41. See note 32, supra. And also, from a vast bibliography, O. Maduro, *Religión y conflicto social* (Mexico: CRT, 1980); V. Lanternari, *Movimientos religiosos de libertad y liberación de los pueblos oprimidos* (Barcelona: Seix Barral, 1965); M.I. Pereira de Queiroz, *Historia y etnología de los movimientos mesiánicos* (Mexico: Siglo XXI Editores, 1969); and D. Lindoso, *A Utopia armada: Rebeliões de pobres nas matas do Tombo Real* (Rio de Janeiro: Paz e Terra, 1983).

42. This does not contradict what I said in note 35, supra. The specific explanations and means (symbolic or otherwise) do vary greatly among the Latino communities, but I would argue that all are placed and dealt with within the religious sphere.

INDEX

Academy of Catholic Hispanic
Theologians of the United States
(ACHTUS): ix; and Espín, x
African population: Catholicism of,
124; Christianity, acceptance of,
122-123; rebellion of, 122
African religions: in the Latino community, 114
Africans, enslaved: 21, 37, 121,
152nn62,63; and the African slave
trade, 68; Christian converts of, 70;
defeat of, 25; and the Iberian
Reconquista, 22; religious beliefs
of, 123; and Spain, 116-117
American Catholicism: 96-99. *See
also* Euro-American Catholicism
American society: church, role of, 99-
104; Latino community, role of, 94-
95, 99-104, 102, 139; Latino
popular Catholicism, role of, 99-
104; post-World War II, 139-140;
religion in, 97
Americas: Christianity in, 69;
Christian Trinitarian monotheism,
introduction to, 57; European invasion of, 69; Latino community in,
21; missionaries in, 69, 120-122.
See also Latin America; Latino
community
Amerindians: abuse of, 43, 121, 123;
Catholicism of, 124; and Christian
converts, 57, 70; Christianity,
acceptance of, 122-123; *cofradías*
(religious fraternity), 49, 141; and
colonial Christianity, 130; colonization of, 37; defeat of, 25; *Encomiendas*, 37, 59n11, 68, 85n25;

and friars, 43; and God, 55; and
the Iberian *Reconquista*, 21-22;
and the *Libro de Oraciones*, 55;
rebellion of, 122; and Spain, 46,
116-117
Anglophone Church: 91, 99, 101. *See
also* Euro-American Catholicism
Arawak (Antilles): religious beliefs of,
123
Augustinians: 69

Bañuelas, Arturo: ix
Baptism: and missionaries, 131
Barth, Karl: 15, 16, 19, 24
Bible: 67, 142

Catechisms: pictorial works, 125-126;
Testerian, 48-50; and the Trinity, 41
Catholic Church: conservatives and
liberals, xix-xx; and the Council of
Trent (1545-63), 117, 120, 124,
174n15; definition of, 4
Catholicism: authority in, 4, 113;
conservative and liberals, xix-xx;
and the Council of Trent (1545-
63), 117, 120, 124, 174n15;
excommunication, xx; in Latin
America, 69; and Latino theology,
xvii-xviii; and Latinos, 3; and
Mary, 129; polarization of, xx;
popular Catholicism, conflict with,
3-4; and the poor, xiv; pre-
Tridentine Iberian popular Catholicism, xviii; symbols in, 134, 142;
and Tradition, 64-68; and the
Trinity, 33